Palgrave Studies in Minority Languages and Communities

Titles include:

Glyn Williams
SUSTAINING LANGUAGE DIVERSITY IN EUROPE
Evidence from the Euromosaic project

Forthcoming titles:

Anne Judge
LANGUAGE POLICIES IN FRANCE AND BRITAIN

Máiréad Nic Craith
EUROPE AND THE POLITICS OF LANGUAGE

Vanessa Pupavac
LANGUAGE RIGHTS IN CONFLICT

Palgrave Studies in Minority Languages and Communities
Series Standing Order ISBN 1–4039–3732–X
(*Outside North America Only*)

You can receive future titles in this series as they are published by placing a standing order. Please contact your bookseller or, in case of difficulty, write to us at the address below with your name and address, the title of the series and the ISBN quoted above.

Customer Services Department, Macmillan Distribution Ltd, Houndmills, Basingstoke, Hampshire RG21 6XS, England

Also by Glyn Williams

THE DESERT AND THE DREAM: The Welsh Colonisation of Chubut, 1865–1915

THE WELSH SETTLEMENT IN PATAGONIA: A Bibliographic Review

THE WELSH IN PATAGONIA: The State and the Ethnic Community

SOCIAL AND CULTURAL CHANGE IN CONTEMPORARY WALES

CRISIS OF ECONOMY AND IDEOLOGY: Essays on Welsh Society, 1840–1980

THE SOCIOLOGY OF WELSH

SOCIOLINGUISTICS: A Sociological Critique

EUROMOSAIC: The Production and Reproduction of Minority Language Groups in the European Union

FRENCH DISCOURSE ANALYSIS: The Theory and Method of Post-Structuralism

LANGUAGE USE AND LANGUAGE PLANNING: Welsh in a Global Age

Sustaining Language Diversity in Europe

Evidence from the Euromosaic Project

Glyn Williams

First published 2005 by
PALGRAVE MACMILLAN
Houndmills, Basingstoke, Hampshire RG21 6XS and
175 Fifth Avenue, New York, N.Y. 10010
Companies and representatives throughout the world

PALGRAVE MACMILLAN is the global academic imprint of the Palgrave Macmillan division of St. Martin's Press, LLC and of Palgrave Macmillan Ltd. Macmillan® is a registered trademark in the United States, United Kingdom and other countries. Palgrave is a registered trademark in the European Union and other countries.

ISBN-13: 978–1–4039–9816–3 hardback
ISBN-10: 1–4039–9816–7   hardback

This book is printed on paper suitable for recycling and made from fully managed and sustained forest sources.

A catalogue record for this book is available from the British Library.

Library of Congress Cataloging-in-Publication Data
Williams, Glyn, 1939–
    Sustaining language diversity in Europe : evidence from the Euromosaic Project / Glyn Williams.
        p.   cm. – (palgrave studies in minority languages and communities)
    Includes bibliographical references and index.
    ISBN 1–4039–9816–7 (cloth)
    1. Linguistic minorities – Europe.   2. Language planning – Europe.
    3. Multilingualism – Europe.   4. Europe – Languages.   I. Title.   II. Series.

P119.315.W543   2005
306.44'94–dc22

                                                        2005050389

10   9   8   7   6   5   4   3   2   1
14   13   12   11   10   09   08   07   06   05

Printed and bound in Great Britain by
Antony Rowe Ltd, Chippenham and Eastbourne

Contents

U H University of
Hertfordshire

College Lane, Hatfield, Herts. AL10 9AB

Learning and Information Services

For renewal of Standard and One Week Loans,
please visit the web site **http://www.voyager.herts.ac.uk**

This item must be returned or the loan renewed by the due date.
The University reserves the right to recall items from loan at any time.
A fine will be charged for the late return of items.

Figures

Tables

Series Editor's Preface

Worldwide migration and unprecedented economic, political and social integration in Europe present serious challenges to the nature and position of language minorities. Some communities enjoy protective legislation and active support from states through policies that promote and sustain cultural and linguistic diversity; others succumb to global homogenisation and assimilation. At the same time, discourses on diversity and emancipation have produced greater demands for the management of difference.

This book series has been designed to bring together different strands of work on minority languages in regions with immigrant or traditional minorities or with shifting borders. We give prominence to case studies of particular language groups or varieties, focusing on their vitality, status and prospects within and beyond their communities. Considering this insider picture from a broader perspective, the series explores the effectiveness, desirability and viability of worldwide initiatives at various levels of policy and planning to promote cultural and linguistic pluralism. Thus it touches on cross-theme issues of citizenship, social inclusion and exclusion, empowerment and mutual tolerance.

Work in the above areas is drawn together in this series to provide books that are interdisciplinary and international in scope, considering a wide range of minority contexts. Furthermore, by combining single and comparative case studies that provide in-depth analyses of particular aspects of the sociopolitical and cultural contexts in which languages are used, we intend to take significant steps towards the fusing of theoretical and practical discourses on linguistic and cultural heterogeneity.

Gabrielle Hogan-Brun
University of Bristol

Preface

> Democratic culture is defined as an effort to combine unity and diversity, liberty and integration. That is why it has been defined here from the start as the association of common institutional rules and the diversity of interests and cultures.
>
> (Touraine, 1994, 29)

This book is about the capacity of the European Union to sustain its linguistic and cultural diversity as it moves towards a federalism based upon principles of democracy. European liberalism and democracy have always emphasised the importance of a civic virtue constructed out of the full participation of citizens in public discussion and decision making. They should encompass individual liberty, cultural diversity and pluralism.

The intention is to indicate where the ability to produce and reproduce language actually lies by exploring how European minority language groups are incorporated into the different agencies of language production and reproduction across the private and the public sphere. How diversity is given a material importance within current thinking about knowledge and the economy means that diversity is of value to everyone, and not merely to those who speak minority languages.

Between 1992 and 2004 the European Commission contracted a study of European minority language groups (EC, 1996). The data is now publicly accessible and is used to explore the relationship between diversity and democracy within the European Union. The work was undertaken by three institutions:[1] Institut de Sociolingüística Catalana, Generalitat de Cataluña; Centre de Recherche sur le Plurilinguisme, KUB, Brussels; Research Centre Wales, University of Wales, Bangor. This data is the basis for the analysis.

I owe a particular debt to three people, all of whom were an integral part of the Euromosaic project, the project manager Olga Profili, and my colleagues Peter Nelde and Miquel Strubell. Working with them was not simply a learning process, but also an enormous pleasure which has led to an enduring friendship. While I do not wish to hold them responsible for the views presented here, it would be disingenuous of me not to acknowledge their part in developing many of the ideas which the book contains.

---

[1] A fourth participant in the initial part of the work was Henri Giordan of Fédération National des Foyers Ruraux, Paris. Ultimately M. Giordan chose to submit his own report to the European Commission.

Introduction: the Minoritisation of Languages

1 Introduction

Minority language groups are social groups that lack the political, institutional and ideological structures to guarantee the relevance of those languages for the everyday life of their members. The prefix 'minority' pertains to power rather than numerism. Only in recent history have ethnic and national minorities become a 'permanent institution' in the sense that they have become juridical categories under law (Arendt, 1968). An account of that process of minoritisation is a prerequisite for a sociological analysis of minority language groups.

Poststructuralism denies the Cartesian focus on the rational human subject as the determinant of all social activity, of Sociology as the study of associated patterns of human behaviour, and societies as collectivities produced by the intentional action of individuals. Rather, the focus is on how subjects and objects are constituted in and through discourse. Individuals are transformed into subjects in their engagement with discourse. As subjects of discourse they are aligned in particular ways with other subjects, as well as with objects. This sets limits on their ability to act as independent beings. This approach suspects any sociological theory that claims to be the meta-narrative and claims a superior grasp of truth and reality.

Treating the social sciences as practices that systematically form the objects of which they speak, Foucault (1972:49) challenges the epistemology project wherein knowledge is to be seen as the correct representation of an independent reality. This obliges us to consider how the normative changes across different historical conjunctures, and how this involves a destabilisation of objects within discourse – Foucault's concept of event. Ideas that we take for granted are social constructs serving as the basis for the production of a normative order within which objects and subjects exist in specific and particular relationships, one to the other. In his genealogies Foucault sought to delegitimise ideas by showing them to be deeply implicated in multiple relations of force. He displaced the participant's perspective with an externalist perspective from which the claims of reason are not engaged, but are observed at work in the constellation of power in which they function.

These objects and subjects, and the role of the disciplinary meta-discourses in legitimising such objects and subjects are considered, and the meaning of notions in real situations, partly determined by enunciation acts and the interdiscursive, are discovered. How does Linguistics construct language as an object, and speakers as subjects that relate to that object? How does Sociology operate objective concepts that obscure the normativity of its own practices, how does Political Science take the products of its own practices as objective realities (Williams, 1999b)? The social sciences draw upon their founding fathers as the foundations of their discipline – in the case of Sociology, Marx, Durkheim and Weber, and occasionally Comte – but the explicitly political proto-Sociology from which the work of these 'discoverers' derived constructed a set of meanings which would legitimise and justify political goals and ends. We must establish how the entire concept of Europe is structured and conditioned by specific discourse subjects and objects that are socially constructed.

The relationship between objects such as language, nation or community are stabilised within discourse to the extent that they become institutionalised as the taken for granted, or as a form of normativity that goes unquestioned. This involves what is common to all discursive domains – constitution, stabilisation, and the setting of boundaries. Thus, by reference to the political, there are two key elements: stabilisation involves the relationship between the state and the institutions and individuals which are contained within it; while the setting of boundaries pertains to the relationship between the group that is circumscribed and other groups. The issue of constitution can oscillate between these two elements. The setting of boundaries involves differentiating those on the interior of the boundary – 'us' – from the 'them' who are outside, even though they lie within an alternative boundary.

Political activity relies on the presupposition of appropriateness of the relationship between *locuteurs* – who speaks?, and *enonciateur* – which discursively constructed social place does one speak from? The concept of 'place' derives from how the individual becomes the subject of a discourse through the anchorage of time, person and place, and in relation to other subjects. Certain places are opened up for the individual to occupy in becoming the subject of the discourse. Consequently, the deictic relationships largely determine what can and must be said from a given place (Williams, 1999a). A member of society is discursively defined as anyone who can legitimately occupy the place of *enonciateur* in the field of politics, taking the parole as a 'we'. This leads to articulating with the diverse places that s/he occupies, and within which s/he is situated in relationship to the power of the state.

The legitimate member of the political community is the citizen, but the relationship between the citizen and the national dimension is never expressed directly, even if the space that articulates the political and the private sphere already predetermines the relationship between state and culture so that the preconstruction of what is political and what is private inscribes the conditions of legitimacy. It is here that we encounter the state/civil society distinction. It is also the place where we encounter the relationship between the individual and the state, and how this relationship is legitimised through the social construction of the 'nation'.

Stabilisation involves what Seriot (1997) calls *demos*, where the political involves social groups that are constituted around the regulating activity of the state. The discursive structure is one in which the representation leads to formulating the problem in terms of the right of the collective to intervene in the individual or private space – the idea that what is not forbidden is permitted, or the distinction between the moral and the legal. This *demic* dynamic involves a progressive disengagement of the private sphere, by a distinction between morality and law, and by a limitation on the extent to which the private sphere crosses the political.

Ethnos involves how the political constructs a group within the political dimension in contrast to a group of 'strangers'. The focus shifts from internal organisational problems and the content of the political, towards the group itself and to its definition. Where, in the *demic* dynamic, the specific project and legislative practice are at the heart of the organisation of discourse; in the ethnic dynamic it is belonging and identity that dominate. War and conflict reinforce the ethnic dynamic, whereas economy and science prevail for the *demic* dimension.

These two dimensions are not opposed, but are co-present in the construction of contemporary politics, being the analytic notions that words such as 'people' convey. Both represent the field of legitimacy of political discourse. *Demos* presupposes the group without questioning it, while posing the question of the legitimate field of political activity. *Ethnos* presupposes agreement on political activity, and poses the question of who belongs to the group. Whereas *demos* privileges the rights of the soil, natural frontiers and accepting the rules of citizenship; *ethnos* emphasises birth, faithfulness and 'cultural' modes of life – what the *demic* conception relegates to the private sphere – and the impermeability of groups by reference to one another.

It is conceivable that whatever will be said about any part of Europe will be applicable across Europe. There are internal variations, and the relationships between the global and the local gives them their distinctive contexts. The global and local are historical constructions within which tension is manifest. They are constructed as a singular means of constructing human groups in interaction with others, within a dynamic where the relationship to the others guarantees the originality of a specific comparison. The meaning of the notions of 'nation' or 'national minorities' varies considerably, even though the discourses that construct these notions appear 'natural' to different constituencies. Each state locally regulates the relationship between *demos* and *ethnos* as a feature of its normativity and sense of social order, even if the nation constitutes a local compromise between *demos* and *ethnos*. It also relies upon its insertion within a global context. The *demos/ ethnos* relationship constitutes a dialogism, not only by reference to the play that focuses upon the local, where the 'we' of political practice pertains to the *a priori* legitimacy or non-legitimacy of specific actors, but also because these local relations link to the global as a particular actualisation of a common rule of legitimate power. It is this that constitutes the legitimacy of Europe.

Language emerges as a specific object within the discursive formation that links nation and state, involving the institutional structure that can legitimise or de-legitimise discourses and who has the right to speak about specific issues, and the role of language as an object in such 'speaking'. The issue of what is, and is not, a language, is a political issue that constructs speakers and non-speakers as political subjects. It pertains directly to the setting of boundaries. The relationship between language and territory is established in the concept of autochthony, where the spatial boundary also becomes the boundary that distinguishes the 'us' of the language group from the 'them' of 'other speakers'. There may be 'other speakers' within that territory, but autochthony involves laying claim to the territory in the name of the language group. Where the autochthonous language is also the state language there is no tension, the citizen is also the subject that belongs to the language group that lays claim to the autochthonous territory. *Ethnos* and *demos* overlap. Where the state lays claim not only to the territory that defines the spatial extension of the state, but also to the territory within that space which is claimed as the autochthonous of a different language group, the tension is over space and the identity that accompanies it. *Ethnos* and *demos* may be in contradiction.

At particular historic conjunctures the discursive conditions arise that allow certain things to be said, and limit other thing from being said. These conditions involve how objects and subjects are aligned so that certain things can and must be said in order to be the subject of specific discourses. This involves classes of objects with essentialist categorisation, with a discursive and performative order, involving individual *locuteurs* in identity and solidaristic groups. It is the discursive universe that assigns value to these objects. It is necessary to consider the different forms of discourse, for example, the political discourse that assigns value to notions such as 'nation', but only in relation to other objects such as the 'state'. It pertains to a far broader register that we call 'modernity'. For Foucault, history is a study of the relationship between discursive formations, subjects and objects across such wide registers. It is in the specific of the discursive-practical register of politics that we encounter the production of meaning within the various national categorisations of each specific case, making it possible to outline the relationship between the emergence of the modern European state and the relevance of language for this development.

2 Language and the state in pre-modern Europe

In the eighteenth century, that which gave life to the world was held to derive from God, whose Word or *Logos* was the source of creation. The individual possessed free will to obey God voluntarily, and thereby had choice, but reason depended upon *logos*, thought being signified through language. Mind leads to thought, which leads to action as the practice of bringing thought into action. Speech was an ordering of thought in that it was the basis for distinguishing the myriad of things stored in the mind. It was also how the meaning of things was signified. Languages derived from reason, since God willed that humankind, through reason, had the liberty to formulate arbitrary sounds in making their meaning more intelligible. All humankind agreed in their knowledge of things, even if they differed in their naming process.

By the end of the sixteenth century Reformation became part of state politics, and was often the means of linguistic and cultural planning. The translation of the Bible into Irish by Queen Elizabeth I of England was an explicit part of a policy of conquest and destruction, and was contrary to a long native Christian-literary tradition. The Reformation insisted on translating the Bible and imposing so-called 'Biblical' values, destroying most of popular culture over Northern Europe. Among the Catholics, the retention of the Bible in Latin served its purpose for the French, Italians and Spanish, who saw it as the classical form of their own language. For the Celtic Catholics the Bible did not have the same importance as did, for example, the lives of the Saints. Translated into the vernacular, it was claimed that the Bible must constitute the standard form of language, since it was a text that everyone should be able to understand. It was the imposition of a 'standard'.

The concern with grammar derived from the pedagogy of the vernaculars that began to contest the space occupied by Latin (Auroux, 1994). The focus upon formalisation, on establishing form in language, was linked to standardisation, and early European vernacular grammars insisted on the notion of rule through paradigms, which did not exist in classical Greco-Roman grammars. Regularity was imposed on language, leading to reduced variation within any language group. Alphabetisation involved the transcription of language into Latin characters, and assigning letters to the sound of a language. The letter played the role of the nineteenth-century phoneme. Much of the writing reflected variation in speech, but alphabetisation did correspond to standardisation where the effect is reinforced in print.

As the focus of university learning, Latin and logic resulted in an abstract and theoretic discipline associated with argumentation and science. Relating grammar to Latin leads to an abstract economic language lacking distance between the language as object and meta-language, in that meta-language is internal to language. The grammarians or logicians who defined the linguistic units and their relations were not interested in classifying the forms, and A 'mode of interpretation' in which the analysis of order, identity and difference is not a fundamental mode of knowledge transpires from this (Foucault, 1966:17–45). This has far-reaching implications for any sense of nation and of the relation of language to that notion. Interpretation is central. Knowledge of the world consists of interpreting signs and, thereby, of the ability or capacity to recognise signs. One enters knowledge through divination and not through analysis. As a sign, natural language could not be a system of signs. How the word resembled the thing in a clear way had to be reconstituted by interpretation. Language was a text to be deciphered like anything else.

A relationship between the state and nation, and between language and nation was impossible. Language did not represent anything and was not a symbolic or subjective representation of anything. The state, such as it was, was subordinate to a European universalism that related to a sense of classicism, while the university was a feature of that same universalism, even though contributing to the local context.

The Port Royal Grammar of 1660 refutes the claim that language is a mark upon things; above which is a commentary that assigns to those marks a relation to a level below language – the text. Language is constructed as a relationship of representation. Things and words become separated from each other, and seeing becomes different from reading. It raises the question of the relationship between the sign and what is signified, or how humankind uses signs to signify thoughts. The focus shifts to the mind, to conceiving, judging and reasoning. Permanence becomes the fixing of thing by thought (Descartes, 1979:260), and 'mental vision' is directed to discover truth as '. . . the order and disposition of objects' (Descartes, 1970:14). Intuition and discursive reasoning serve as the basis of method. Any grammar analysing the order of language must be prescriptive, it must order correctly. Linguistics becomes a description of how there is an integration of how discourse represents thought in different ways. There is a proximity between grammar and truth. There is also a shift from interpretation to analysis.

Grammar ensures the correct correspondence between words and ideas, and that the sequence of words correctly represents the sequences of thought upon which it is based. This guarantees the fulfilment of the communicative functioning of words. Truth is more than individual opinion, and rests upon general agreement or normative consensus. It is logic and reason that accesses the truth that gives the consensus that is essential for the creation of a collectivity. Truth becomes the moral basis of community and nation, and good language is responsible for good thinking as the essential precondition of any access to truth. The groundwork for the moral basis of Durkheim's *conscience collective* and for Condorcet's drive to educate through French as the language of reason for the greater good of the nation *qua* state was set. These conceptions of language ran parallel with political developments. The political 'we' consisted of 'domestic greatness', where power is exercised by the household (Thevenot and Boltanski, 1987). Royal power depended upon domestic greatness that extended to the economic dependency of the nobility, and the industrial greatness that was subordinate to royal charter. By the beginning of the seventeenth century French absolutism was in place. In England the sixteenth-century triumph of royalty over the Church dismissed the duality of spiritual and worldly power, and the king received a greater degree of sovereignty than any other monarch in Europe. A challenge to the traditional, immanent fundamental of royal power in the form of a 'we' based upon the civic domain of the ancient *cité* emerged. The hierarchical mode of enunciation gives way to symmetrical, egalitarian relations based upon discretion and distance. In the social realm there was a reduction of hierarchy.

The heightened constitution of the collective 'we' of the people led to the nation emerging as an extension of domestic greatness, involving an elaboration of the *Ancien Régime* meaning of race as a family, with descent linking to language, which thereby becomes an object of speculation around the Babel thesis, and the relationship between forms of government and the legitimacy of dialects appears. The enunciative structure places language and nation in parallel – people and use.

Nation is conceived of as people defined by reference to a territory whose unity is guaranteed by government, and whose essential attribute pertains to language. Unity is manifested by 'character'. These five notions – 'people', 'territory', 'government', 'language' and 'character' – pertain to the notion of a protected nation that transcends all local situations. In eighteenth-century France the discursive space of politics is European, whereas the idea of nation is far from salient. The unity of Europe involved a kinship system constructed around the exchange of women within the royal line, uniting the various kingdoms by blood and territoriality. The end of the seventeenth century experienced a passage from an essentially European political space to one that focuses upon a Europe of nations, from a practice of an open sense of nation to a closure of national space.

In the French *Encyclopédie* the idea of nation carries little relevance, being outside of representation (Achard, n.d.). It merits a few lines, compared with more than 30 pages devoted to 'language'. There is an opposition between people and the lords, or between the king and his subjects, linked with an external opposition between the French and 'other peoples'. The French nation pertains to 'character', allowing an internalisation by reference to 'other people', while maintaining subordination to power. While a nation has a 'character' much like 'men' (*sic*), the nation is not 'people', but that which is common to many people. It relates to Rousseau's 'general will', and does not oblige an individual to relate to either a people or a nation since they are different entities at the same level. Neither is there anything that suggests that a nation 'belongs' to a government or state, where the nation is constituted by the submission of territory to the same government. A nation involves many 'peoples'.

'Character' pertains to *ethnos*, and 'government' to *demos*. However, the distinction between *ethnos* and *demos* made in the Greek city cannot prevail since 'the people' pertain to a feudal context. France emerges as a political territory that constitutes a virtual *demos* occupied by plebeians or peasants. The emphasis is upon the political rather than the subjective element of nation. From a political perspective, the origin of enunciation presupposes a location where the opposition between 'people' and king is neutralised, and anticipates a *demic* position. The idea of the 'French nation' is a notion in a syntagmatic relation with the power to which it is submitted, and is only paradigmatic by reference to 'other people'.

Until the eighteenth century cultural differences were treated as being among the natural order of things. Despite the existence of the procedural verb '*civiliser*', it took many decades before the noun 'civilisation' was used in French and English (Febvre, 1930). '*Civiliser*' referred to the pliability of the social environment which could be manipulated by planners, while '*civilité*' was used to denote the judgement associated with a superior life-style manifest in courtesy, good manners, mutual reverence and so on, and linked to specific rules of behaviour.

As content, the verb '*civiliser*' is similar to a longer established verb '*policer*' which connoted 'the idea of preservation of order, elimination of violence (or, rather, the monopolisation of violence in the service of state-supported law), safety of public space, a public sphere closely supervised and kept within well-defined, easy to decipher rules' (Bauman, 1987:91). They involved something that was performed on human relations, while '*civiliser*' and '*civilité*' both referred to reforming the individual in achieving a desirable pattern of human relations – to achieve a peaceful and orderly society through education. Where '*civilité*' referred to that which hid the underlying passions, a set of rules for the select, civilising reached directly to the individual, seeking to suppress the passions – enforcing reason at the expense of emotion. For Diderot instructing or educating a nation was to civilise it, drawing it out of primitiveness and barbarism.

Originally culture referred to gardening, involving selecting the right seed, employing the right techniques, and rooting out the weeds in order to reap a rich annual harvest. The analogy with civilising is obvious, culture becomes a tool in the state's objective of achieving social order and harmony through education in creating cultivated men (*sic*). The language of reason and the associated capacity for clear thought was essential for education.

The triumph of progress, opposing traditional and modern cultures, involves removing the weeds that conform to what was previously regarded as culture, in the sense of a natural order of things that had to be eliminated by a higher order of culture whose aim was to civilise. These two senses of culture lie side by side, being divided by the distinction between emotion and reason.

Analysing people in terms of their 'character' now becomes possible. It involves moving from a visible structure to a taxonomic character, under the assumption of the continuity of nature. This constitutes the *a priori* that governs arguments concerning the problems of genera, the stability of species, and the transmission of characters. The conditions of existence of nations and languages had changed.

It can be claimed that the number of languages within Europe in the seventeenth century was either large or small, depending upon how one conceives of language. Traversing the space within which the masses were located involved a subtle change from one language variety to the other. This is the essence of the concept of Ausbau languages (Kloss, 1967), or of geographical dialect continuum (Chambers and Trudgill, 1980). Those located at either end of a journey across Europe would not understand one another, but neither would they recognise what they spoke as distinctive languages in the way that became common in the nineteenth century.

The world of learning was moving towards the universalism of *universitas*. Voltaire refers to '. . . une républic litteraire établie insensiblement dans l'Europe, malgré les guerres et malgré les religions différentes' (Voltaire, 1879). The closure of the 'us' and 'them' for those involved in the world of learning did not correspond to state boundaries:

> Vous êtes Anglais, mon cher ami, et je suis né en France; mais ceux qui aiment les arts sont tous concitoyens; les honnêtes gens qui pensent ont à peu près les mêmes principes, et ne composent qu'une république.
>
> (Voltaire, *Zaire*, Épitre déclare à Falkener)

What Voltaire refers to is the *'civilité'* of the judgement associated with a superior life-style and the reforming of the individual in order to achieve a desirable pattern of human relations. This is expressed by Balibar:

> L'élite des savants et des écrivains se pensait comme 'la républic des lettres' selon une locution humaniste; marquant une appartenance des lettres à un univers comparable à celui de la chrétiente our de la nation.
>
> (Balibar, 1985:97)

Their republic was defined in terms of the space of government which governed people, with an analogy between the Christian republic and the European Republic where the men (*sic*) of letters were considered as a nation.

3 Modernity

Between 1775 and 1825 the change in the mode of knowing led 'languages' rather than discourse to become the objects of study (Foucault, 1966). Domains of knowledge become independent entities, being seen as structures or organic unities whose elements work together to fulfil functions. Life, labour and language become the new positive regions of knowledge. A new space opens up between philosophy and biology, economics and philology, making possible the appearance of the human sciences, replacing the general domain of representations. Humankind is not the subject of history, but is determined and subject to limits – s/he is subject to the laws of biology, of production and language. Biology, economics, linguistics and philology have disengaged from the classical uniformity of creation.

Positive knowledge is reorganised in terms of domains, objects, concepts and their relation to one another. This includes grammatical systems. The objects of knowledge become a structure; knowledge of them is a knowledge of their causality, their history and their origin. 'Discoveries' such as Sanskrit grammar or the economic function of capital must be seen not as causal factors, but as the results of this new episteme.

A new basis for social order was based upon the fundamentals of reason, governed by natural laws to which reason itself submitted. The people, the nation as a collective humankind constituted a social body that also functioned according to these natural laws. Rational society involved the extension of scientific and technical reason to encompass the government of humankind and the administration of things – society and the state encompassed overlapping interests, and were coterminous. Thereafter, it was inconceivable that anyone could lie outside of either society or the state, which became centrally involved in the construction and conservation of a creative social order conditioned by reason.

The nation in eighteenth-century France was a territory whose unity is guaranteed by government and with an essential attribute of language. The five notions of people, territory, government, language and character, pertain to a nation that transcends all local situations. The discursive space of politics remains essentially European, and the idea of nation is not salient. The shift in modernity focused upon the relationship between political participation and citizenship, linking the masses to the space of power.

In the *Encyclopédie* the notion of 'nation' involves a juxtaposition of an intentional definition that carries the clause 'obey the same government' with an extensional list of cases Achard (n.d.). There is an analogous extensional list of 'languages', together with reference to certain nations not being united by reference to government, but still achieving legitimacy.

The issue of nation becomes a local issue. Nonetheless, the stable designation is 'French' or 'British', so that whether or not there is a one-to-one relationship between nation and that stable designation, the nation cannot exist outside of it.

The new Enlightenment 'view' of politics involved transferring allegiance as subject to the king who held divine right, to being a citizen of a state governed in the name of the people. The discourse on the people and the nation intervenes in sociopolitical practice – the 'people' assume power and the definitions of nation shift to an intellectual condition at the point where the effective legitimacy of the political apparatus is confronted. The 'people' becomes the object by reference to submitting to the same government, and involves knowing who would govern in the name of the people, how the people see government across their *porte-parole*, and how these are legitimated. A debate over language ensues, one side exaggerating diversity and the other minimising it. One side deploys the discourse of evolutionism and universalism by reference to language – *patois* are different not because they are 'strange', but because they are retarded, and bear no kinship by reference to French; whereas the other side merely focuses upon difference. Both view access to politics as the basis of citizenship, language not being the essence of the people. People should accede to French since, as citizens, they already have that right. French becomes the language of reason in that its form leads to clarity, and its syntactic form betrays a direct relationship to the 'natural' order. Distinctions emerge between logic and passion, between reason and emotion, between languages of reason and the languages of emotion. The latter are languages which name the objects which strike the senses, whereas the former are languages in which one first of all names the subject, then the verb and finally the object, as in French syntax. There are languages that follow the order of sensation, their syntax being corrupt, and languages that respect the logical order:

> Le français, par un privilège unique, est sul reste fidèle à l'ordre direct . . . la syntaxe française est incorruptible. C'est de la que résulte cette admirable clarté, base éternelle de notre langue. Ce qui n'est pas clair n'est pas français.
>
> (Quoted in Calvet, 1987:74)

It is only when this notion of a logical order is linked to the people writ large that it becomes a basis for articulation with 'people', 'nation' and 'character' in a politics of language. In the nineteenth century the nature of languages became embroiled with a social science based upon the centrality of superiority and inferiority through the doctrine of evolution. Christianity was the civilising force that tamed the emotions in favour of reason, and conversion to the languages of reason was an essential part of that process. Normativity is the norm of the political order which, when expressed in terms of language, leads to polarising those subjects marked as normal by reference to the language of reason, against the deviants signified by reference to their possession of non-state language, who are, as a consequence, labelled as 'ethnic'. The overlap between state and society closes the space within which the difference is established.

Ethnos, involving how the political constructs a group in contrast to a group of 'strangers', does not explicitly pertain to the political dimension. Neither does it involve the construction of the 'us' against 'strangers', but involves dividing that orthodox or normative 'us' in such a way that it constructs part of the 'us' as strange or deviant, if not as 'strangers'. The concept of 'stranger' confirms the normative, and the political 'we' is consolidated. It leads to a suspicion of the internal deviant. An overlap is created in which the 'us' is exclusive for one group as the normative which defines inclusion. The relevant subject position is unitary, leading to a single, exclusive identity. For the other group, one subject position pertains to the same normativity of the defining group, and the other to the deviance of the ethnic. Thus a dual identity, which can be ambiguous, exists for the subject. These subject positions are linked to the space through the overlap between the defining criterion of the subject – language and the territory related to the language – autochthony. This is achieved by strictly defining the cultural that links with the faithfulness that is required by the state as normative. The normative group is simultaneously defined by reference to language, culture and reason. In a sense *ethnos* and *demos* overlap, since it is the same regulating activity of the state that constructs the language group as the social group. This is achieved by referring to the defining criterion of normativity by reference to both the moral and the legal domain, by appealing to the link between science, or more specifically, linguistic science, and reason within the context of a space that can no longer be either individual or private space, since it pertains to everyone.

Through legislation, the state could eliminate any interference to progress, making progress inseparable from the polity. The state was the custodian of the search for perfection through progress. Some languages were constructed as the languages of reason whereas others, somehow, lay outside of reason (Calvet, 1974). State languages were deployed in pursuing 'modern' activities demanding the essence of reason – administration, education, science. The other languages could be deployed for the emotive context of the 'traditional'. This language planning made language use the prerogative of the state.

The relationship between 'modern' and 'tradition' was one of antagonism, with 'tradition' being seen as the 'Other' of the modern. This was the central thrust of a political antagonism, and it was only towards the end of the eighteenth century that it was divested of its political essence, through the extension of the principles of science to accommodate society, giving birth to the proto-sociology of Saint Simon, Comte and Condorcet. 'Tradition' was denigrated by placing it in terms of the converse of reason – in the world of uncontrolled emotion, involving the raw materials of human nature which reason was striving to control.

Society was conceived of as an order, with reason as the instrument of creative order. This has been the cornerstone of the social sciences, which have retained the inherent biases of that political statement which aimed at displacing 'tradition' in the legitimation of the modern state. Ethnicity, defined in the social sciences as 'part society and part culture', involves the subjective elements of identity, community and so on rather than the parameters of the social and the rational. Ethnicity is defined by default, by its difference or deviance from the normative which is society.

The ascendancy of the modern involved the equation of progress and development as 'modernisation'. Reason was reified as the agent of all development, leading to a perfect society vested with the good life for all worthy citizens. The divine was replaced by the political as the expression of the sacred in social life. Society became the field of social conflict between past and future, interest and tradition, public and private life.

The inevitability of progress related to the evolutionary argument that claimed that reason led to the movement of society towards perfection. Evolutionism constituted the 'discovery' of the laws of progress. Darwin claimed that a genealogical arrangement of race would equate with a classification of the different languages of the world. He also claimed that the splitting of the proto-language into different languages was the consequence of the civilising force of 'co-descended races'. For Darwin the Indo-European philologists were practising the paradigm of scientific method, with historical comparison equating to genealogy. Similarly, Saussure emphasised the contribution of the neo-grammarians whose focus upon normativity is deterministic. Cartesian rationalism transforms natural selection into rational selection. The status of 'language' was reserved to those forms of speech that had a corpus of rules similar to those relevant to Latin, distinguishable from 'savage languages devoid of rules', or 'imperfect languages'.

The fundamental principle of modernism, the separation of language and thought, led to a suspicion of language. If thought was the basis of reason and if language was the transmitter of thought, a match between thought, reason and language was essential. A weakness in one betrayed a weakness in the others. It led to a focus on political evolution, being the basis of the claim that non-civilised societies were incapable of developing polities and, conversely, that those linked with the languages that stood outside of reason, the stateless languages, constituted a threat to the state. Social order derived from a general will that was reflected in a social contract, the basis of the nation based on reason. 'Modern' state languages became 'languages of development', with the notion of 'language' being politically signified (Achard, 1982a:419). Linked to the state and to commerce, they become objects engaged in development, preventing the use of other languages for administrative purposes.

The ideal conception of language is attained in its link to law, with law crossing the symbolic unity of the language, rather than law in terms of the state's legislature. In renouncing all distinction between human and divine law, the modernist state substituted absolutism, with its political duality, by the monist totalitarianism of one law for all. There is no place for social organisation, nor for any incompatibility of points of view, in the space between the individual and the state–nation–society relationship. Linguistic diversity becomes the obstacle to development. This totalitarian construction of language as the basis of unity overlaps with the conception of the economy as a market that has a similar unifying force.

The discourse on normative and ethnic in French discourse evidently contrasts with the discourse of Germanicism. The French conception of nation, based upon free choice and upon the revolutionary affirmation of national sovereignty against royalty, contrasts with the conception of nation as a community of destiny. Herder's conception of reason and religion were far removed from those of Rousseau or Voltaire. The relationship between language and people are evident. As early as 1767 he speaks of a 'culture of the language', a perspective assumed in the twentieth century by the Prague Linguistic Circle. His views are heavily influenced by French intellectualism. He elaborated his argument from an enunciative displacement where he placed Germany as the prototypic nation, at a time when Germany was not united through governmental politics (Achard, n.d.). Unlike the French case, linguistic unification preceded the construction of the state. In order to place the people at the centre of social and political functions he did not follow the French example in referring to *the* political power *of* the people simply by substituting the nation for the king. He developed a theory of the artificiality of the political, a declaration of the naturalness of people, and a naturalist and anti-political theory of their existence. Within this meta-discourse the notion of nation-state does not appear, except as an intermediary in the drive for a *'fin du politique'* based on a concept of general will which lacked Rousseau's contractual element, while involving a moral, communal state which spontaneously led to an organic agreement. Language is the intentional criterion of people at the centre of the argument, and involves a familial rather than a contractual unity, a unity that ultimately rests on the land that is preconstructed as an essential criterion. The individual is a crucial notion, but within the context of humanity rather than by reference to *Volk*.

Imposing state structure on this conception means there is no deviation from the normative. The normative is defined as ethnic and since the normativity of the state, and thereby of society, is a subcategory of the ethnic space, there are profound implications for *ethnos* and *demos*, as well as for the deictic and for subject positioning. The 'us' of state normativity is contrasted with the 'them' of other similar normativities, some of which may be part of the inclusive 'us' of the ethnic or *volk*. Thus the dual identities are normative in two senses – by reference to state normativity and by reference to the supra-state ethnicity. The associated subjects overlap so that identities are not in conflict as in the French model. Both identities are normative, and no sense of denigration associated with deviation from the normative is constructed. It is a pluralist view of politics.

Herder condemns expansionism, colonisation and conquest, making the issue of closure very clear. The problem is not seen at the level of a closure of the political, where the political itself appears as a global mechanical device that disappears, but only to permit the organic reality of nations to express itself. The consequence of the privileging of the concept of *volk* is that unity transcends the eventual political frontiers and their overlap with societies. The relationship between the state, the nation, the people and language is quite distinctive.

The French and German constructions of nation as an object are opposed, involving different conceptions of society. The French construction equates nation and state, arguing that statehood assumes rationality, promoting a single language of reason to serve the state in the name of the people who must all have access to this single language of reason. The normative consensus pertains to the state and the single society that it contains. Other languages and what they represent are relegated to the rubbish heap of deviance from the norm, where they become labelled as *patois* or ethnic, concepts that rest on an acknowledgement of cultural deviation from the norm. Since the norm pertains to reason, cultural deviation pertains to a domain outside of reason, to the realm of nature and the emotive, somehow being 'not quite civilised'.

The German construction acknowledges a similar link between language and reason, but claims that all languages have the capacity to develop reason. Furthermore, each language equates with a nation, regardless of the political space that it occupies. That is, the construction of space incorporates the duality of nation and state as separate objects. Reason and the cultural are not distinct, and nation conforms with ethnicity. Stateless nations occupy a space within states. Normativity pertains to the nation, and even though nations are ranked in an evolutionary continuum, it remains possible for all nations to develop their character in the direction of reason, and even to lose that character and regain it once more.

These developments had a long history, involving the closure of space in relation to common languages long prior to the existence of the modern nation-state (Baggioni, 1997). In the sixteenth century attempts to promote the various vernaculars against Latin led to an argument in favour of the equality of all languages, even if proximity to the original language did carry its influence. By the eighteenth century the point of closure was Europe, and the relevance of French as the universal language of Europe

(Calvet, 1987:70–3). A new stabilised position emerged in which the people gained a new space of legitimacy across Europe, but with the political European space fractioning into potentially separate units.

4 Meta-discourse

The preceding maintains that the social sciences constitute meta-discourses which played a role in the legitimation of discourse on uniformity and state construction. Where sociology was conceived of as an explicit political science in the eighteenth century, during the following century it developed its autonomy from the political, an autonomy that is questioned by reference to all the social sciences. If language is merely an object constructed in and through discourse, then it is essential to consider how that object is constructed, demanding a focus upon the emergence of the metaphysics of its construction, and of the relevance of grammar and lexicography for meta-linguistics. Grammatisation is the process that leads to describing and using a language based upon the technologies that are the basis of meta-linguistic knowledge – the grammar and the dictionary (Auroux, 1994). It is never based on the totality of language, but rather on selected representation. It has independence *vis à vis* theory in that it rests on language before there is a meta-language.

Formalisation involves imposing form on language, and is linked to standardisation. The question involves the extent to which such a process discovers a pre-exisiting form in language, or merely imposes such a form through its practice. Is it the form that emerges, capable of accommodating variation, or is it merely a technology that allows control over language, converting speech into a political object? Grammar is not a simple description of natural language. Auroux (1994) maintains that while it constitutes a normative order, spoken language does not have rules. This does not refer to languages perhaps not having known rules, and that establishing such rules involves passing from the epi-linguistic to the meta-linguistic, but that the language spoken prior to grammatisation had far less unity than thereafter. Within a linguistic space devoid of technological intervention, the freedom of variation is considerable, and dialectical discontinuities are evident.

We think that variation is secondary, that variation is a deviation from some pre-established norm, implying that some primitive and homogeneous entity existed, and that variation derived from this entity. The idea of languages as entities which we consider homogeneous, everywhere identical to themselves, independent of space, circumstances and speaker, is a consequence of the appearance of grammatisation. It is this that lies behind the tendency for the Comparativists to conceive of an original language that was fragmented. Schleicher's work on proto-languages is a case in point.

At the beginning of the nineteenth century language becomes a thing with its own form, time and laws, not the exemplar of a general domain of representation. Simultaneously, representation changes in becoming what determines humankind, while eluding consciousness. The human sciences seek to present language and representation as a general relation, inferring the unconscious from the fact of representation – Durkheim's social facts, Marx's account of ideology, Saussure's account of language and so on. The unknown of representation can now be revealed by the human sciences.

The form of the word's existence is no longer given in its representative and analytic functions, but is determined by something beyond representation. Different languages are characterised by reference to grammatical principles that are not reducible to discursive means, to signification; each language has an autonomous grammatical space. Languages can now be compared without reference to signification, becoming objects that are analysed according to an internal structure.

The dictionary and the grammar remain the pillars of meta-linguistic knowledge (Auroux, 1994:12). These linguistic tools lie outside of the speaking subject and modify the space of communication by stabilisation and standardisation of the means of expression: the basis for establishing a normative communicational structure, controlled by sources beyond the reach of the public to which they pertain. It contributes to the homogenisation of the relationship between language and space.

General grammar as the science of what was common to all languages produced the science of the laws of language to which all languages were submitted. Kantian idealism led to an *a priori* deduction of grammatical categories, leading to most general grammars being supported on the edifice of the written language, and on the two classical languages (Kant, 1946). Defending universality and the assertion that some categories exist identically in all languages inevitably led to creating a language tree, so that the categories susceptible to being optional in the different languages cannot branch into any of the universals.

Applying the genealogical system of kinship to language led to a networking of languages on the basis of a common Latin origin of grammars. The general grammar and the genealogy of language is a response to the problem of relationships. In both cases the network is transformed into a tree as a consequence of a commonality of roots, of the general category of the 'mother language'. Furthermore, each node is accessible from each one of the others. Language becomes explicitly political, and the argument of what is and what is not a language within the general typological taxonomy of Indo-Europeanism relates to the emerging political taxonomy of Europe. Grammar and standardisation were powerful tools that allowed the boundaries of languages to coincide with the territorial boundaries of states.

Indo-Europeanism was founded upon Eurocentrism. Greek heritage predisposed Europe to rationality, the motor of progress, and nineteenth-century Romanticism inspired 'Hellenomania', resulting in linguistic 'creativity'. While up to half of the Greek language derived from the Egyptian and Phoenician languages, a mysterious 'Proto-Aryan' language was created to protect the 'Aryan purity' of Ancient Greece. Classifying languages derived from the biological sciences, implying that the unique character of 'peoples' bore a relationship to the characteristics of their languages. Renan made claims about the 'monstrous and backward' character of Semitic languages that contrasted with the 'perfection' of European languages, claiming that the distinction was 'scientifically established'.

Usage is the final arbitrator of the rules of language. The nineteenth-century practice of Linguistics, in which use is observed and rules developed from normative practice in establishing the form and boundaries of languages, is put in place. The perfect state was premised upon a single language, the language of reason (Baggioni, 1997). What was to be defined as a language, or was rejected from such a definition, was based upon political normativity. The Indo-European project of establishing a kinship of languages across Europe that paralleled the kinship of royalty, was also fuelled by the need to encompass the political needs of sustaining new state boundaries premised on the relationship between people, language, nation and state. Language was firmly involved in governmentality.

Indo-Europeanism led to a taxonomy of reified state languages as related objects on the basis of a kinship analogy. This work relies upon historical linguistics or philology and the comparative method. Three points have to be made both by reference to Germanism and Indo-Europeanism:

1 how there is an explicit focus upon the relationship between language and space as territory based upon a strong kinship analogy;
2 how the argument inevitably leads to a conception of what is and what is not a Language,
3 how there is a sense of Eurocentrism associated with the closure of relationship between languages, people and states, and the boundaries of 'the family'.

The link between Indo-Europeanism and Eurocentrism established a kinship of language while retaining the autonomy of state languages. Linguistic science was serving the political order of the time, while simultaneously claiming to be a new discipline premised upon principles of objectivity and political neutrality. Linguistics became the basis of evaluating the correctness of language *vis à vis* the standard as norm. This norm defined inclusion not merely within the state to which that language pertained, but also by reference to the reason that defined such inclusion. Linguistics, like Sociology, speaks from the place of the state, and serves as its legitimising force. In so doing it defines the legitimation of what is and what is not language.

Language does not represent thought, but a subject or a nation. This leads to analysing linguistic roots, and to a kinship of languages. A language is bound to other languages by reason of the general function of representation; a language is like or unlike other languages in its means of representation. The work of Grimm and Bopp leads to the historical comparison in the Indo-European 'family' of languages. Here language no longer represents thought by analysing it; it becomes thought, determining the expressive possibilities of thought through the structure of sound in history. Nations and history express themselves in language, at the point where the act of the speaking subjects is determined.

Thereafter standardisation became political, with the goal of promoting a standard form that conformed with the goal of promoting reason and correct thinking, deriving from an exposure to correct language. Languages which were not languages of reason were minoritised. They hindered correct thinking and the development of reason because they pertained to 'the sensuous and the unrefined in the state of nature' (Herder, 1966:139), and therefore had to be outlawed: 'the more primordial a language is, the less grammar must there be in it, and the oldest language is no more than the aforementioned dictionary of nature' (ibid:159)

The kinship analogy legitimates the concept of 'Europe', and the independence of the new nation-states as the parts of a greater whole. It prioritises European unity, while conceding autonomy to its constituent parts. It establishes links of blood through the language of kinship in establishing the kinship of language that consolidates the European family unit. This unit is constituted of the languages of reason, the state languages, together with a few residual anomalies. The exclusivity of reason and rationality asserts the superiority of Eurocentrism, establishing the boundary between Europe and the rest of the world. It replaced the historic distinction between Christian Europe and Infidel externality with the difference between languages of reason and those that stood outside of reason. It was the basis for a hierarchical evaluation of culture, and established a 'connection between languages and the mental capacity of nations' (ibid:217). Comparative grammar demonstrated that the Germanic languages had the same level of paternity, and thereby of dignity, as the classical languages – Greek and Latin, the source of reason, and the repository of Western cultural heritage.

Language becomes explicitly political, linked to the idea of popular sovereignty and the emerging emphasis upon democracy, with popular sovereignty pertaining to the sovereignty of nation-states, even if it had to be constructed out of diversity. It involved the will of people, defined by language and culture. The boundaries between the languages as objects are pre-constructed, with the analogous basis for description – kinship and territory – assuming such boundaries. Kinship units are separated by different patterns of residence that create the distinctiveness of sub-families, whereas within each kinship unit there are individual differences. It is all defined around the boundary between families rather than within families. It is no coincidence that these families, and thereby languages, tend to overlap with the emerging European states. It could have been possible to claim that there were only three languages in Europe, or indeed any number, but that would have required a different conception of the boundary that both separated and confirmed language as an object.

In the relationship between nation and state, an artificial, authoritative entity – the state, governs in the name of 'the people', giving rise to the need to foster the consent of the people thus to be governed. If *ethnos* and *demos* overlap and are jointly implicated in the concept of 'people', the social groups constituted around the regulating activity of the state become the same groups that unite in contrast to the outsider or 'stranger'. The nation is then either the basis for creating unanimity, or it is a manifestation of that unanimity. If an overlap between language and nation *qua* people can be demonstrated, there are grounds for appealing to that overlap as the basis for a consent constructed out of a common orientation based upon similarity. An overlapping boundary between people, nation and state must be created, and the definition of what is and is not a language is a key feature of that boundary construction, in that it is a ready means for establishing the 'us' and 'them'. When a common identity is constructed around a 'we' that derives from a conception of language that distinguishes this 'we' from a 'they' that is similarly based upon language, it becomes the basis for a political identity. Indo-Europeanism is closely linked to state construction in Europe because of the particular historical conjuncture at which they both occur. What is and is not a language is a political rather than a linguistic question.

Language became the marker of boundaries between one state and another, and between one society and another. The entire edifice of the social sciences, founded upon the idea of society, was imbued with a statist bias which has coloured the subsequent study of society. Social groups were always identified by reference to the state that included them, either as normative entities as in the case of social classes or as deviant elements as in the case of ethnic groups, which were characterised by the features that differentiated them from the normative, while still insisting upon their inclusion within society.

Linguistics sought to remove itself from the explicit political concerns of the Comparativists and neo-grammarians by claiming a concern with the elements of language and a focus upon syntax. However, the object at the root of contemporary Linguistics was constructed long ago. The boundaries between the different objects that allow claims for universalism were constructed as political entities, and were manipulated through standardisation. The political goal was to create a specific form of relationship between this object and the subjects to which it pertains. It persisted in linguistic practice along with concern for the relationship between standardisation and normativity. Chomsky's logico-formalism relies upon the competence of the rational human subject as speaker who selects what reflects a norm or sustains a particular model of competence from among a series of possibilities.

It is hardly surprising that both the political process and the meta-discourses of the disciplines that support it have created certain languages as minority languages. As such, these objects are either outside of the normative order of the state, or are marginal to that order. This relates to the parallel construction of the speakers of these languages as deviants, who have been historically regarded as either dangerous or irrelevant. The arguments used to support these constructions may appear absurd to us now, but their effect remains far reaching.

1
Conceptualisation, Data and Method

SECTION I CONCEPTUALISATION

1 Introduction

Minority languages are constructed as non-normative objects that lie outside of the normative context of the state. The language-object relates to an epilinguistic activity that correlates historically with the emergence of the modern state. During the past two centuries, the state was premised upon universalist principles involving linguistic uniformity, so that the agencies and institutions responsible for the reproduction of most language groups remain unquestioned.[1] A consideration of the ability of different European minority language groups to reproduce themselves must make institutional agencies explicit within an explanatory framework.

Sociology and Linguistics are meta-discourses rather than knowledges that lead to truth or reality. Both incorporate the interests of the state in constructing their theories and concepts, and speak from the place of the state in elaborating societal subjects and objects. Concepts were based upon the legitimacy of a normative order that left little room for deviation, and relied upon a homogenous conception of the relationship between citizens, culture and language. Both were part of the supporting meta-discourse that legitimated non-normative language groups as deviant and pejorative. Sociology was also the mainstay of a particular conception of liberal democracy, becoming the ideological means of incorporating the individual in the consent that sustained the legitimacy of the state. The social science disciplines assumed radical political perspective, but failed to develop such a radicalism without speaking from the place of the state.

Orthodox sociology developed the methodological individualism of liberal theory. The social is a stable element relevant to all human populations, where the general will is the sum of individual opinion. Each individual rationally seeks her own individual interest, and the general will becomes the consequence of that which allows collective good to be maximised

22

through serving the advantage of the individual. All interventions of inter-mediary bodies isolated from this ideal, and the local effects which clarify the 'ideology' – conceived of as the adhesion of false or doubtful ideas – can simultaneously be viewed as part of this intermediary body. The question is one of theorising global society in terms of the normative model which conditions its effective functioning, and dysfunctions become artificialities. The social sciences, as practices, systematically form the objects of which they speak (Foucault, 1972:49).

It is now common currency to regard this fundamental philosophy as wrong. The shift accommodates a broader conception of equal treatment, opening the space for a re-evaluation of the value of diversity. However, the apparatus continues to operate as the effects of a discourse premised upon these ideas. To that extent the philosophy is not 'wrong'. We can still main-tain that it is not 'right', but how can we give an account of European minority language groups if we maintain that such an account can be no more than discursively constituted? How can it lay claim to any superior sense of truth or reality if we deny the link between the social sciences and such truth and reality? If the two main frameworks which account for the nature of language in society lack their claimed interpretive scientific status, what can replace them in describing and accounting for the nature of lan-guage in society?

The answer lies partly in considering how minority language groups can reproduce themselves. The language-object and the associated subjects must be constituted in particular ways within the order of discourse. The state plays a central role in this respect, and the different European states have been subject to different conditions by reference to the production and reproduction of the minority language groups within their territory. If a model of how languages in general are reproduced is available, then we can elaborate the extent to which these circumstances pertain to the various minority language groups. We can establish how the minority languages are constructed as objects within the discourses on the social forces relevant for language production, and the implication of such construction for the speaking subjects which constitute the minority language group. This does not refute the independent existence of subjects and objects, but claims that they are brought into play not through the rational action of human behav-iour, but by the relationship between the individual and the discourse into which s/he is interpolated (Williams, 1999a). Different discursive formations construct different meanings for the same objects, and meaning is always a contested field.

Different discourses convey different statuses through the way they relate to institutional settings that convey different degrees of power. The official discourse, including discourses on social policy and public management, carries institutional legitimisation, assuming a position of dominance. It extends across all of the areas which will be discussed in the following chapters. It organises all the objects of the discourse, not merely language. The analytical model does not seek to encounter a 'truth', but merely serves as a template against which the circumstances of each language group can be compared. It can legitimately be claimed that the model of the official discourse and its effect upon social and economic process presented below is far too general, or that it rests on a conception of the state as intervening in the planned economy rather than emphasising the market economy, and, in this respect, it is not 'up to date'. In the democratic, interventionist model which informs this analytic model, the market and the state are distinguishable in the sense that the state involves the organisation of economic practice and the distribution of profit as sociopolitical practice within the context of liberalism. It can be argued that the process of globalisation, the emergence of the Information Society and the evidence of the New Economy renders the model obsolete. However, the concern is with the discourses which have shaped the current situation.

While there has been an increasing tendency for the modern state to appropriate private space into its domain, culminating in the welfare state and the predominance of public sector employment, minority language groups have been excluded from the discourse on public policy, administration and the economy. Regardless of the language of the home or the community, the state insures that every citizen masters the state language. Yet language groups whose languages are restricted to the private sphere are unable to reproduce themselves. This observation informs the model of language production and reproduction.

This relationship between the state and public order on the one hand, and social reproduction on the other, informs how the various institutional structures of society play a role in language production and reproduction (Williams and Roberts, 1982). The discourse which sustains the normative order incorporates the centrality of social institutions involved in highly formal planning orientations. Language plays a central role in this structure. The normative interpolates individuals as subjects which operate within the context of the institutions. The stabilisation of these discourses is fragmentary, but is sufficient to accommodate both social change and continuity within the overall process of social reproduction. While the state effectively regulates the economy, education, social administration and other functions which influence the lives of individuals, it constitutes the social groups through the effects of discourse. It is the progress of the *demic* to the point where it is virtually all inclusive. It is reinforced and sustained by the meta-discourse of the social sciences. The private sector can contest the *demic* by constituting *ethnos* in rejecting how the political constructs the 'us'/'them' opposition. Traces of prior discourses constitute subjects and objects which influence meaning systems that relate to contemporary discourse. The symbolic nature of language is important in this respect, since it conditions difference, and also highlights the 'other' of the 'us'/'them' relationship. The struggle over normativity is an essential feature of minority existence.

The relationship between *ethnos* and *demos* involves different discursive formations which speak from different places, constructing subjects and objects in different ways. State discourse constructs *ethnos* as all inclusive, the 'us' pertaining to every citizen, not one of whom can lie outside of this subject position, and whose border overlaps with the state's territorial border. The same is true of communities, the sum of which, within the state discourse, constitutes the state. In contrast, the minority language group-will speaks from a place which is self-ascriptive, in that it speaks in the name of the entire group. It contests the all-inclusive ascription of the state discourse by laying claim to an 'us' which is internal to the state, and which contrasts with the 'them' which is also internal to the state, but which is opposed to the 'us' of the language group. This may or may not result in polarisation, since the possibility of an overlap of the two forms of 'us' is possible. This largely depends upon the space that the discourse of democracy allocates to accommodating plurality and diversity. There is a strong dialogical polarity, where the author of the same concrete referent – the 'people' – involves two modes of apprehension, involving the oppositions 'people/government' and 'people/stranger', as unrecognised. The normative order constructs 'the people' in the same way, as the same subject, whereas the discourse of the minority language group constructs them as different subjects. The mode of understanding is discursively heterogeneous, and the resultant polarity involves 'bifurcation' where the symbolic unity of the people, which is assumed in the subjacent notion of 'nation', may or may not overlap with the state. Where this involves labour-market segmentation there can be considerable conflict. The boundary between 'us' and 'them' pertains to language within a state which constructs all of the 'people' as uniform.

A reflexive position whereby we understand how language groups have been constituted as minority groups, and how the associated practices have become institutionalised, is required. We must place the language groups that are addressed in the context that constructs them, involving how modernist society is constituted. The goal is to investigate the empirical nature of the constitution of minority language groups within the society in which they are located. Such state societies involve describable institutional structures – education, the family and so on. The first task is to evaluate the extent to which minority language groups have been accommodated into these structures, or have been eliminated from them, by different state discourses. That is, to consider the nature and extent of the space that opens up for minority language groups within modernist Europe. We then consider the implications for language use as a measure of institutionalised language behaviour. This obliges a discussion of society by reference to the orthodox parameters of modernism, for it is here that we witness both how society is constituted and how it operates within the modern state. No claim is made about the superiority of this account over any other of how minority language groups are produced and reproduced. It is one way of ordering ideas about how modernity operates by reference to society. As a sociological account it is open to the critique outlined above.

Sociologists often assume that social groups exist outside of discourses, as things that are already there to be studied. Yet Marx claimed that capitalism organised the relationship of production so that the individuals involved in these relations occupied similar places that opened up for them to move into (Tucker, 1972:146–200), and this similarity of positions gave the commonality of the social group. In structural terms the individual had no choice other than to be assigned to the class position, but the subjective relationship was the consequence of assuming or rejecting that place. Language groups are constituted in the same way. The space opens up for the individual to either take in charge by responding positively, or to reject by not responding. These subject positions, however, are not separate from other subject positions and objects within the same discourse. Thus the subject position of the minority language speaker clearly relates to the language as an object, but it may also relate to gender or social class and the associated multiple identities. The individual evaluates whether or not 'taking in charge' the relevant subject place is desirable. Within stable discursive contexts this happens without reflection, and the context is institutionalised as common sense or the taken for granted.

The model involves three related processes. First, the legitimation of language groups involves the extent to which language and the associated group is incorporated into the state's discourse on social policy, or the extent to which the minority language group is incorporated into the democratic process as a language group. This would involve a democratic pluralism that opens the space for minority language groups to be constructed as normative. The extent of this development is, of course, limited in that language planning (LP) marks the language group as deviant, even if it is acceptable.

The structures which exist to allow a language group to be reproduced partly derive from policy in that it involves the willingness of the state to make the necessary resources available. It also involves civil society and the state, since some of the agencies of language production and reproduction exist in civil society. Unless these agencies of language production and reproduction can operate effectively, the language group is unlikely to survive. Here we refer to the family, the community, the economic order, education and the media. Each pertains to a discursive formation which constitutes a particular meaning of 'language'.

The extent to which language use is institutionalised within the society to which the language group pertains involves language use as social practice. The rules of formation for the language object involve what Foucault

(1972:45) calls the space which articulates 'institutions, economic and social processes, behavioural patterns, systems of norms, techniques. Types of classification, modes of characterisation.' It involves Foucault's concept of 'orders of discourse', or the sum of discursive practices within any society, and the relationship between them. The interdiscourse which spans the structures, integrate the different discursive formations associated with each structure. While each discursive formation plays a role in constituting the language object within each of the different structures or domains, institutionalisation refers to the relationship between the interdiscursive and language use as social practice.

These three processes provide an indication of prevailing diversity in Europe. They indicate the nature of the democratic process, and the associated structures which exist across the respective states. For linguistic diversity to prevail within democracy, the language object and the associated subjects must be constructed in particular ways within the order of discourse. In the subsequent chapters I construct a picture of the relevance of each of these processes for the different European minority language groups.

2 The production and reproduction of minority language groups

What follows is not a quest for 'truth', but an attempt to develop a model of how the orthodox discourse of the state involves a specific understanding of society, the economy and social policy. It is a model that accommodates significant variation and exists at a high level of generalisation. It also considers the relationship between the state and civil society.

The analytic model draws heavily on the biological analogy of social and cultural reproduction, common to the meta-discourse of Economics, and involving a metaphor with the social body as a 'global society' having a formal structure that implicates the state as a social apparatus which is self-evident in the discourse (Achard, 1982b). This flows over into discourse on education and on society in general. There is a direct link between the social policy and economic management of the official discourse and the disciplines of Economics and Sociology in that the meta-discourses of the two disciplines condition the application of public management. Sociological theory is metaphorical, deploying an ontology of collective subjectivism, with 'society' being constructed as a living, conscious being. Its organicism combines materialism and idealism, society being portrayed as a collective organism capable of displaying collective consciousness. It also emphasises an evolutionism that is held to be common to all life. The epistemological structures of Sociology and Economics have been at the heart of the state's legitimation of social policy. However, within the discourse of Economics, the 'economy' involves a continuous process of economic restructuring, and the structure and dynamics of labour-market organisation. The same claim is made of conceptions of social change. This link between the state and society involves treating language groups as social groups, without reifying language and disassociating language from social action.[2]

The focus involves how a social group is reproduced or not reproduced, and how social change influences language groups as social groups, something that is often taken for granted by reference to language. However, treating minority language groups as non-normative within the relevant discourse means this is not possible, since the language group changes demographically. The implicit is made explicit. Our concern is with the dynamics of the relationship between production, reproduction and non-reproduction processes, which may well coexist by reference to the same language group. This is schematically represented in Figure 1.1.

This model allows us to consider the relevance of different agencies for production and reproduction. These are institutions conditioned by the function that is assigned them by the modern episteme. Some of them are unique to one process rather than the other, whereas other agencies serve both processes. Despite the universal competence of nuclear family members, it may be that the family plays no role in reproduction, but that other agencies such as education are capable of ensuring that reproduction takes place. These processes also relate to the more general processes of social and cultural reproduction. This is clear if we recognise that a language group is only one among several social groups which overlap in relation to membership. Each social group has the capacity to serve as the basis of social identity, individuals being interpolated as subjects of the various social groups, either as individual or as overlapping components. Culture is the means whereby meaning is a structured, symbolic constitution relying upon such structuring. It has relevance for the reflexive process associated with language use.

This links with economic restructuring and economic change, including globalisation. Between this higher order process that determines social change and the local community is the policy framework. This involves a much broader context than that of LP. Indeed, there is a grave danger in isolating LP from more general social policy prerogatives and processes, since language groups fit into the more general processes of social change which LP rarely addresses.

Changes in the language group relate to the more general process of economic restructuring. Globalisation and the Single Market limits state regulation, realigning the relationship between the state and its economy. There has been a profound shift in the meaning of the spatial components of the discourse of economic regulation. 'Regional' development no longer refers to state regulation and a labour market no longer pertains to a single state. Labour markets now assume local and regional configurations. A dynamic factor of this development involves the relationship between the public and the private sector, a dynamism that has particular significance for minority

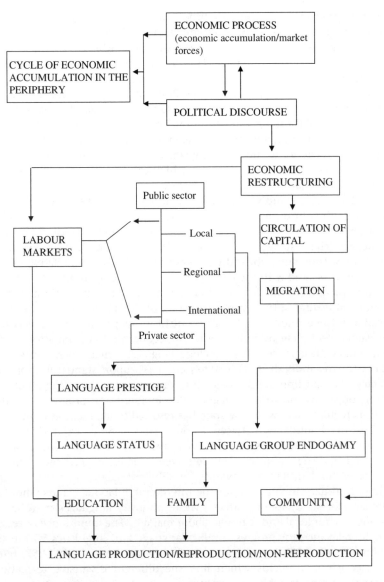

Figure 1.1 Schematic representation of language production, reproduction and non-reproduction

language groups as a consequence of how LP is conceived of as a feature of social policy.

Language prestige is introduced to designate the value of a language for social mobility. This is the primary motivating force for those interested in language production, as well as reproduction. Constructing language as an object that has relevance for economic gain maximises the likelihood that the individual will take in charge those situations where the subject place involves the use of that language. This does not only involve the speaker of this language. The commodification of language makes it desirable in the sense that it signifies a positive value. Prior discourse has linked language and economic position since the importance of standardisation – 'good' language, 'good' thinking and educational success – was formalised through compulsory education and its relationship to economic success. It is far less tangible by reference to the state language which the individual speaks than it is by reference to another language which can be 'gained' by learning it, or by insuring that one's offspring learns it.

The centrality of individual mobility and self-improvement within the modernist discourse gives social mobility a particular importance within Western society. It constitutes economic actors as subjects with possibilities for action. These subjects' places are reflexive in that they involve a life trajectory within which the individual assumes different, but related, subject positions associated with the concept of 'career'. The opening of the subject position pertains to the individual's relationship to the institutions that are an integral feature of the entire structuring of the relationship between the social and the economic order. These institutions provide the objects that are valued positively by reference to the economic transformation of the individual's life chances. They include language which opens up subject places for the individual. The state's emphasis upon standardisation and literacy plays an important role in the constitution of language as an economic object within its discourse on development and progress. Together with its regulatory powers, the state has resorted to language as a means of establishing boundaries between labour markets. Since capital does not recognise state boundaries, *lingua franca* transcend individual labour markets. Language and the labour market are linked by language prestige. Different languages hold different relevance for different labour markets, English being of primary importance for the international labour market, the state language for state labour markets, while minority languages may have a significance for local and regional labour markets. The importance of reason and its relevance for progress unifies language and linguistics within the economic order. The interdiscursive reveals what Foucault (1972:57) refers to as concomitant fields which link the different discursive formations where these objects achieve meaning.

Where all members of the labour force speak the same language, that language becomes the means whereby each individual takes in charge the various subject positions that constitute interaction in the workplace, but only when everyone has the same competence in a single language and only one language is used within the labour market. Within the workplace, constraints on interaction are imposed by language competence. The relations of production, and their relationship to language use and language group membership, become relevant. This involves the cultural division of labour, where there is a restriction of specific social places within the economic order to subjects who pertain to one language or culture group, and others to a different language or cultural group. It also involves how the economic discourse divides geographical space.

The insistence on the free mobility of labour, together with the spatial division of labour, links the circulation of capital and the circulation of people. Social policy in the form of regional planning and regional development relates the variable process of economic restructuring and the variation in these mobilities over time. The profound influence which the in-migration of non-speakers into the autochthonous territories of minority language groups has upon language group reproduction derives from the different cycles of economic change. In-migration influences language group endogamy and, in turn, the ability of the family to serve as an agency of language reproduction. It also has a profound influence upon the relevance of community as an agency of both production and reproduction.

Within the current process of social and economic change, the family is the social unit responsible for economic subsistence. It shares with the educational institutions the responsibility for socialising the individual into the social and economic order. How the economic and educational discursive formations operate in constructing the language object influence how the family also is constituted. Individual freedom encourages the individual to select a partner on the basis of factors independent of family interests or local interests. The 'partner' as subject is constructed in a particular way. How society organises interaction on a local basis results in highly localised marriage patterns, while the economic discourse and its relationship to subcultures also determines the interaction that leads to union. How the social discourse sanctions language group endogamy is less evident. Populations from outside of the autochthonous territory influence the rate of language group endogamy. Of course, even a high rate of language group endogamy does not guarantee a high incidence of language use within the family. However, the focus of interest is upon the structures which make language use possible.

Community often remains a major agency of both the production and reproduction of the minority language group. The normative context of language use and its institutionalisation in community activities allow in-migrants to learn the minority language. However, there are considerable differences in the demographic, institutional and language competence structures across the communities in Europe. How these structures relate to the other agencies, especially to family and education, is important in understanding the processes of language production and reproduction.

In all states, regardless of the home language, the school is the main agency whereby the production of the state language is guaranteed. This

universal function of education can also apply to the production and reproduction of minority language groups. The interrelationship between this
agency and those of the family and community is emphasised. The function
of education has always been both to inculcate a sense of normativity associated with state nationalism, and an adequacy in relation to the economic
needs of the state. Thus the entry of minority languages into the labour
market is paralleled by their entry into formal education. Viewing education
as a primary agency of language production and reproduction also links with
how economic process is achieved within the schema. The extent to which
the minority language is incorporated into education is indicative of the
different meanings that accrue to the language object.

3 Language use as social practice

The focus thus far is on the process of generating 'ability' or competence.
The relationship between ability and use is of a different order. Much of
Sociolinguistic theory, such as it is, focuses upon the issue of motivation
and use, rather than on the structuring of language groups as social groups.
It is conceptualised by reference to two key variables – institutionalisation
and legitimation.

Every language group is subject to planning and social management.
Public management is where the state encounters the interface between the
government and the citizen. Through language planning or other forms of
social policy, both the minority language and its speakers are constituted as
subjects and objects in specific ways within the discourse on public management. The language is constituted as an object within a sphere of legitimacy
that derives from the state. The speakers are constituted as subjects which
carry status. The legitimacy of the language partly exists to insure the con-
tinuation of this status.

Legitimation incorporates constitutional and social policy, and different political levels (Williams and Morris, 2000). Neo-liberalism involves
'enabling' principles, and the freedom to pursue certain forms of action
rather than the rights-based emphasis of legislation. It involves educational
policies and the differing extent of the legitimation of language use in the
public sector, where the policies of the different authorities play such a
significant role.

Institutionalisation refers to non-reflexive, patterned behaviour. It pertains to the stabilisation of discourse. Language use becomes the taken-
for-granted use of one language rather than the other within a bilingual
setting. 'Institutionalisation' rather than 'domain' is used because it extends
beyond the relationship between context and use to encompass both interactional capacity, and 'taken for granted' behaviour. From the individual's
viewpoint, the subject position does not pertain to any marked feature of
the associated discourse (Williams, 1999a:209). Thus meanings will tend not

to be contested. The concept rejects action as being conditioned by the centred human subject, and involves how social practice exists at the point where the human subject is constituted in and through discourse. It is the relationship between institutionalisation and legitimation that plays the main role in transforming structure, ability and motivation into actual language practice as stabilised social practices.

Institutionalisation involves language behaviour as part of the common sense of life within the community. This taken for granted is destabilised in social change, and the associated symbolic elements are reorganised. This is not a reflection process where whatever happens at the behavioural level is a manifestation of social change as a reified process. Institutionalisation is not only manifested in language use, it is also stabilised in language. Language is so complex that it is impossible for any individual to be reflexive about every word stated, how it is said and when it is said. There are recurrent pieces of discourse which bear a direct relationship to social practice. These often rely upon prior discourses which become stabilised in current language practice as traces of prior practice in relation to prior social contexts. The relationship between object (language) and subject (speaker) within these discourses is stable. The use of different languages does not relate to a reflexive code-switching premised upon rational action nor to such static concepts as domain or diglossia, but is linked to institutionalised behaviour associated with discursive structures. It is part of the social and institutional context. Language is social behaviour. The respective use of one language or another depends not merely on ability, but on how language use is institutionalised or stabilised as language practice.

Institutionalisation is not a normativity where social norms are automatic processes associated with consensus between rational actors. Normativity is ingrained with power, and there are different struggles over normativity. At the local level, the process operates in a way different from the link between the state and normativity. Language use within the community involves how meaning is socially constructed as institutional behaviour, and how social change undermines the social and institutional contexts supporting stabilisation. There is a symbolic component to language which signifies meaning within social practice, and the use of one language rather than another becomes part of that signification. The social constructivist view of social reality replaces the passive, perceptual models of the subject–object relationships of positivism.

The institutionalisation of language use is understood as activity that is structured in and through language by how different subject positions in relation to different objects produce specific meanings, of which 'Welsh' or 'language' is one. Thus it conditions the use of language as stabilised discourse, but always with the possibility of destabilisation of the relationship between subject positions and language as an object among other objects.

4 Conclusion

Most of what has been said above pertains to the production of competence rather than language use. The relationship between the structure responsible for the generation of competence, and the use of that competence in social life is questioned. A Sociology which sets store both upon elaborating the social as patterned behaviour which transcends face-to-face interaction and upon the actual implementation of the same behaviour between social actors is problematic. Outlining how competence is generated within society before elaborating how individuals become social actors through the resolution of the ambiguity of meaning in interaction provides the solution. The generation of competence and the conversion of the individual into a social being are both inherently linked to discourse. The decentred approach of social action theory links with a structural approach that is equally decentred (Boutet, 1994).

The following describes the context of language use rather than language use itself. It allows a demonstration of where use is possible and where it is not, making tentative suggestions concerning the link between that possibility and the tendency to use the minority language, at least as it is reported by those using the language. The normative effect, or how people report what they feel they should say, is resolved by asking respondents to report on what happened in concrete situations.

SECTION II THE DATA AND METHOD

1 Introduction

The data drawn upon to explore the extent to which the different European minority language groups are capable of being reproduced derives from the EC-commissioned Euromosaic study (European Commission, 1996). Such a comparative survey was obliged by constraints of time and resources to adopt an empirical approach, obliging the researcher to ensure that the measures deployed derive from a basis and orientation that is common to all cases.

The objects of the study were autochthonous minority language groups – language groups which claimed a territorial base that links language and society. This raises the question of what are the entities to be compared. The acceptance of one linguistic form as a 'language' and another as a 'dialect' is a political and not a linguistic decision. Linguistics has sought to appropriate this issue, using linguistic theory to establish typological systems of form involving categories and subcategories, including language and dialect. The meta-discourse of Linguistics constructs a language as an object by reference to certain parameters, while the relevance of such a construction for social practice is constrained by the political discourse and how it constructs language as an object which may, or may not, relate to the object constructed by Linguistics.

Some state languages vary in form, but are still classified as a single language, for example German in Germany and Switzerland. Their distinctiveness is addressed by reference to the political, which precludes their being classified as variants or dialects of a single language, independent of political affiliation. Dialects of a state language within one state might be included as a language in another. The political element is not static. The realignment of political space within Europe means that forms which, hitherto, might have been regarded as a dialect of the state language suddenly become promoted as regional languages. The overlay between language and politics that is based upon the principle of difference is clear.

Distinctions between 'national', 'official', 'regional', 'lesser used' languages and the like are social constructs. Negative connotation of such classifications had to be set aside. 'Lesser used languages' allows powerful state language groups, such as Irish or Luxembourgese, to be compared with extraterritorial state language groups such as German or French, or a variety of stateless languages including Ladin, Welsh or Catalan, each with different degrees of power and a vast range of language density and numbers of speakers.

'Language group' viewed as a social group was a defining criterion. Language can structure aggregates of individuals into a self-conscious social group which involves commonality of orientation or perspective within the overall social system. Each state has a single society so that a language group in one state, even though it uses the same language as a social group in another state, is regarded as a distinctive social group. There are several German language groups within Europe.

The state might seem an unambiguous concept involving the various Member States of the European Union. On the other hand the extent of political function that is allocated to regions within federal systems in Spain or Germany means that institutions and legislative bodies which are of relevance to the minority language group are prescribed by reference to these 'autonomous governments' rather than the central state. As referents to which the social groups pertain we consider these as 'societies'. Thus the Catalan language group in Spain is fragmented into different language groups which are located in Catalonia, Valencia, Aragon or the Ballearic Islands. The power to legislate by reference to the institutions and agencies relevant to the language and the language group lies with the regional government.

2 Data sources

The goal was one of collecting valid and reliable comparative data associated with the different variables that derive from the concepts which formed the corner-stone of the study, and with the various hypotheses that derived from using these concepts. The fewer the number of respondents contributing any single piece of data, the more difficult the task of establishing reliability and validity for that data. Once these fundamental principles of empirical research can be guaranteed the investigator is in a position to move to a consideration of data sources.

Five main sources were exploited in collecting relevant data and information:

1 Secondary sources. The studies in the various minority language data banks can be of a very high quality but, unfortunately, most of them provide little reliable data. Even when reliable empirical studies are available, the theoretical, philosophical and methodological context might be removed from those of the Euromosaic study. Nonetheless, such secondary sources do have some value.

2 The official authorities in the Member States. These include the permanent representatives of the Member States of the Commission, the various consulates, and local and regional governments or authorities. They completed a specially designed questionnaire which covered official policy, data sources and factual information about the various language groups. This represents the official position *vis à vis* the language groups.

3 Language group correspondents. For each language group, one regional researcher was allocated the task of gathering a diverse nature of data based on another questionnaire. Each language group correspondent was asked to provide 'key witnesses' who were experts in the various fields which the questionnaire addressed. These 'key witnesses' were, in turn, asked to answer a lengthy and detailed questionnaire that was standardised across the various language groups.

4 Other experts and well-informed professionals. In order to check the validity and reliability of the data collected a range of other contacts were exploited, these people being asked to complete yet another questionnaire and to comment on the various pieces of information collected.

This data set was employed to generate measures for each language group on the analytic variables and to create a series of reports for each language group. These reports constitute the most detailed and up-to-date information concerning the various language groups currently available.

5 Language-use surveys. The fifth source of data consisted of a series of empirical field language-use surveys on a carefully selected sample of speakers for 18 language groups. The focus was on the institutionalisation of the respective languages within the different societies.

It is surprising how few language-use surveys have been constructed by reference to the rigour of survey research. They tend to be a check list of language-use contexts, sprinkled with questions concerning attitudes which are not adequately contextualised. They are characterised by intuition and induction, partly because of the inability to conceive of such groups as social groups.

Resource limitation restricted the language-use surveys to 18 language groups and to 300 interviews in each case. This constitutes a particular problem in that the margin of error is drastically reduced compared with the customary sample size. This is partly accommodated by restricting the analysis to frequencies and by restricting the variables so that the number of cases in the relevant cells is adequate. Careful attention had to be given, first of all to the selection of cases, and then to how two quite different sets of data could be related in order to create valid empirical measures for all language groups.

The selection of the 18 cases was based upon common-sense principles:

- The best of the language-use surveys that had already been undertaken – the Frisian language group in the Netherlands, the Irish and the Basque language groups in the Autonomous Community, Navarre and France – were not replicated. While the interview schedule of these surveys was by no means identical to our own, the topics covered in the surveys and the statistical validity of the data was such that they could, nonetheless, be used as valuable data sources for our purposes.
- No more than two cases were chosen from any single state.
- Survey work allows the investigator to generalise from a large population while also permitting the investigation of a range of issues. It would have been futile to deploy the large-scale method of survey research for small language groups.
- There were also good reasons for avoiding the more contentious cases – the limited time scale, the newness of the approach and so on.

Age, gender, social class, and different sampling points informed the sampling frame. Decenial census data for Wales and Scotland and a prior survey of 40,000 respondents for Galicia were used to develop proportional, representative, quota samples. Elsewhere the 300 cases were distributed into ten locational subsets, with cases then being selected by reference to the social variables. The locational quotas were randomly selected.

The interviews were undertaken by a supervised, trained, team of native speakers. Each interviewer was allocated a randomly selected quota within the location for which they were responsible. This is time consuming, but is an essential prerequisite. The interview schedules were coded, data entered and analysis undertaken.

Each interview took between 45 minutes and an hour and covered basic demographic information, information about language use by reference to family, education, work, community activities, leisure, religion and related contexts. It sought to cover most of the interpersonal contacts which most people within the various communities would encounter. These items were constructed to provide measures on the relevant variables. Opinion and attitude scales referred to the degree of commitment of various agencies, institutions and social actors by reference to the language in question and items were based on the Semantic Differential Scaling Technique. Each respondent kept a week-long diary of contacts about the context of the contact, language use and the nature of the relationship with the contact. This covered the normative factor (Achard, 1993).

3 Scale construction

The variable nature of the data made comparison problematic. The subjective data for the language group reports had to blend with the more objective data of the language-use surveys. Qualitative data had to lie with the quantitative data. The use of scales for comparative research facilitates abstracting from a series of data sets to develop single scales across all cases. Properly designed and employed they enhance comparison. However, they do demand attention to a number of technical issues relating to design and validity.

Among the fundamental principles of scaling considered were the following:

- The scales had to be sufficiently broad to encompass the entire range of cases to be included.
- The distance between the respective scores had to be uniform.
- The scales had to be internally consistent.
- Some measure of validity and reliability had to be incorporated, both by reference to the scales themselves, and by reference to the scores that derive from their use.
- For the scales to be integrated, the same range of scores had to be deployed for each scale, and no more than one scale could be employed for each dimension of the integration.
- Only one scale could be employed for each dimension, but more than one dimension for each variable was possible, leading to sub-scales which had to be correlated by reference to the degree of relationship between them.

This made it possible to score each language group on the key variables, and, by adding these scores, to generate an overall score for each language group. This process was undertaken independently by several analysts, the comparison producing measures of inter-rater reliability for each scale and each case. These measures were then employed in order to generate reliable figures. Disagreement was resolved by discussion and arbitration. Content validity was established with colleagues.

Generating universal scores for each case does overlook variation within the territory of each language group. This was the source of much of the disagreement among those responsible for creating the various scores. The highly general nature of the scales is inevitable given the need for comparability, and the level of generalisation must be similar across all cases. Each person responsible for allocating the various scores did so by reference to the same information sources which consisted of the various language group reports and the 18 language-use surveys. The relationship between these two data sets is important. For the 18 cases we had two sets of data, and these were the cases where there was the greatest degree of agreement among the evaluators. The 18 cases served as a standard against which the others were measured by, first of all, scoring the 18 cases from the survey data on each of the scales, and establishing a satisfactory level of agreement by reference to these scores. Second, by independently scoring the same 18 cases on the same scales, using the respective language reports as the basis for this task, and establishing agreement on these scores, it is possible to compare the respective sets of scores on all scales. We were then able to evaluate the level of comparability of the two data sets. Where comparability was low, it was possible to ascertain the reason for the lack of comparability, and to build this knowledge into our general approach to validity and reliability across all of the cases.

4 Conclusion

This chapter has outlined the decentred approach as the basis for the subsequent analysis. The analytic model focuses on the conditions necessary for minority language groups to be reproduced. The focus was on how subjects and objects are constructed in discourse. It has also discussed the analytic data that derives from an already completed study (European Commission, 1996). The present work involves a re-evaluation of this data. This involves recursivity and recursive reading (Seriot, 1996; Valku-Poustovaia, 1997), involving the contextualisation/decontextualisation of any discourse, thereby admitting the multitude of possible contexts. Valku-Poustovaia (1997:86) defines this as an:

> operation of localisation (positioning) of a point of view of the observer, allowing a reconstitution (a calculus) of a series of discursive events, recontextualising this or that discourse.
>
> (1997:86; my translation)

The recursive reading of a text presupposes an earlier reading which it questions, and recentres the viewpoint of the reader from a supplementary knowledge of that text and its conditions of production. Involved is a consideration of the orthodox discourse on social policy, public management and economic development by reference to the implications for the production and reproduction of minority language groups in relation to this official discourse. This observation of a particular object of study rests in a more or less stable management paradigm. The analytic reading of a research is an act of discourse that reactivates prior work.

In the following chapters the various strands of data are considered by reference to the various topics which, together, constitute the interdiscourse of public management and the relationship of language use to this order of discourse. The next chapter considers the issue of legitimation. The data for this chapter derives not merely from the information gathered in the various language group reports, but also from a close analysis of those cases which do indicate a degree of incorporation of minority language groups in the social policy principles of the respective legal authorities.

2
Legitimation

1 Introduction

The separation of language from the social in the eighteenth century created language as something to be studied and manipulated, while the human control over the future through reason, and the ability to plan that future, led to language planning (LP). Linguistics involved the separation of language and nature, and of representation and fact. Sociology and Linguistics became different objects, sharing a central place in the preoccupation with the rational state and the state of reason.

As social policy, LP supported the creation of a culturally and linguistically homogeneous state. It encompasses two different conceptions, one associated with standardising the state language, and the other promoting minority languages. Conceptions of democracy that encompass ethical principles of rights, led to extending these rights to include the rights of minority language groups, but only when the central state became sufficiently self-confident of its hegemonic control. Initially, liberal democracy left minority languages and their speakers outside of reason and any sense of 'rights'.

LP initially emerged by reference to the Third World, as a feature of social policy only by reference to language. LP developed as a discipline remote from the more general principles of societal development. Those to whom LP is applied were from a part of society with a culturally distinctive context, the basis of 'ethnicity'. As 'ethnic' groups, minority language groups are beyond the parameters of normative society, its promotion and development. All issues pertaining to minority languages relate to languages and not to social groups, and normativising language practices as social practices is ignored.

LP relates linguistic functions and their relationship to a conception of the social and to claims about how the social operates, before linking the two in promoting the linguistic function. It links a sociological orientation with linguistic aspects of language use. Social and linguistic dynamics relate to interventionist policies not being allowed to inhibit what is regarded as 'natural development'. The emphasis is on the construction of typologies, and on how language is modified or promoted (Montgomery, 1998:49).

The law specifies the ultimate conception of a desired outcome, and policy derives from the legal context, but implementation may fall short of the policy statement, or it may go further. The relationship between the legitimation conferred by law, and the institutionalisation of policy as social practice means policy can operate without recourse to legislation.

Colinguisme is: 'the association of certain languages of the State in an apparatus of language where they find their legitimacy and their material practices' (Balibar 1985:14; my translation). It involves 'language apparatus', concerning how the interests of the state penetrate a variety of social institutions (Althusser, 1976). The association of languages and their relationship to corresponding practices, such as translation and grammatisation, institutionalises the linguistic norm, constructing language as a specific object by reference to state and society. Legitimation is much broader than the concept of LP allows. It deals with social policy by reference to the interests involved, raising doubts about the extent to which LP serves the interests of the minority language group. Consequently, the goal of developing parity of use across both the minority and the state languages is missing. It lacks direct reference to the general principles of democratic society, and rights are not seen by reference to the wider parameters of the relationship between citizenship and constitutional issues of the state.

Citizenship is constructed out of the rights and advantages of certain categories of subjects (Dahrendorf, 1974). The rise of the modern state saw the recognition of minorities in law. Human rights became the prerogative of the nation-state, 'the emancipated sovereignty of the people, of one's own people . . .' (Arendt 1968:171), involving the 'us' of the state insuring the creation of a culturally homogeneous citizenry. Any community of identity was subservient to the normative 'we', and the state was constructed as a community made up of the sum of all communities within its territory as the basis of social order, a community of law that determined the rights of participation. The qualities of 'birth, political, ethnic or religious denomination, mode of life or occupation' (Weber 1978:695–6) relate such rights to status. Capitalism shifted the onus of law from status to contract, and the emergence of state welfarism means rights are increasingly claimed on the basis of ascriptive criteria:

> disadvantaged ethnic minorities do not simply or necessarily acquiesce in their subordinate position but clearly organise themselves to promote and improve their position in society. That is, minority groups appeal to citizenship rights in order to draw attention to their disadvantage on the basis of their ascriptive ethnic status.
>
> (Turner, 1988:59)

Neo-liberalism has replaced struggle with a focus upon partnership, responsibility, accountability and enablement. 'Citizenship' pertains to a range of different status groups, or groups with ascriptive traits that cut across social class. It is also about collective mobility within both the state and its labour market (Montgomery 1998:72). 'Rights' are defined by reference to the collectivity rather than the individual. It is not validated within the legal framework of the state, but as a challenge to the normative order. The priority of institutionalisation over legitimation makes it a forceful challenge that leads to destabilising discursive subjects and objects.

In formal equality individuals have equal access to the means of personal achievement and satisfaction, whereas substantive equality involves the creation of equality through state intervention (ibid: 78–80). These different orientations towards liberal democracy make equality a contentious issue. Formal equality reinforces the advantages of the normative structure by limiting non-normative structures and recognition to abstract principles devoid of operational principles. These two forms derive from two distinctive democratic discourses – liberalism and social democracy. Many of the social-democratic European states do little to promote the interests of minority language groups, emphasising unitary forms of inequality rather than the pluralism that is essential for substantive equality (ibid.).

Organisations theory relates to constraints and opportunities generated by organisational environments, deriving partly from institutional or organisational structures, and partly from discursive formations which determine what can and what cannot be said from a given place. LP must be seen as discourse, as a practice that only becomes possible at particular historical conjunctures when the space opens up for the destabilisation of the converse discourse of state promoted cultural homogenisation. The concern is with the extent of LP that exists for the various minority language groups, the historical context which established these processes, the nature of the supporting discourses, and how they relate to implementation.

Planning agency models that link the change orientation with the planning orientation focus upon the customary social science concepts of community, the market and the state. In Europe, the search for different models of service delivery extends to an attempt to establish how its diversity can be sustained by developing a universal LP. It demands knowledge about how policies and institutions work. Forms of neo-liberalism vary, but there is little doubt that it has had its effect upon policy across Europe writ large.

Bossuyt (1975) distinguishes between civil and political rights on the one hand, and 'social, economic and cultural rights' on the other. In civil and political rights the state makes no financial commitment, intervenes only when there is a violation of rights, and they are seen as civil rights in the sense that they pertain to the individual. 'Social, economic and cultural rights' involve financial investment by the state, require state intervention for their promotion, and are accorded to the individual (ibid.).

This distinction overlaps with a legitimacy associated with a series of Border Treaties which differs from more recent forms of legitimation which are associated with quite a different understanding of the relationship between the state and the individual. Legal discourses within modernity are constructed around the rights of the individual citizen. It is difficult for any state to accommodate the simultaneous definition of a social group constructed out of cultural distinctiveness, and the conferring of rights on such a group, when its embodiment as a state relies on the conception of social groups as conforming to the state's identity as a stable and homogeneous cultural entity. The focus on individual rights avoids such issues. The guarantees to collectivities that was evident in the Peace and Minority Treaties after the two World Wars have given way to legislation pertaining to individual rights as members of minorities, emphasising individual guarantees rather than collective guarantees. These polarisations are currently being reconstituted within neo-liberalism, with rights giving way to enablement or empowerment.

There are three configurations of LP in Europe – state border cases which have a fairly long standing history of LP; minority language groups which have achieved planning status during the second half of the twentieth century; and language groups which still have no LP of any significance. The argument presented below is that the meaning of LP varies historically. Consequently, the Border Treaties are restricted to those created after the two World Wars and the stateless language developments to the more recent past.

2 Border Treaties

The Peace and Minorities Treaties which followed World War I involved the legitimation of 'national minorities' through law (Arendt, 1968:154–5). Legislation established stable international bodies that could safeguard human rights. The five conventions between the Allied Forces and the newly created or expanded states, together with the guarantees imposed through the peace treaties with the four conquered states of Austria, Bulgaria, Hungary and Turkey, included reference to language guarantees. The boundaries of European states should correspond with 'nationality' in order to secure 'the rights of the small nations' (Hobsbawn, 1992), a definition of nation that involved a formal recognition that minority rights should exist. The Treaties of St Germaine and Versailles, and even the Treaty of Lausanne of 1923, recognised that some states were created on the back of 'nationalist aspirations' which were not recognised in the existing polities. This included Finland, Estonia, Latvia, Lithuania and Poland.

The new political map of Europe consolidated political borders while recognising the needs of extraterritorial language groups. In Greece particular attention was given to the Turks; in Finland the Swedes gained a relative autonomy, and both Swedish and Finnish were recognised as official languages; Alsace was returned to France, but with recognition as a distinctive language group; the same applied to the German language group in eastern Belgium; the Danes in Germany and the Germans in Denmark were constituted as minority language groups in the Treaty of Versailles; in Italy the German language group of South Tyrol, and the Slovenes and Croats in the north-east of Italy were recognised. These 'national groups' were constructed in a particular way within the political discourse.

After the Second World War further legislation was aimed at sustaining the interests of the same language groups. We find a process of revision in operation in Finland and in relation to the Ladin, the German language group, the French and Franco-Provencal group of Val d'Osta, and the Slovenes in Italy; the Ethnic Law for language groups in Austria; the Danish group in Germany and the German group in Denmark. There is a reaffirmation of the principle of belonging, where a language group is permitted a degree of non-normative independence within a state.

The Treaties contained four types of language guarantees:

1 Freedom of language use in private, in commerce, in religion, for publication and in public meetings.
2 Provision to use the group's language in the law courts.
3 Primary educational provision where the use of a minority language was justified.
4 Public funds should be allocated to support educational, religious or charitable activities in those languages where justified by numbers.

The focus was on non-discrimination, rather than on the promotion of language group production and reproduction. This has implications for how legal strictures are translated into policy and implementation. There remained reluctance to conceive of minorities as culturally distinctive social groups, because of the prioritisation of national sovereignty.

2.1 Austria

The Treaty of St Germain oversaw the break up of the Habsburg Empire and replaced the State Act of 1867, but some of the language groups influenced were more favourably placed under the Habsburgs. During the Nazi regime the guarantees of the St Germain Treaty were ignored, minority language groups were persecuted, and the 'line of blood' between Germanic and non-Germanic linguistic 'families' was established. The concern of the occupational forces lay more with resisting Communism than with negating the effects of Germanicism.

All language group became equal in law, legitimised the use of the language, and allowed the use of minority languages in the law courts (Austrian Centre for Ethnic Groups, 1996). Where the numbers were sufficient, it guaranteed public education in the relevant language, but with German taught as an obligatory subject. An equitable proportion of public funds allocated for educational, religious and charitable purposes should be used for minority language groups where their numbers are 'considerable'.

The 1955 Treaty gave the Slovene and Croat minorities in Carinthia, Burgenland and Styria the right to their own organisations, meetings and press in their own language; to have elementary instruction in the Slovene or Croat language; and a proportional number of their own secondary schools. In these administrative and juridical districts, the Slovene or Croat language is accepted as an official language in addition to German.

Since the 1976 Act, Ethnic Advisory Councils acting as consultative authorities can submit proposals to the Federal government as well as to the regional government. The language groups are also funded. Half of those serving on these Councils are appointed by the representative organisation of the ethnic group, and the other half either by the political parties or the Church respectively, providing they are members of the ethnic group.[1]

While legislation outlines the general conditions concerning rights, implementation is another matter. Often the infrastructure to cope with the implementation of these rights is not in place. Materials have to be translated, leading to delay and inconvenience. Exercising the right demands considerable perseverance and self-confidence, and a staunch unwillingness to take the easy route of opting for a German language service. Translation becomes a solution rather than insuring that service provision can cope with the demand. Enablement does not accompany rights. A trained lawyer appointed to safeguard the interests of minority language speakers is herself obliged to resort to translation in order to insure that these rights are preserved! A variety of agencies which have authority, but no power, are called to act upon any complaint.

The relationship between legitimisation and institutionalisation is weak. The solution involves the cultural groups informing their members of their rights. There are as many as 80 state institutions where the right can be exercised, but they rarely advertise their obligation. There are a few institutions which use minority languages as a public display. Local knowledge of their neighbours, including their extent of language ability, is used. The Slovene newspapers often report about the success of Slovene speakers in certain offices. It is this knowledge and not legitimation that informs this aspect of language use. While legislation and legitimation seek to generate change, some process of implementation which leads to institutionalisation is essential. Rights have to be enabled and not merely granted.

Contradictions between giving freedom to language groups and assimilating such groups are resolved by reference to individual freedom, whereas in practice the resources and state normativity are orientated towards assimilation. There remains a concern about the internal deviant, and the threat to the integrity of the state. There has been a gradual retreat from the dogmatic discourse on state homogeneity of the previous century, but the Germanic emphasis on the territorial imperative, and its relationship to autochthony was retained. It obliged a distinction between 'native' language groups and 'immigrant' groups. The 'us'/'them' distinction and its relationship to the stabilisation of boundaries lead to a liberalisation of the definition of the subjects that becomes inclusively associated with the 'us', while immigrants replace the minority language groups as internal deviants.

In contrast to the Slovenes and Croats, the Hungarian language group in Burgenland, and the Czech and Slovak groups cannot base their demands for equal treatment upon the constitutional Vienna State Treaty, but rely on the Ethnic Group Act. The Slovene language group in Styria is treated differently from the language group in Carinthia. They belong to the same language group within the same society, yet are treated differently.

2.2 Italy

The Treaty of Rapallo of 1920 passed the cities of Trieste and Gorizia, and their surrounding areas which included the Slovene language group, to Italy (Carrozza, 1992). Legislative authority was confirmed in The Osimo Treaty of 1975. The Paris Peace Conference of 1947 conferred the right of the Slovenes of Gorizia to use the language in their personal affairs and with the regional authorities (Heraud, 1982). This included the right of reply. An act of 1967 provided translation and interpreter support facilities. Demographic limitations were placed in signage. Slovene language schools were reopened in 1945 and became state schools in 1961, becoming compatible with Italian educational structures in 1963. One seat on the National Council for Education is reserved for a representative of the Slovene teachers.

In Valle d'Aosta French and Italian have equal status in administrative, but not in legal documentation. Members of the French language group are recruited into administrative positions, and French language qualifications relate to certain civil service positions. French language education and a modified curriculum are provided. No reference is made to Franco-Provencal.

In Trentino Alto Adige the Paris Agreement of 1946 and the subsequent special statute preceded the new statute of autonomy approved in 1972 (Carrozza, 1992). German was allocated equal status with the state language. Legislative texts and other administrative documents were to be produced bilingually, and German able to be used with the regional police and public sector institutions. Representative assemblies use both languages, and communication with them will involve either language. Proportionality in local offices of the central government, and the need for civil servants to have an oral competence in both languages were conceded in 1976. The statute also accommodated the Ladin language group, but the main emphasis was on education and culture, and on the use of Ladin in dealing with the public sector in general.

Media services were to be provided for the German, French and Slovene language groups in Italy. This included re-broadcasting the services provided by neighbouring states. This was additional to indigenous provision in German, French, Slovene and Ladin, and was among the most extensive of minority language provision in Europe.

2.3 Finland

Sweden held autonomy over Finland until 1809, and when the Finnish state was established in 1917, side by side with Finnish, Swedish became its national language. The province of Aland has enjoyed an internationally guaranteed autonomy under the Geneva Convention of 1921 (Pentikainen and Hiltunen, 1995). Regional citizenship only applies to those who have an adequate knowledge of Swedish. Within this region, Swedish has dominance over Finnish, being the only official language of administration. Elsewhere municipalities are marked as unilingual or bilingual, dependent on 6–8 per cent of the population speaking either of the two languages (Liebkind, Broo and Finnas, 1995).

The Language Act of 1922 insured that the public can use the language of its choice, qualified by the designation of municipalities as being monolingual or bilingual. Higher level officials must have competence in the relevant dominant language. Oral and written competence in both languages is required of officials in bilingual municipalities. In 1993, only 21 of the 460 municipalities were designated as 'monolingual Swedish', and a further 43 were designated as 'bilingual'. Furthermore, only its inhabitants are allowed to own land or to establish enterprises in Aland.

The interface between the state and the language group is undertaken by a political party – the Swedish People's Party – whose membership spans the range of political positions united by language-related issues. Its activities cover not only education, but also the economic support that derives from central government.

2.4 Germany and Denmark

The Bonn/Copenhagen Agreement of 1955 provided public sector services and education in the minority language (Christiansen and Teebken, 2001). For the German language group, Danish remains the language of the legal structure, but interpretation is guaranteed. While a permanent office located in Copenhagen is supported, it has no LP function. The situation in Germany parallels this situation.

The recent German Unification Treaty emphasises 'freedom' and individual liberty from direct impediment deriving from the state, its function or associated legislation. The constitution of the Saxony *Lander* makes reference to a 'guarantee' and 'cultural independence', suggesting a much more active role for regional government in educational, media and place-name provision in Sorbian. The right to speak Sorbian in the courts runs parallel to the insistence that German is the language of the courts (Elle, 1995).

The 'Foundation for the Sorbian People' and the associated Treaty seek to promote Sorbian interests. The literature places a heavy emphasis upon art and culture. Sorbian is constructed as an object that has value outside of the normative context of German language use, as an emotive rather than a rational object. Other references are to 'identity', 'coexistence' and 'co-operation with other ethnic groups'. The Sorbians are treated as a non-normative anomaly, rather than as a mainstream aspect of German life. Culture marks difference and constructs Sorbian 'identity', and involves difference from the norm as opposed to integrating Sorbian into the normative structure.

2.5 Greece

Members of the Muslim religion, rather than a language group, receive legal protection in the region of Thrace, which includes Turkish, Pomak and Romani language groups (Christopoulos and Tsitselikis 1997; Trudgill, 2000). The Treaty of Lausanne, a trans-frontier agreement between Turkey and Greece, mentions 'freedoms' and 'rights', including 'the right to use their minority language', and 'the right to primary education offered in the minority language'. The relevant articles are recognised as 'fundamental laws' which cannot be superceded.

The emphasis is very much on the provision of education, but by reference to a Greek curriculum, and with minority language textbooks. Provision also covers Turkish language print and broadcasting media. Reference is to the Turkish language being justified by the claim that Pomak is 'not a written language', constructing Pomak as a Greek language, while rejecting its relationship to any other language.

2.6 Belgium

There is a considerable degree of autonomy for the culturally based communities in Belgium. They have a relatively high degree of power by reference to education, culture and the general aspects of social administration. These powers deal only with matters assigned to them in the Constitution, but the communities are the only ones who have these rights within their territories. Regions are higher level authorities that are economically defined and territorially based. They have associated powers that refer to such areas as economic development, labour market affairs, environment, housing and so on.

2.7 Summary

All of these international treaties or agreements confer rights on language groups and provide associated facilities, but do not develop the structure whereby they are integrated into a formal conception of planning. They only insure the provision of services that are restricted and static by reference to their implementation. It requires political pressure to extend the initial policies into new social and economic contexts. In the absence of any formal state authority that can monitor and police the existing legislation, the onus is on the voluntary aspects of minority language group activity to apply pressure to grant further concessions. The only formal relationship between the language group and the state authorities is through channels which exist for the population in general, making it difficult to use the existing structures to develop non-normative policies. The language groups sometimes turn to the neighbouring state to obtain the resources and modicum of support that their own state's social policy will not provide. Where guarantees of language use are accompanied by the insistence on language competence for service providers, the situation is stronger.

Legitimation is limited by this failure to integrate LP into social policy. The main focus is upon the relationship between legislation and institutionalisation. There will always be concern about the extent to which the authorities will insure that what is provided for in legislation is translated into effective policy that results in the institutionalisation of language use by reference to relevant institutions and agencies. The treaties have succeeded in extending the relevance of the language beyond the private world. What is missing is a willingness to conceive of language not merely by reference to reproduction, but also as a feature of production. The Swedish language group in Finland and the German language group in Italy have the political power to develop policy formations of their own. This is not the consequence of devolved power, since Finland is highly centralised, and Italy has failed to implement its legislative decentralisation. Rather, it is the consequence of the treaties.

3 Stateless languages

These cases involve a link between legislative principles and policy measures concerning an LP agency that promote the production and reproduction of the minority language group. They include language groups in Spain, the UK, Ireland and Scandinavia. Some would include Luxembourgish here. However, according to the Constitution of Luxembourg, the national language is Luxembourgish but legislation and the regulations concerning their implementation are drawn up in French! The local and the central state accommodate the use of French, German and Luxembourgish in administration and legal affairs. This is a matter of stabilised discourses which cut across status associated contexts. Some of these comments also apply to Irish. Perhaps the Frisian case could be included, but is not, since even though it does have official status in the Netherlands this is not expressed in a specific law and LP is dispersed across several agencies.

A new form of governmentality is involved. There are specific historical conditions associated with each case, and there is no specific historical conjuncture that covers all cases. Stateless languages once remained on the margins of what was conceived of as essential to sustain the drive towards modernity and progress. A break in the relationship between progress and the exclusivity of state languages was necessary before stateless languages could be drawn into the policy frame.

Stateless language groups lack the kind of support which extraterritorial languages can solicit or obtain from other states. The language group may aspire to a nationalism which draws on the past in signifying its aspirations, but it is also a nationalism that is constructed of its own time. Language is often central to how this nationalism is signified.

3.1 Spain

The brief Republican period prior to 1936 generated aspirations that could not be realised until the death of Franco in 1975, which opened the door to a decentralised political regime. The new constitution constructed Spain as a plurilingual, pluricultural state (Alcaraz Ramos, 1999; Siguan, 1993). It retained the primacy of the state, and the priority of its universal language – Castilian – but constructed other languages as objects related to Spanish subjects who occupied particular spaces within state territory. These spaces were constructed as 'communities', and were allocated a degree of political autonomy. The eighteenth-century conception of the state as the sum of its constituent communities, and as the basis of social order and normativity, persisted. The nation is Spain, an object that remains a construction that conceives of the entire population of the state as expressing allegiance to that state. No one can construct herself as anything other than Spanish, except by being both Spanish and Catalan or Basque and so on, with the proviso that priority is accorded to the relationship between the individual subject and the state. This is clearly expressed in the introduction to the Spanish constitution:

> The Spanish nation . . . proclaims its will to . . . protect all Spaniards and Spanish territories in the exercise of human rights, their cultures and traditions, languages and institutions.

Article 2 of the constitution states:

> The Constitution takes the indissoluble unity of the Spanish Nation as its basis . . . and recognises and guarantees the right to home rule of the nationalities and regions which form it . . .

A distinction is made between 'Nation' and 'nationalities', priority being accorded to the former. A subordinate nationalism can pertain to regions.

It is axiomatic that a region is part of some greater entity and, in this case, it is made explicit that these are Spanish regions.

3.1.1 Castilian

Article 3 clearly constructs Castilian as the official state language, and as an obligatory aspect of citizenship:

> Castilian is the Spanish language that is official in the State. All Spaniards are obliged to know this language and have the right to use it.

Furthermore, Castilian no longer pertains merely to the region of Castile, but to the entire territory – Spain. The obligatory clause is missing by reference to other languages:

> The other Spanish languages will also be official in their respective Autonomous Communities, in accordance with their own Statutes of Autonomy.

These 'Spanish' languages belong to the state as 'variants', they are not normative. This non-normativity, in turn, is constructed as a 'cultural heritage'. That is, they are also constructed as objects which derive from the past and are in need of 'protection'. They are not seen as functional prerequisites.

The state retains the right to intervene in the legal status of the various languages, even if this contradicts the legal strictures of the Autonomous Communities. The meaning of 'official language' is given in the following statement by the Spanish Constitutional Court:

> a language is official irrespective of its reality and weight in society, when it is recognised by the public powers as a normal means of communication in and between said public bodies and in their relationship with other individuals, with complete validity and legal effect.

Legitimation derives from a normative context defined by use among public bodies, and relies upon public policy and its translation into practice. This normativity, supported by legislation, is an expression of overlap between legitimation and institutionalisation. It is assumed education ensures that everyone in Spain has a competence in Castilian. However, where relevant, all school pupils should have equal command of both Spanish and the regional language.

A model dictated by Catalan and Basque demands/desires has been extended to encompass all of Spain. The Constitution offered this possibility, but did not mark out the territorial boundaries of the Communities, nor the form of organisation of each element. The final 17 Autonomous

Communities evolved rather than being the result of a preconceived plan. The state's attempt to develop a modicum of coherence for the different statutes failed.

The legislative powers of the Autonomous legislature, created a space within which regionalism assumes a distinctive meaning, linking the identity and subject places constituted out of the nation object in relation to a particular geographical space. Multiple subjects are forged out of a political condition which, hitherto, had insisted upon the singular nation and singular citizen. The status of 'language' can apply to what was hitherto regarded as a 'dialect' of the state language. 'Language' is reconstitution as an object in relation to the subjects that speak it. There remains the struggle over the meaning of such objects.

The 'us'/'them' relationship is no longer defined and legitimised by reference to the state, and consolidated by spatial boundaries that are simultaneously state boundaries. Internal parameters of 'us'/'them' are legitimised, and can achieve more salience than those that pertain to the state. The prior discourse of history conditions the meanings assigned to contemporary subjects and objects. This interdiscursivity can have a powerful impact upon the social construction of meaning. Subject places are legitimised, and the associated identity institutionalised, becoming a new aspect of state normativity. The territorial fragmentation involves both the historical nations and the rest of Spain, tending to break up the entire conception of an integrated nation.

The Autonomous status was conferred on the 17 different regions between 1979 and 1983, the Spanish authorities dealing with each case separately. Six regions make reference to languages other than Castilian in their statutes, the language being constructed as the 'ownership' of the territory and its people; together with Castilian, it is an official language within the territory, and it is the right of all members of the Community to 'know and use their own language', and refers to the fact that no one should be discriminated against on the ground of language. A distinction is made between a language that 'belongs' to the territory and its people, and the state language which only has relevance for the Community as a consequence of it being part of the Spanish state. In Catalonia, Catalan is referred to as the *'lengua propia'* or the language of the people, conferring on the language a territorial integrity that contributes significantly to its legitimation.

Language acts confer and confirm the responsibility for language policy to the Autonomous Government. Legislation is much broader than language policies, laying down the basis whereby public administration must be conducted bilingually, the need for bilingual educational provision, and rights and responsibilities *vis à vis* culture and the media. Regions approach these issues differently, with the law in the Basque Autonomous Community and Navarre, for example, making explicit reference to translation where civil servants are not familiar with the Basque language, whereas a bilingual civil service is taken for granted in Catalonia, Catalan as Catalonia's rightful language being the norm for administrative purposes. This seeks to prioritise Catalan over Castilian, and also either advocates a bilingual normativity, or contests a Castilian normativity, in administrative affairs.

The traces of the prior discourse from the pre-Franco period influences institutionalisation, carrying a strong signification by reference to legitimisation, especially in Navarre and Valencia where competing discourses contest the relevant meanings.

In the following discussion three cases are left aside. Asturian is not a language which is referred to in the Spanish Constitution, thereby giving it less claim for authenticity than some of the other language groups. The Catalan language group in Majorca has a greater sense of consensus around the need to promote the regional language than in Valencia. However, there remains contention concerning whether or not that language is Catalan. The internal political struggle in process only in some respects parallels that in Valencia. Finally, Aranese in Val d'Aran questions the extent to which the Catalan authorities apply the same principles by which they have contested the primacy of Castilian in Catalonia, to a minority language within its own administrative territory.

3.1.2 Catalonia

The goal set by the Catalan government for its language planning initiative strives to ensure that Catalan becomes the predominant language within Catalonia. The nationalist parties, which have been in power since 1980, seek to achieve this as part of a process of national reconstruction. LP is conceived of as a political objective and not simply as a sociolinguistic exercise. The different discursive formations construct language so that each meaning reinforces the other.

After 1980, the initiative was one of consciousness raising, to implement the official use of Catalan in the public sector, and to establish the use of the educational structure for the generation of competence (Mari, 1991). More recently, the focus has shifted to extending the use context of Catalan, beginning with all of the government departments and activities. If the Statute of Autonomy claims that Catalan is the 'rightful' language of Catalonia, then it should be the normative language of administration:

> Catalan is the official language of Catalonia, as is the Castilian language which is official in the whole of the Spanish state.

The Statute proceeds: 'Catalonia's own language is Catalan.', Catalan is the 'proper language' and the Generalitat has the mandate to insure the normal use of the two official languages, to adopt the means necessary that will guarantee a knowledge of them, and to create a condition of equality between them by meeting the rights and obligations of Catalan citizens. 'Proper language' constructs Catalan as the unambiguous language of preferred use in Catalonia. 'Normal use' relates to the key concept of normalisation rather than to normativity as institutionalised social practice. The reference to 'Catalan citizens' sets the 'us/them' boundary by reference to the polity. Being non-marked, this does not exclude the possibility of the same individuals also being Spanish or European citizens. The points of reference are Catalonia and Catalans, welding citizenship with a knowledge of Catalan.

During the 1980s the Socialist Spanish government was critical of the need for Catalan civil servants to display a knowledge of both official languages. The recent entry of Catalan nationalist parties into an alliance that supports the ruling party in the Spanish government has, temporarily, silenced such opposition. Extending use to include the right of Catalans to use Catalan with any agency, public or private, in the 1990s has been interpreted as a measure of the success of the educational-linguistic immersion programme for the younger generation during the preceding decade. This led to research into the existing use structures, and the possibility of restructuring them; the development of a new organisational structure capable of implementing the new stage of language policy; and the development of a general plan of linguistic normalisation which would promote normalisation across the public and private sectors. A new language law reserved the status of 'proper language' to Catalan, while allocating the role of official language to both Catalan and Castilian. It prioritised Catalan, but in making both languages official, it also ensured the goal of a bilingual society devoid of linguistic discrimination. Strict guidelines regulated the promotion and monitoring of the use of Catalan across a wide range of activities. The interests of individuals was insured by making the use of either language possible in all contexts.

The General Plan, based on research results, integrated language policy with the process of social and economic restructuring, and the promotion of language use. Language is now a social entity responsible for cultural reproduction at the community level. Only if language is a feature of social normativity across all social activities will the free choice of language use by individuals be possible. A balanced relationship among languages that derives from the equality and reciprocity of the rights of linguistic communities and the language speakers is necessary. Without access to the entire range of civil society activities within a particular language, the referenced language group is endangered. The Plan is monitored constantly and modified accordingly.

Side by side with this social science orthodoxy are elements of neo-liberalism which, to an extent, clash with it. 'Ownership' transforms the language through reification into a commodity – the language belongs to the community. Choice is possible by enabling and empowering the citizen to use the respective languages in their dialogue with the public and private sector. Despite the continued emphasis on rights, we find reference to equalities of opportunities through enablement. The end goal is institutionalised communications. The distinction between 'its own language' and 'other languages' overlaps with the state/civil society distinction. Universal competence in the language means that choice pertains only to which of the two state languages is to be used in official business.

Political inclusion has focused upon public intervention rather than on social consensus and grass roots implementation. The authorities have been sensitive to public opinion, and have even tried to manipulate it, but policy has, by and large, been driven by the various public authorities. This can lead to a dependency relationship between language promotion and language use which can fluctuate with changes in political power holders, as has happened in neighbouring Valencia. The massive financial support afforded to Catalan language services within the public sector is rationalised by arguing that if the language can be institutionalised within these agencies, the support is for the services and not for the language within which they are offered.

Catalan language planning has been conditioned by the strength of the nationalist vote and the liberal democracy of the centre-right. Yet it was the left which gave the main impulse to incorporating Catalan in the statute as the proper language of Catalonia, and in extending Catalan language use. The nationalist centre-right has been most sensitive to the fear that public opinion did not support such an extension. The right is relatively weak in Catalonia. This LP discourse makes it difficult to establish a place to speak from which opposes the institutionalisation of the Catalan language because of how Catalan and the state are constructed. Opposition becomes an external rather than an internal marker.

3.1.3 Valencia

Within the Valencian Autonomous Community language legislation merely sets the parameters within which policy can be developed. How policy develops depends very much upon how different discursive formations construct meanings for the relevant subjects and objects. The same laws can lead to quite different policy objectives and LP formulations. Legitimisation is subject to interpretation. There is a political struggle associated with language, which does not allow subjects and objects to be stabilised.

The constructions 'Catalan' and 'Valencian' relate to the territorial constructions 'Catalonia' and 'Valencia'. Valencia includes the line between historical Spain and historical Catalonia. Almost half of the population speaks Catalan/Valencian, 30 per cent can read the language, 15 per cent can write it and 79 per cent can understand it. Most of the bilingual population resides in the most populous areas, the empty interior being occupied by monoglot Castilian speakers.

The confrontation between pan-Catalanism and pan-Castilianism revolves, on the one hand, around the construction of Catalonia as a historic nation that transcends any contemporary subdivisions, being the homeland of the Catalan people; and on the other hand the proclamation of Castilian as the language of a single and indivisible Spain. Both discourses seek to transcend the current division of space into Autonomous Communities. Pan-Catalanism constitutes a direct challenge to the integrity of the state, and the struggle over normativity involves issues of space, polity, subjects and objects. Language becomes the marker of unity, being constructed as a feature of the commonality of people which carries a 'coherence and substance' (Marin, 1996). Linguistic science is the arbitrator of what is and what is not a language.

The pan-Catalan discourse constructs Catalan as the official language spoken in northern Valencia. The territory consists of two linguistic zones – a 'Catalan/Valencian-speaking region' and 'Castilian-speaking areas'. In the former, 14 per cent do not speak Catalan, whereas in the latter 74 per cent do not speak Catalan. On statistical grounds, priority is accorded to the former which is claimed to constitute a 'territorial, economic and cultural unity' that is under threat from the central state. The Catalan/Valencian language is constructed as a dialect of standard Catalan, the basis of 'linguistic unity' and a legitimacy which has implications for other spoken forms which must be compared with it and linked to it. The mother idiom with which minor forms relate, integrates other members of the 'family', thereby consolidating the 'us'/'them' boundary. Standadisation is linked to a spatial, political and social agglomeration, thereby representing a 'community' defined by reference to a 'Catalan space' which has political aspirations. It raises the question of whether those in Valencia who speak the dialect are Catalans, or Valencians, or something else? Being Spanish cannot be questioned. Territoriality involves autochthony and the relationship between 'people' and 'territory', subject to an 'enforced Castilianisation' which precludes Castilian having an autochthonous status.

The alternative discursive formation constructs Catalan/Valencian as unambiguously Valencian, refuting the concept of a Greater Catalonia. The language of Valencia – Valencian – pertains to Valencia and nowhere else, and cannot be a dialect of anything, but becomes an 'idiom'. There is an overlap of territory and language, not only by reference to Valencian and Valencia, but also of Valencia as an integral part of Spain. It sits side by side with Castilian, which is also Spanish. Spain is thereby constructed as an inclusive concept, the spatial closure not equating with either social or linguistic closure. Valencian is neither Catalan nor Castilian, but is unrefutedly Spanish. The 'us' of Valencia is opposed to the 'them' of 'Catalan', but is accommodated into the 'us' of Spain.

This process of construction is expressed from the place constructed by the Catalan discourse as follows:

the right-wing forces in Valencia, centralist from time immemorial, have discovered a trick by which to ensure their survival in the face of the threat posed by this democratic interlude. A 'Valencian language' has been invented, which all Valencians must defend against Catalan.

(Aracil, 1983:131)

This text constructs a series of opposing dualisms as follows:

Catalan	Centrist
Democratic	non-democratic (non-marked)
left-wing (not marked)	right-wing
Catalan	Valencian
Catalan	Castilian (non-marked)

It constructs a threat – Greater Catalonia – that is balanced against a state centrism that equates with a particular political philosophy and serves as a bulwark against the threat. 'Valencian' is presented as a social construct that defends centrist interests. It achieves this end, not merely by opposition, but by 'the disarticulation and dismemberment of its rival, namely Catalan'. It leaves open the possibility of sustaining Valencian in opposition to both Catalan and Castilian.

These constructions of meaning prefigure the object that requires planning, and the nature of the subjects who relate to that object. Both discourses appeal to History and Linguistics as the basis for their respective claims. They pertain to the polar extremes of political ideology, forcing an intermediate discursive place that conforms, in its entirety, to neither of the two extremes. In the Statute of Autonomy and the legislation that pertained to teaching and using Valencian, the second official language is 'Valencian', the 'own' language of the Valencian Community. The ambiguity by reference to what 'Valencian' consists of and how it should be standardised remains, and it is the space that such a construction opens up that has been filled in different ways by the different political parties which operate LP as social policy.

The right seeks to confirm Valencian as a unique language by establishing linguistic norms for it. The Socialists construct Valencian as a dialect of Catalan, subject to Catalan linguistic standardisation. Neither side has paid much attention to language status, and the promotion of its use, even where it has been treated as the signification force for Valencian unity. How the object is constructed limits how it relates to the subjects that associate with it. It is difficult to construct a policy of unity out of such different subject constructions.

3.1.4   The Basque Autonomous Community

Within the Statute of Autonomy Euskera is described as 'the language of the Basque people', claiming that all residents of the region will have the right to know both Spanish and Euskera, public bodies guaranteeing the use of both languages. This is an enablement statement rather than a measure of compulsion by reference to Euskera. However, there is a rider that is not made explicit in the form of the statement 'bearing in mind the Basque Country's sociolinguistic diversity' (Cenoz, 2001).

The language planning agency of the Ministry of Culture co-ordinates and monitors the regional government's language policy, and co-ordinates with the local councils as well as with the voluntary and private sectors. The joint budget of the public bodies associated with LP is of the order of $\in 10$ m. Its actions are conditioned by the need to insure public support for its actions, to develop policies which do not infringe the rights of anyone, and to develop a grass-roots approach to policy formation. Policy was preceded by extensive research, focusing largely on a survey of competence and use which acts as a benchmark. Corpus planning runs parallel with the ground that has been gained within the educational sector through status planning.

Since 1989 extending the Basque language competence of civil servants has involved in-post training within the administration itself. Between 1990 and 1995, almost 9000 civil servant positions – 34 per cent of all civil servants working for the regional government, the internal councils and the local councils – carried a Basque language qualification. Subsidies and monitoring plans are offered to companies to integrate the Basque language into the private sector.

The current concern is that those who have been subject to the production process, learning the language within the community or at school, retain the level of competence as adults. In this respect they are moving towards a higher degree of collaboration across institutions and across the public, private and voluntary sector.

About a quarter of its population is born outside of the region, and a similar proportion speaks Euskera. The majority of the population is from the region and this is reflected in political affiliation. The polarity and contestation of the situation in Valencia does not apply. The autonomous government has general support for its language policies, largely because the opposition which accrues to centrist parties is weak. Euskera is an unambiguous concept, and the language is constructed as an object which bears an equally unambiguous relationship to that conception. The emphasis on enabling principles carries the support of the majority.

3.1.5 Navarre

Historically, Navarre has had some degree of continuous autonomy since the Middle Ages. The northern part is occupied by the Basque language group, and Basque nationalist parties contest the hegemony of the Spanish Socialist Party (PSOE). Two extraterritorial units – Spanish and Basque – are contesting their legitimacy *vis à vis* territorial rights within an autonomous community. Political separatism becomes significant since the autonomous status of the community implies a unitary conception of the relationship between people and territory.

Basque is an official language within a defined area of the territory. When this was debated, the Basque nationalists refused to vote, preferring to construct Basque as the language of the Basque nation. The concept of a 'Basque Country' parallels that of the 'Greater Catalonia'. The other parties construct Basque as of relevance to Navarre rather than to the 'Greater Basque nation', a concept which they reject. Referring to the language as Basque acknowledges its signification by reference to a distinctive population which may not be only of relevance to Navarre. No attempt is made to construct the Basque language as the Community's 'own language'.

A percentage of the civil servants that conforms with the percentage of the local population that speaks the language must have a knowledge of Euskera. These figures are reviewed each five years. The regional government determines which of the jobs advertised carry a Basque language qualification. For the other positions a knowledge of Basque is treated as desirable. Despite the existence of legislation to the effect that similar codes should be used by reference to the offices of the central state, these have yet to be put into practice.

3.1.6   Galicia

The first controlling party in autonomous Galicia was the Spanish Conservative Party whose right-wing views have never been accommodative of linguistic and cultural diversity. Later they shared power with the regionalist and nationalist parties of Galicia, leading to legislation associated with 'Linguistic Normalisation' and to the establishment of a formal language planning agency (Garcia Negro, 2000).

Legislation gives a central place to language:

> The 1978 Constitution, on recognising our rights to self-government as a historical nationality, made possible the initiation of a constructive effort aimed at the full recovery of our collective identity and its creative potential. One of the basic factors in this recovery is the language because it is the vital nucleus of our identity. The language is the greatest and most original creation of the Galicians, and the true spiritual force which grants internal unity to our community.

This statement speaks on behalf of all 'Galicians' as a 'nationality', lacking a 'collective identity'. Language sets the boundaries of 'us' and 'them'. The recovery of identity must involve the recovery of language which is constructed as a 'collective creation', and a 'spiritual force' that unifies. Language links with the construction of Galician subjects, and of the community they belong to. It is reminiscent of the Basque and Catalan laws, both of which reflect a similar centrality for language. It does seem at odds with the views of a right-wing Spanish party – Alianza Popular.

The 'us'/'them' duality intensified after the creation of the Autonomous Community, and part of the opposition to the centrism of the right has involved a radical nationalism. The legitimation of the autonomous status, together with the status confirmed on the various defining objects and notions, has linked with the prior discourse to confirm a distinctive signification of which language is part. Language is established as a symbolic object of considerable significance. Even the centrist parties are adopting an exclusively Galician platform and a Galician structure for their own administration. The regional political platform allows all political parties to develop a truly regional orientation without centrist constraints.

The *Sociolinguistic Map of Galicia* published in 1996 (Galician Regional Government) and the survey on which it was based identified a low level of literacy and a widespread use of the language. The associated low status of the language was redressed through legitimation, a literacy campaign and an extension of use. This does generate an internal division which does not involve a rejection of regional identity as in the Valencian case. It is a statement about language status, and how the respective language objects are constructed in the respective discourses.

3.1.6 Conclusion

The constitutional emergence of autonomous authority was linked to the salience of the prior discourse. The devolutionary process was the means whereby the goals of the pre-Franco aspirations could be met. Language became the defining force of the autonomous status for several of the communities, even if it was constructed by reference to the needs of existing administrative structures and conceptions as it developed into policy strictures. The reformulation of administrative priorities, and the understanding of the nature of the relationship between policy, administration and planning has incorporated language planning. The prior discourse, how it constructs language and its entry into the interdiscursive context which links it to current administrative needs, accounts for the variation in language planning across the various communities.

3.2 The British Isles

There are two cases where there has developed a fairly coherent language planning orientation aligned with the creation of associated agencies – Ireland and Wales.

3.2.1 Ireland[2]

Irish has been at the heart of how Ireland has been constructed as an object since the rise of modernism. During the nineteenth century language symbolised the Irish quest for independence from an English-dominated British

state. Following independence in 1922, the Irish state sought to re-establish Irish as the national language. Irish was constructed as 'the national language', but with English being constructed as an 'official language' on a par with Irish.

Policies implemented in locations where there was sufficient density of Irish speakers for communities to conduct their affairs largely through the medium of Irish – the *Gaeltacht* – sought to link the reproduction of Irish with principles of regional development to prevent out-migration. Outside of the *Gaeltacht* the focus was upon language production or 'revival'. Education was to proceed by gradually replacing English with Irish in all Irish schools. Establishing Irish language services implied public servants should use Irish in their work. However, no steps were taken to incorporate non-Irish speakers already in the civil service into the language group. Creating a body specifically designed to deal with the language was resisted for fear of creating Irish as deviant.

In 1969 the Irish Language Council was established, *Bord na Gaelige* which was responsible for language promotion in 1975, *Udaras na Gaeltachta* responsible for economic development and language production and reproduction within the *Gaeltacht* in 1978, the Irish Language Institute responsible for research in 1972, and *An Gum* responsible for Irish-language publishing. Despite the persistence with economic planning, Irish has tended to be marginalised within the overall governmental structure, being associated with culture and the Irish periphery rather than with mainstream Ireland.[3]

Udaras na Galetachta focused on 'integrated rural development'. Its mission statement is: 'To develop the economy of the *Gaeltacht* so as to facilitate the preservation and extension of the Irish language as the principal language of the region.' This is achieved by promoting employment, partly via inward investment and community development. However, it lacks a clear conception of the link between language and work, and inward investment has given way to the concept of sustainable indigenous growth. It has been sensitive to local labour-market penetration as a consequence of inward investment, and insists that enterprises have a language-practice code that enhances the status of Irish within their business operations. It provides Irish language courses for in-migrant employees who do not speak Irish, and promotes community co-operatives.

Bord na Gaelige involved a shift from obligatory to enabling measures. The goal of the Irish state was European economic and political integration through 'modernisation', rather than a focus upon the basis of its distinctive cultural and political identity. Planning involved the consent of the citizenry, gained through monitoring and shaping attitudes. Attitudinal factors placed the onus on the citizen and contrasts with the directive approach of planning that relies upon state intervention. This was a manifestation of the state's frustration with its inability to advance the goal of regeneration, and it opted for policies that placed the onus on the citizen. Social and political administration was subject to substantial restructuring based upon rationalisation, both by distinguishing between policy and implementation, and involving a highly hierarchical responsibility structure.

Bord na Gaelige sought to institutionalise language planning within state administration, by developing planning initiatives which would be translated into policy and implementation (O'Riagain and Tovey, 1998). Language was constructed as a feature of society, rather than being reified as an object that was of importance to Ireland and its people. The Act of 1978 states its primary function as 'to promote the Irish language and in particular its use as a living language and as an ordinary means of communication'. Nonetheless, the emphasis was on the promotion of language use rather than on the planning function.

The goal of *Bord na Galeige* was to enable people to use Irish within Irish society writ large, while insuring that both languages had equal status. The concepts of domain and diglossia were central to these ideas. Currently *Bord na Gaelige* espouses the goal of promoting 'a society-wide individual bilingualism', but its *de facto* goal is that of maintaining 'the language rights of Irish-using groups and communities', and enabling Irish speakers to use the language (ibid.).

The three-year Action Plan of the early 1980s involved the monitoring of measurable goals. The Plan rested on two assumptions – that general support for Irish emanated from 'the national community' and that public services had to be available in Irish. Language is commodified within a neo-liberal discourse, and voluntary associations were implicated in promoting Irish. Tovey (1988:65) describes the plan as follows: 'The survival of Irish gives the consumer more choice . . . but . . . choice can only be guaranteed through some degree of state protection in a basically *laissez-faire* situation.' Language use is institutionalised practice, and enabling people does not guarantee change in practice.

This neo-liberal rhetoric emphasised public-private partnership formation. The choice of language in relationships with the state was guaranteed, each state department developing proactive planning to meet this goal. *Bord na Gaelige* was deeply involved. Research demonstrated that state provision in Irish was totally inadequate. These initiatives involve the provision of quality services that meet the needs and expectations of the consumer, and discussion on moves to sanctions for non-compliance.

The distinction between status planning and use planning implies that *Bord na Gaelige* should be seen as a language promotion agency rather than as a language planning agency. Neither *Bord na Gaelige* nor *Udaras na Gaeltacht* are language planning agencies in operational terms (O'Riagain and Tovey, 1998). The latter operates by reference to the discourse of regional and rural development without a conception of how these relate to institutionalising the use of Irish. The former operates as a promotional enterprise, again without any conception of what it could achieve as a planning agency. The institutional and political structures in Ireland construct the language and the language group in specific ways *vis à vis* the different political and administrative functions and organisations, making language planning an open option for either agency. This merely depoliticises language, constructing it as an object that relates to either population maintenance or consensus promotion. The new govermentality associated with the 1990s merely intensifies this tendency.

3.2.2   Wales[4]

Prior to 1967 Welsh had no official status, and the 1967 Welsh Language Act merely legitimised Welsh as a minority language (Williams, 1987b). Welsh had been standardised at an early date and corpus planning was thereafter an on-going process. The process of institutionalising Welsh as the language of education and learning had proceeded throughout the twentieth century. The 1967 Act did not recommend establishing a formal language planning agency and did not lead to establishing one. It was innovative only by reference to constructing the language as a legal entity, and was merely a prologue to language planning *per se*, and as an adjunct to existing social policy as it pertained to the Welsh language (Williams and Roberts, 1983). This was characteristic of how the liberal state addressed its relationships with its constituency – concessions to minority groups are possible, and even desirable in so far as they do not prejudice the nature of the dominant/subordinate relationship. Drawing Welsh into the legal framework was a recognition of the state's responsibility for issues pertaining to it, while also signifying the language group's subordination to the state. This duality is the consequence of legitimation.

The 1993 Act involved taking the same neo-liberal principles as in Ireland much further as a consequence of the extent to which neo-liberalism has become the main edifice supporting the political philosophy in UK politics. Neo-liberalism claims that state welfarism has fettered individual creativity by creating a paternalistic, dependent relationship between the individual and the state. A different form of democracy, based upon enabling rather than upon citizen rights, or universal ethical principles, is required. States should respond to the needs and expectations of the citizen rather than directing them towards certain ends. The animator state responds to problems via organisation, co-operation and confrontation between public services, elected administration and associations, with social actors playing a more active role in the solution of social and economic problems. Society is replaced by a focus upon the individual, the family and the community.

The Welsh Language Board administers the 1993 Act and is accountable to the Welsh Assembly Government, operating policy determined by the Assembly which appoints Board members who provide guidance and direction. The Board has a degree of authority over many public sector agencies, including the local education authorities, who are obliged to address how they intend to conform with the demands of the Act via the Welsh Language Board.

The Board's (1993) document *A Strategy for the Welsh Language* states:

> The Welsh language is the common property of all Welsh people, whether they speak the language or not. It is part of a cultural heritage of all the people of Wales, indeed of Britain, of Europe and beyond. The same is true of the English language.
>
> The Board aspires to see the day when those in Wales whose preferred language is Welsh will have the same rights as those whose preferred language is English. In a world and continent which are still divided by ethnic and national differences, this is an ambitious aim. But there are encouraging signs as well, as multilingual and multicultural frameworks are increasingly accepted in society. It is within such a framework . . . that we must now consider the future of the language.

Language is reified and commodified, establishing it as an object separate from its speakers, as something which can be operated on, as something which can be given value, as a property, involving ownership, and incorporated into an economist discourse. It does not pertain to individual ownership, but is of relevance to the entire world. The value of linguistic diversity is contextualised by making a similar claim for English – the 'Other' of language in Wales. Sustaining diversity is in the interest of everyone. It is impossible to lie outside of a field of interest.

The 'people of Wales' links subject and object, whereas 'Welsh people' pertains merely to subjects. The object 'Wales' is a geographical space that is not circumscribed, but is part of an ever-larger geographical space. The subjects become 'those in Wales' being constructed as part of 'Welsh people' which is not marked. Welsh and English in Wales are objects that relate to subjects who are conceived of as having both preferences and rights. Those who opt for one preference have different rights from those who opt for the other preference. This dissymmetry is the focus of the Board's concern. The difference of rights relates to 'ethnic and national differences' which hinder the aim of equal rights, and are counterposed to 'multilingual and multi-cultural frameworks' which are 'accepted in society'. 'Ethnicity' and 'nation' are divisive. Since the converse of multilingualism and multiculturalism pertain to society, the reference is to social divisiveness. Imposition gives way to persuasion in resolving division. Any sense of nationalism is refuted, thereby negating any explicit political involvement. Language is depoliti-cised. Where ethnicity and nationalism are correlates of identity, language and culture are objective dimensions. The author is distanced from any emotive context.

Enabling and grass rootism as dimensions of non-directionality link with the political objective of achieving goals through placid means, relating to the commitment of the individual to the greater good of the community, uniting the essential principles of the individual, the family and the community. Protest, or direct action, merely alienates. The involvement of other agencies which are the main providers leaves the Board with a strong mandate but a weak involvement. Consequently, partnership of co-operation leading to consensus is a means of uniting everyone 'working for the benefit of the language' who will agree to pursue the Board's strategy. It results in 'taking the language out of politics' and divesting the language of any moral or ethical context. The onus is on the individual and the state is divested of any responsibility – if the individual does not avail herself of the opportunity implicit in the enabling process, then the consequence is her own fault.

The shift from the world of ethics to the world of technology negates concerns with the morality of minority status, people are enabled to exercise their preferences by reference to goals and values within an asocietal context. In LP, self-regulation is implemented via a behaviourist model of action. The goal is 'To enable the Welsh language to be self-sustaining and secure as a medium of communication in Wales'. This is to be achieved by increasing the number of speakers, expanding the possibility of use, changing use structures, and strengthening the use of Welsh in the community.

Changing language behaviour invokes the punish/recompensation principles of neo-liberalism and the reasonable, rational subject. Enabling involves using 'the language naturally when conducting their business or when receiving bilingual services from bodies or companies operating in Wales', and is distinguished from the interactional use of language and, presumably, the means of 'persuasion' varies accordingly. The 'natural' use of language contributes to the 'natural life of Wales', and derives from the regular use of the language in 'everyday life'.

The Board seeks to develop partnerships with private sector companies, selected by reference to relevance and potential for co-operation. Language is a commodity that can enhance the business potential of the company. Within the market, the cost of developing an adequate policy will pay off by the increase in business. Cost derives from implementing the company or agency's language policy, benefit in terms of language, and profit in terms of public satisfaction and effectiveness. The relationship between cost and benefit must result in profit through a service content that is commensurate with the needs and expectations of the consumer, leading to enhanced efficiency and satisfaction.

The needs and expectations of the Welsh speaker will be met by Welsh language service provision. This involves changing the consumer's attitude to language use. Attitudes are held to be manifestations of values. If values can be changed, then so can attitudes, and thereby, needs and expectations. This behaviourism involves 'marketing the language in order to change attitudes, raise the confidence of Welsh speakers, or improve the image of the language'. It blames the victim via a deficiency argument, and views the problem, not by reference to structural causality, but by reference to the individual psyche.

The stabilisation or institutionalisation of language practice makes this goal difficult to achieve. Changing individual behaviour must derive from grass rootism. Companies may respond without any associated response from the Welsh-speaking customer. A misplaced understanding of the reason for the consumer's non-compliance can lead to the private sector interpreting their own action as a waste of time, and of the Board interpreting non-compliance as non-rational behaviour!

Welsh is not treated as a 'national' language with all of the moral and emotive implications, but as a language that can be used with some institutions, in some places, at some times, and never outside of Wales. Geography and not speakers becomes the measure whereby needs and expectations are measured. Equality is used by reference to treating the two languages equally rather than to the equal use of the two languages. This fails to accommodate the normal context of equality in language group relationships, where reference is to institutionalisation and how it constrains language use. Equality or inequality by reference to language groups as social groups is missing, and the Act, like the previous Act, merely confirms and legitimises the minority status of Welsh.

'Normative' pertains to the goal of 'making normal' rather than institutionalised social practice. As a Welsh speaker, the individual is obliged to mark him/herself as such in order to be enabled by informing the organising body of a public meeting of a desire to use Welsh, leaving the decision as to whether or not this will be possible to that body. The Welsh speaker marks herself as a deviant from the norm. Welsh is marked either as deviance from the norm or as a 'first language', but never as a principle. The enabling principle implies the existence of deviant practice – it is never necessary to enable the normative – so that the entire Act merely serves to confirm this deviance. There is a confusion of normal as 'not being deviant', with the idea of norm as prioritising.

3.2.3 Sweden and Finland

There are an estimated 40 000 Sami in Norway, 17 000 in Sweden, 6000 in Finland and 2000 in Russia, being subject to four different legislative and administrative systems. They consist of different language groups, both within states and across states. We are discussing a number of different language groups, but the Sami regard themselves as a single cultural group, subject to the legal and administrative strictures of the states where they reside (Aikio and Hyrvarinen, 1995).

Much of the Sami discourse on their existence as a 'people' revolves around a non-capitalist mode of production, with ownership pertaining to the group rather than the individual, and territoriality becomes a central component of identity formation. Rights, including economic rights, are conferred by reference to descent and group membership. Identity is based upon a particular configuration of time, place and person. This is at odds with the modernist state, its legal strictures and the associated focus on individualism and private property.

Sections 14 and 51a of the Finnish law of Fundamental Rights of 1995 involves a right where the responsibility is imposed on the language groups themselves, but this will involve interaction between the state and the language group, and this demands a response from the state. No mention is made of the exclusivity of Sami languages and Finnish is present, but unmarked. An autonomous status by reference to culture would 'permit the Sami to live in a multilingual, multicultural Finnish society in accordance with their own identity and way of life' (Aikio and Hyrvarinen, 1995:98). The focus is upon the emotive world of 'language and culture', and the document is comparable to the various postwar Border Treaties. The 1991 Sami Language Act did not grant the legal status accorded to either the Finnish or Swedish language group, and focused upon the use of Sami with state officials. A further Act of 1993 created three research centres for Finnish, Swedish and Sami as the 'domestic languages' of Finland.

Language is linked to economic practices – fishing, hunting and herding – the associated terminology involving the relationship between corporate rights, territory and descent. The Sami discourse on language and being conflicts with that of the state whose discourse focuses upon the customary relationship between citizenship, rights, the free mobility of labour and individual access to economic resources.

The Sami Parliament established in 1973 has no independent decision-making powers deriving from the relevant Act, but is responsible for 'promoting Sami cultural conditions'. It appoints members to other key agencies that cover economy, media and education. It distributes funds assigned by the state for promoting Sami culture in Finland. The 20 members of the Parliament are elected from a Sami list every four years. Yet it has no authority to represent the Finnish Sami, even though it is accountable to the Ministry of the Interior, and its staff consists of civil servants. It is consulted by the government and has helped draft relevant legislation.

Democracy implies that whoever holds responsibility and accountability should have a say in the decision that affect it. In practice central government treats consultation in a *post facto* manner, drafting legislation by reference to centrally defined needs before seeking consultation. This is not akin to having a direct say in policy. Moves are afoot to replace the Parliament by an Assembly, thereby giving it the power to initiate, petition and to make public statements.

As 'the only indigenous people in Finland', the Sami are a special group. Parliament hears their views on matters affecting them. This concession merely pertains to the Sami people rather than the territory and its occupants, partly a consequence of the Sami being a minority within their own territory. State ministries, other than the Ministry for Forestry and Agriculture, the one Ministry whose responsibilities pertain to their economic activities, regularly consult the Sami. This Ministry is obliged to recognise the Sami as 'indigenous people', but in practice refuses to do so because this could involve conceding them special rights to water, land and livelihood.

Any definition of 'Sami' must encompass much more than language. The relatively small percentage of the population which speaks a Sami language, and the inclusion of Finnish in-migrants constitutes a dilemma for those Sami promoting Sami languages within the context of collective rights and identity.

Legitimation and the associated policy implementation in Sweden is somewhat different. The distinction remains between one conception of being which integrates time, space and person, economy and language, and another which separates language from being, obliging it to be a feature of a rationally constructed identity. Swedish authorities use only Swedish, and are only obliged to provide a Sami interpreter when the protagonist has no knowledge of Swedish.

The Social Democrats drew on the 1983 report on 'The Status of the Sami in International Law' to establish new policy by reference to the Sami. They have yet to acknowledge Sami as a people, treating them as Swedes and nothing else, and the Sami languages are not recognised in Sweden. The Swedish Parliament rejected the Report's recommendation that the Sami be recognised as an indigenous people and treats them as 'ethnic minorities'. Litigation in the Supreme Court confirmed Sami interests on the basis of occupation and immemorial rights, but Parliament rejected any conception of special Sami land rights and has nationalised Sami hunting lands, making them accessible to all Swedes in the name of 'Swedish public interest'. Reindeer herding rights are restricted to the Sami, with almost 40 per cent of Swedish territory being allocated for such use.

In 1993 a Sami Parliament of 31 members as an advisory body to the central government was created. It takes decisions concerning the distribution of state and other funding that pertains to Sami culture and institutions. It appoints members of the School Board, and leads the work on the Sami languages. It represents Sami interests and provides a research/information function. The presidency is the prerogative of the government and not of the Parliament. It is difficult, if not impossible, for the Parliament to enter litigation against the state in national and international courts. Despite misgivings on the part of the Sami, the Parliament has become operational.

The goal of the Sami is to establish a pan-Sami Parliament, maximising the gains by reference to land rights, and confirming measures to promote the language group. The pan-Sami Parliament would consist of members drawn from the four member states, and would acknowledge the existence of the Sami as a single people. The Nordic Sami Council is important in this respect.

4 The political spectrum and diversity

The right in Europe has always favoured the homogenous state and opposed the concept of cultural diversity. The conception of domestic grandeur and how it separated the ruling class as aristocracy from the remainder of the population continued to influence modernism (Boltanski and Thevenot, 1991). The European left has been equally influenced by the evolutionist discourse, and has tended to draw upon the importance of the international class alliance and the drive for world hegemony in order to argue against diversity.

If a centrist party has sufficient confidence in its regional power base, it can develop regional orientations that are constructive, since the discourse of devolution legitimises the regional without it being conceived of as a threat to the integrity of the state. Achieving a truly regional identity, even to the extent of becoming regional parties, leads to the promotion of the regional language becoming a marker of that regional affinity. It proclaims the 'us' of the region against the 'them' of other regions rather than against the 'them' of the centre and the totality.

Few states have adopted a uniform position *vis à vis* language groups and language planning by reference to all of the language groups within their territories, but have responded to the different language groups and to the strength of the 'voice' that they have used to express their needs. Blanket policy perspectives similar to how, say, human rights have been conceived, are missing. A devolved democracy sometimes gives language groups responsibility; in other cases as little as is necessary is conceded in achieving political stability. There is a resounding silence by reference to many states and minority language groups.

All LP frameworks reveal a direct relationship between education and language planning, involving the state's obligation by reference to the production of competence. Often this is the consequence of obligations that derive from international treaties, which are frequently seen as the limit of the state's obligation. Other cases encompass the relationship between the state or the local state and the public, through the idea that public service provision must response to the needs and expectations of the consumer. Neo-liberal forms of governmentality do generate uniformity.

The relationship between legitimisation and the institutionalisation of language use as social practice demands a clear understanding on the part of legislators of how language planning leads to language use. Practitioners must have a clear understanding of the relationship between legitimation and institutionalisation. There must also be a positive relationship between the polity and the planning agency. Where the polity has a clear and positive understanding of the goals of language planning, it becomes a positive exercise. If the polity is less than enthusiastic, there is the clear danger of either limiting language planning to legal implementation, or of undoing work that may have been undertaken under a previous regime.

Language planning is a long-term process that requires either a long-term political stability, or a new form of consensus politics if it is to be productive.

3
Education

1 Introduction

Omitted from the preceding discussion was the tendency for LP agencies to incorporate work on education, the media and culture. Education has tended to be seen as the means whereby language group production and reproduction proceeds. Within the modern state, education has two goals; labour market integration and the ideological aspect of citizen production. As such it is the means of generating reason among the citizenry. Relating minority languages and education implies accepting their relevance for reason and for the labour market.

This economic model of education involves a search for a uniformity of 'quality', measured by qualifications across all scholarly institutions. The link between language, society, reason and educational achievement was one of mutual dependence. Within pedagogic discourse development is linked with 'failure' in terms of the goals of the educational institution and any discordance with its function. Failure is 'explained' in terms of language, society and reason, and usually leads to a 'new' discourse which focuses upon a shift in pedagogy.

Again, incorporating minority languages in state education happens when the state is sufficiently self-confident by reference to its hegemony. During the nineteenth century states were being consolidated, and the link between normativity and social order was being established. Techniques of governance focused on security. This remains the case for some European states. The school individualised the pupil and brought her within the normative order. The regime of supervision and judgment involved norms of scholarly and moral behaviour related to reason and the social norm. The individual was judged, and also judged herself by reference to the social norm. The child was to conduct the rational behaviour of being a citizen by reference to a rational language. A single, exclusive language of reason operated, regardless of social and family practice:

Subjects such as English were to be introduced into the curriculum, not for purely 'aesthetic' reasons so beloved of those who defend 'liberal education' today, but because they would provide a language for speaking about them, they would provide criteria for judging them: in short, they would actually create new civilised sensibilities.

(Rose, 1995:220)

The end result was self-governance through introspection, the formal link between language, education and democracy.

The relationship of the polity to constitutional and demographic processes has some bearing on the extent to which minority languages are introduced into schooling and the curriculum. Federal states delegate responsibility to constituent units in a way that centralist states do not, but the regional state must always defer to the integrity of the overall polity. This partly explains variation in minority language educational policies within Europe.

States legitimising minority languages have tended to use education as the *raison d'être* of language production and reproduction. Yet, if a knowledge of the language taught is a necessary qualification for teaching it, which is not always the case, the language does pertain to the labour market. Similarly, a language will not have an impact on the labour market unless it plays a role within the educational structure.

Considering education and the labour market involves social reproduction and the class structure of any society (Williams and Roberts, 1982). Language assumes a crucial intermediary influence (Bourdieu, 1982, *inter alia*). The focus has been on varieties of the state language, those concerned tending to disregard minority languages as having little relevance for social reproduction,[1] perhaps because of the limited extent to which such languages have entered the education system. This betrays an unwillingness to consider the range of subject positions and associated identities which influence social inequality.

The advent of compulsory primary education for the citizen served the two primary purposes of education within the rational state. It was inconceivable that, at the initial stage of such compulsory action, the ideological role could yield to the economic (Boltanski, 1984). Currently, however, neoliberalism emphasises the importance of learning as opposed to education, and the importance of reflexivity for learning extends to accommodate the significance of language for this process.

As the understanding of the relationship between language, education and society changes, so too does the relationship of the language group to the different functions of society. Linking language and education merely to produce or reproduce that language is to construct both language and education in a particular way. The Philosophy of Education as a meta-discourse involves how minority languages have or have not been incorporated into state systems of education.

Establishing the extent to which a minority language is used in education within any state is not easy. How languages are introduced into the curriculum at different levels of the education system, for different subjects, or for different time lengths varies considerably. A simple example is illustrative. Welsh has tended to be restricted to the arts subjects, with even Welsh-medium schools often preferring to teach the sciences through the medium of English. There is also a tendency, across Europe,[2] for males to be encouraged to study the sciences and for women to focus upon the arts. Orthodox discourse has constructed the arts as the field of emotion, demanding emotive expression and creativity, and involving poetry, music and so on, while science is constructed as the domain of reason *par excellence*. Educational practice constructs the sciences as rational and the arts as emotional. Consequently, women are constructed as emotional subjects, and men as rational subjects. Welsh is emotional and English is rational! This does not operate at the level of consciousness or open discrimination, but is institutionalised as social and educational practices. There are schools which teach both the arts and sciences through the medium of Welsh, but none which teach science through the medium of Welsh and the arts through the medium of English! The meanings of the disciplines, the genders or the languages are not stabilised in a universal way within the educational discourse.

Access to minority language education, by reference to level and location also varies. It tells us how the language and the associated language group are constructed, and about the relationship between the state, territory and nationhood. Is everyone exposed to minority language schooling as with state languages, or is it available only to those who seek it? Closure tells us about how the configurations of 'us' and 'them' are institutionally constructed. Relationships of educational administration and policy between the state and its regions can be delicate, while the state may prevail in how educational policy is developed and schooling is administered. They involve different philosophies of political administration.

State education provision reveals how the minority language has been seen as the means of sustaining a language group. The state's curriculum has been presented in the minority language as in the state language. Education, regardless of language, facilitates entry into the labour market. Unless the labour market is open to the minority language, and this must involve post-primary education, it cannot be claimed that there is a direct link between minority language education and the labour market.

Where legislation for minority languages exists, there is also an attempt to accommodate such languages within education, public services, media and culture. Legislation, and some form of language planning, will inevitably involve minority language education. The absence of legislation, and planning, make it unlikely that the relevant minority language will be accommodated in the state's educational provision. This is true of several language groups, but there are exceptions. The state can ignore minority language education, deciding that the relevant language is not appropriate for schooling. At the other extreme, it can make minority language education mandatory for every pupil within the public sector within a specific territory. This territory will not involve the entire territory of the state. Between these two extremes a number of strategies are possible. Where educational administration is devolved, the relevant decision will tend to be made at the regional level, but other territorial units may be pressured to adopt the same role for minority language education. This decision might be made by each school board, or it might be at one or other of the administrative levels of governance. Provision may cover the entire territory, but will not be mandatory for everyone, requiring special provision as a deviation from the norm within special educational units, be they schools, school classes, streaming or any other institution. Variations may involve levels of education, a mix of the possibilities being applicable for different age groups. This tells us about the administrative structure, and how the relevant minority language is constructed by the relevant authorities. There is also a qualitative difference between teaching a language as a subject and using a language as the medium of instruction, and the relationship between the social and administrative use of the minority language within the school as an institution is also instructive.

2 Centralisation and devolution[3]

The state centralisation of the eighteenth and nineteenth centuries, and the link between education and citizenship remains evident in several European member states, especially in Greece, France, Finland, Italy and Portugal. This centralisation has loosened in France during the 1980s and also in Portugal. Only Higher Education has decentralised in Greece. The town councils and regional governments in Italy have a limited autonomy.

Federal systems may devolve responsibility for educational policy, but the territories are not necessarily treated as language territories. The devolution of power and administration to social groups which may contest the normative structure of the state do not necessarily coincide. The central issue involves the extent to which concessions made to minority language groups in education are limited by the political prerogative of consolidating the state. Does devolution retain the primacy of the state? The discussion moves beyond the link between education and language prestige to address the significance of linguistic diversity for the political process of European integration.

Central government often co-ordinates the curriculum, finance and general management. In Portugal central government treats co-ordination and legislation as control functions, whereas local and regional authorities have been given additional authority by reference to human resources. In Sweden and Finland responsibility for strategy, infrastructure and financial control rests with central government, while regional authorities assume responsibility for direct contact with individual schools, advice on school work and staffing. In Italy all schools are subject to state regulations, but with public schools being run by the town councils.

In contrast, in Germany the Lander have responsibility for the planning, legislation and administration of the essential components of the educational system. Within the UK, England, Scotland, Wales and Northern Ireland have different, autonomous educational systems. Since 1983, and in some cases earlier, Spain has operated by reference to a fully operational principle of regional autonomy – Catalonia, the Basque Country, Galicia, Asturias, Valencia and Navarre have full rights over educational policy and implementation. Belgium has a federal system of three administrative regions and four linguistic areas, and the three official languages play a central role in educational policy and delivery. Ireland also has a high degree of devolved responsibility. The state often retains a say in such matters as the core curriculum, and will often fund regional education from central funds.

Other states have an intermediate position on devolution. In the Netherlands anyone can establish a school without state funding and, in principle, this sets limits on management by central government. In other respects there is a centralised focus on power and responsibility. In Denmark there is shared responsibility across the central state, the district authorities, town councils and the private sector. Nursery and primary education are the responsibility of local authorities, whereas high schools and other institutions are the responsibility of the 14 counties. All Danish schools and local authorities contribute to planning, educational methods and programmes, but conform with state principles. In Austria any amendment to the legal basis requires a two-thirds majority of the Lower Chamber of the Austrian Parliament. Implementation is the responsibility of each of the Austrian federations. The school authority is the provincial or town council, which has a limited responsiblity for schools and professional training colleges. Luxembourg shares responsibility for education across all of the administrative levels.

Universal principles of state education limit developing minority language schooling. Centralised control and planning sets severe limitations on anything that does not conform with central decisions. Devolved systems create the opportunity for minority languages to become the focus of developments in education and learning, but these are not always adopted. The Border Treaties discussed in Chapter 2 and the special status of extraterritorial languages as 'foreign' or 'modern' languages are important, but this distinction sets the platform for the consideration of minority language provision that follows.

3 Educational levels

3.1 General observations

Minority language education provision, its territorial distribution and the extent to which it is mandatory and for whom varies considerably. Some language groups have no provision in their language. Extraterritorial state language groups subject to the reciprocal treaties discussed above have access only to primary education, This is seen as a concession to retaining ethnic identity. Exposure to the general curriculum involves host-state discourses and significations. There is no continuity to the secondary level giving relevance for state or regional labour market. The EU integration of Croatia, Hungary, Slovenia and Slovakia, involves a slow extension of the associated languages into post-primary sectors (Austrian Centre for Ethnic Groups, 1994). Other language groups appear to be highly privileged. They tend to be those groups who have succeeded in ensuring that the languages operate within the regional labour market.

In the following table I have attempted to summarise the main educational functions of the different languages. This is no easy task and the contents of the table must be accepted as a generalisation. This is because each state or region is likely to have more than one approach for the use of the respective languages in their educational structures. Thus in Wales an attempt is made to provide Welsh-medium education at the secondary level for all who seek it. However, it is also taught as a subject in English-medium schools. In other cases some schools may teach a language as a subject, which for some districts or kinds of schools will be at the discretion of the individual teacher. As a rule of thumb I have sought to record the maximum level of involvement for the different languages.

3.2 Pre-schooling

Pre-school and early primary education are regarded as a prerequisite of primary education, as a means of socialising the child into the ways of the classroom, and of integration into society. Minority language pre-schooling invariably leads to, and links with, primary level education in the same language. Pre-school education has tended to be voluntary and limited to the private sector.

Pre-school education as immersion education also has value for language production, facilitating the transition from homes where the minority language is not spoken into minority language primary education. It also reinforces the reproduction process, especially where minority language primary education is mandatory. Pre-school education involves the relationship between language and education on the one hand, and the family and the economy on the other. There is no direct one-to-one relationship between state policy and the incidence of language involvement in pre-school education. Sometimes pre-school education is the means whereby children can begin to operate through the medium of the minority language within the voluntary sector rather than through the formal educational sector. As state provision extends, doubt is cast on this distinction and on the ability of the minority language groups to operate within the voluntary sector.

Resorting to nursery education to incorporate children into the language group is often thwarted by the state's pre-school activities. Introducing immersion education at an early age involves restricting language use to the minority language, allowing both production and reproduction to occur simultaneously. Insisting on using only the state language in nursery schools makes this impossible. In France the state allows between one and three hours a week of teaching of the regional language and culture (Giordan, 1992; Ar Mogn and Stuijt, 1998). Similarly, since 1985 the Italian state has allowed the regional language to be used in pre-school education (Carrozza, 1992). Other states, including the Netherlands, have taken similar steps (Renkema, Ytsma and Willemsma, 1996). This does not allow incorporating children from contexts which offer little extra-school support for the language. Bilingual schools in Occitan where 15 hours a week are devoted to French medium activities and 12 hours to the minority language, struggle in achieving minority language competence among children whose parents do not speak or use the minority language (Berthoumieux and Willemsma, 1997).

Distinguishing between those cases where no pre-school education in the minority language exists, those where it sits side by side with the state language, and those where the minority language is the dominant medium in schools which offer education at this level, allows us to distinguish between where pre-schooling is a concession to recognising the existence of the minority language and its associated social group, from where the language group is constructed as normative for that particular political space, leading to the assimilation of those who do not learn the language at home into the minority language group. The state language is also viewed as a normative language, albeit that its spatio-political reference is the state rather than the region. This involves accommodating dual identities; the regional coexists with, and within, the state. This issue pertains to state policy, but different conceptions of minority languages within the individual state are also envisaged. Often, status accrues to an extraterritorial language group that has 'rights' as a consequence of interstate statutes. On the other hand there are also cases where this does not entirely explain the variation in policy within the state.

What stands out in Table 3.1 is the limited number of cases where effective immersion education is possible. The groups which have no provision tend to be located in Greece, Italy and France. This does not mean that the state is necessarily opposed to such developments, but that it tends to wash its hands of the responsibility for provision. There are several cases where

Table 3.1   Languages and educational provision

Pre-School

None	Occitan, Friulian, Franco-Provencal, Catalan, Albanian, Turkish, Pomak, Cornish, Slovak/Austria, Frisian/Germany, Dutch/France
Discretionary	Croat/Austria, Catalan/Aragon, Sardinian, Griko
As subject	Not relevant
With state language	Asturian, Czech/Austria, Hungarian/Austria, Alsatian, Mirandes, Occitan/France, Breton/France, Basque/France, Catalan/France, Sami/Finland, Sami/Sweden, Occitan/Catalonia
As medium	Luxembourg, Welsh, Slovene/Italy, German/Italy, Swedish/Finland, German/Belgium, Danish/Germany, Sorbian/Germany, German/Denmark, Irish/N. Ireland, Gaelic, Irish, Galician, Basque/Autonomous Community (AC), Catalan/AC, Catalan/Valencia, Catalan/Majorca

Primary

None	Aroumanian, Pomak, Macedonian, Albanian/Greece, Albanian/Italy, Dutch/France, Friulian
Discretionary	Frisian
As subject	Occitan/Italy, Franco-Provencal/Italy, E. Frisian/Germany, Czech/Austria, Slovak/Austria, Asturian, Sardinian, Portugese/Spain, Mirandes, Basque/Navarre, N. Frisian, Catalan/Aragon, Tornedalen, Dutch/France, Sardinian, Danish/Germany
With state language	Croat/Austria, Hungarian/Austria, Corsican, Tornedalen, Breton, Alsatian, Slovene/Austria, Turkish, Occitan/Catalonia
As medium	Irish/N. Ireland, Welsh, Catalan/AC, Basque/AC, German/Italy, Gaelic, German/Belgium, Frisian, Basque/France, German/Denmark, Sorbian, Ladin, Slovene/Italy, Catalan/Valencia, Catalan/Majorca, Galician, Luxembourgish

Secondary

None	Portugese/Spain, Mirandese, Albanian/Greece, Macedonian/Greece, E. Frisian, Aroumanian/Greece, Albanian/Italy, Griko/Italy, Franco Provencal/Italy, Occitan/Italy, Sardinian, Catalan/Italy, Czech/Austria, Slovak/Austria, Cornish
Discretionary	Dutch/France
As subject	Frisian, Dutch/France, Catalan/France, Corsican, Occitan/France, Catalan/Aragon, Asturian, Tornedalen, Ladin, Friulian, Alsatian, Occitan/Catalonia, Catalan/France, Luxembourgish
With state language	Croat/Austria, Hungarian/Austria, Basque/Navarre, Basque/France, Breton, Gaelic
As medium	N. Frisian, German/Denmark, German/Belgium, German/Italy, Danish/Germany, Swedish/Finland, Welsh, Basque/AC, Catalan/AC, Slovene/Italy, Irish, Slovene/Austria, Sorbian, Catalan/Valencia, Catalan/Majorca, Galician, Irish/N. Ireland

Table 3.1   Continued

Tertiary	
None	Most languages
Discretionary	Not relevant
As subject	Most extraterritorial state languages
With state language	Most cases
As medium	Slovene/Austria, Welsh, Irish, Catalan/AC, Basque/AC, Swedish/Finland, Gaelic, Galician, Catalan/Valencia, Catalan/Majorca, German/Italy

the use of language is the responsibility of the school or the individual teacher, this, in turn, relating to parental demand. It is also clear that there are cases in most states where provision is not available. As the relationship between female employment and nursery and pre-school provision is increasingly accommodated, the issue becomes one of the extent to which the minority language is incorporated into these developments.

It is also questionable if using the minority language side by side with the state language has much of an impact upon minority language production. Several of the cases which are involved in these practices pertain to Border Treaty obligations, but more often than not the tendency is to not regard these obligations as extending to include pre-schooling. Often the use of the minority language is minimal and sometimes it is only available in some locations. This is the case, among others, for the Frisians in the Netherlands and Germany, the Portuguese in Spain, and the Corsicans.

To a very great extent exclusive minority language pre-schooling is available for those language groups where this level of education leads to minority language primary schooling. The pre-school is seen in two contexts. First, the orthodox one of socialising the child into the peer group and authority contexts and, second, as a means of initiating children from homes where the minority language is not spoken into the use of the language. There are examples of cases where the parent who does not speak the language is also offered the opportunity to learn the language side by side with the child.

Where minority language pre-school education is obligatory or readily available, immersion education becomes a real possibility, facilitating the process of language production through schooling. In Luxembourg all kindergartens other than a few private schools provide Luxembourgish pre-school education to over 8000 pupils (European Parliament, 2002). The extraterritorial languages of Slovene and German in Italy, Swedish in Finland, German in Belgium, and Danish in Germany are also well provided for. The provision for these groups is often extensive. Thus, for example, the Slovenes in Italy have 12 pre-schools catering for 252 pupils in Gorizia, 30 such schools catering for 472 pupils in the Trieste region, and one other bilingual pre-school. The Germans in Italy have complete German-medium education at every level within the border regions. In Finland there are over 300 day-care centres that operate through the medium of Swedish, and parents pay according to their income. Finnish speakers use them as immersion centres for their children. Fourteen of the main Finnish cities have Swedish language immersion units.

Among the stateless language groups the provision is variable. Again some states are more generous than others. France tends to make minority language pre-schooling available side by side with a greater use of French within the same unit. Others provide complete systems which operate exclusively through the medium of the minority language, incorporating the language into both teaching and administration. In Wales a voluntary activity has, over a period of 30 years, been transformed into a fully fledged professional organisation with six full-time staff and 29 development officers. Provision includes special-needs units. This model has been replicated for Gaelic. Similar levels of provision exist for most of the language groups in Spain where the autonomous governments assume responsibility for education. In the case of Basque this has extended to accommodate trilingual immersion education.

3.3 Primary

Pre-school immersion education generates language production while secondary education relates to labour markets, but maximum exposure to minority language education is at the primary level. It is the basis for transition from the language of the home to the language of the state, and the relationship between the formality of learning and the informality of socialisation.

Primary level education can either be conceived of in terms of providing the grounding in the minority language to insure production and reproduction or by reference to the trajectory of schooling, as the first stage towards a more complete educational integration with the labour market. Hence the different relationships between primary education and the minority language group. There are no cases where minority language provision within compulsory education is not available until beyond the primary level.

Those seeking minority language education are often seeking an environment within which the minority language is the sole medium of communication. Cost effectiveness leads to providing streams in a school where the state language is the main medium of instruction, having far-reaching implications for the goals and aspirations of those seeking primary level minority language education. Terminology can be misleading. In Austria, Italy and France 'bilingual' education involves the predominant use of the state language with some provision for the minority language.

Again most of the cases where no provision is available are in Greece, Italy and France. However, where provision is available it is often minimal, again in the same states. Treaty obligations tend to ensure provision, but the same language group in locations remote from the border may well receive no provision. The German language group in Belgium is a case in point.

Clearly, the relationship between state policy and provision is often tentative. Apart from a single treaty case, Greece makes no provision for its minority language groups. In Italy the recent regional devolution of educational matters results in regional policy which tends not to provide the service in the minority language. In France the department of Finistère in Brittany and the city of Perpignan in the Catalan region, among others, take steps to promote the respective minority languages. This dates from the 1970s and 1980s when regionalism gained ground in several European states. Often the state provides no funds for minority language provision, shifting financial responsibility to the regional level. The expanding neo-liberalism will extend such tendencies. Initiatives often begin as out of school hours activities and as private ventures, some time elapsing before state aid is received. When mainstreaming does occur, it tends to involve transforming existing initiatives rather than extending provision to the entire population.

Often provision is so limited that it achieves little more than to make non-speakers aware of the existence of the relevant language. The number of such cases is large. Two hours a week of Asturian and of Catalan in Aragon are taught. A fifth of Corsican children receive three hours a week of Corsican. Children of the Dutch language group in France are only given provision of the language as a subject. Often this limited level of provision is complemented by a higher level in some schools for some pupils. In Northern Catalonia there are half a dozen Catalan-medium primary schools, the Breton *Diwan* schools, the Occitan *Calandreta* schools, the *Noveal* schools in Alsace, and the *Ikastolas* of Iparalde exist to provide greater provision than the norm. Even here the use of the minority language is often less than the use of the state language. Sometimes different education authorities within the same territory will apply different policies. Thus in some parts of Wales all public primary level provision is through the medium of Welsh, whereas authorities in other locations make Welsh-medium provision available only in some schools.

It is increasingly evident that if language competence among L2 pupils is to be transferred into language use within society, learning and using the language as the exclusive language for primary learning is necessary. This is best achieved in schools where the minority language is the exclusive language of learning, administration and interaction. The cases where this is available are relatively few and they have a limited reach. There are six Sorbian-medium primary schools, 1200 pupils receive German-medium primary education in Denmark, Ladin pupils receive initial immersion education in the language, and the Slovenes and German language groups in Italy are well provided for. However the best level of provision is to be found in Spain where 89 per cent of the Catalan primary schools use Catalan as the medium of instruction, there are 392 Catalan-medium primary schools in Valencia, and half of the public schools in the Balearic Islands teach through the medium of Catalan at the primary level. Almost a quarter of Galicia's first-cycle pupils receive their education through the medium of Galician, and the percentage is even higher for children in the Basque Autonomous Community who receive their entire primary education through the medium of Basque. Other language groups which have a strong primary provision include the Welsh, Gaelic, Irish and Luxembourgish.

Where education is conducted exclusively through the medium of the minority language there is no need for immersion education, except as an adjunct for those children entering the school from homes where the minority language is not used. Educational authorities tend to divide the territory in accordance with language density of ability and apply different schooling policies for each area. Language groups which have pursued pre-school education as an immersion education continue this practice during the early years of the primary level. Most language groups either have no provision at the primary level, or have such limited provision that it has very little influence on the process of language reproduction, let alone playing any role at all in the process of production.

Apart from where there is a treaty obligation, the various states have made very little effort to sustain diversity. Primary level education has been seen as the basis for socialising the individual into society, and language in primary education has been seen not as a means of sustaining diversity, but as a means of eliminating it. Societies have been constructed as monolingual entities and the associated educational practices have mirrored this conception.

3.4 Secondary

The shift in the meaning of learning between the primary and secondary levels, from societal integration to the formal process of obtaining labour-market qualifications and skills, results in a different orientation towards the use of minority languages at the secondary level. Such use is absent for the following groups: Portuguese in Spain; Mirandese in Portugal; Albanian, Aroumanian and Macedonian in Greece; Albanian, Franco-Provencal, Griko, Occitan, Sardinian and Catalan in Italy; Czech and Slovak in Austria; Cornish in the UK; East Frisian in Germany. Again we note the predominance of language groups in Italy and Greece. However, it is perhaps more surprising that this list includes several state languages. What is evident is that those language groups which have no provision at the primary level are unlikely to have any at the secondary and tertiary level.

Despite the comment above about the absence of some state languages, extraterritorial state languages, often with treaty support, are more widely used at the secondary level. The Danish language group in Germany and the German language group in Denmark each have a single secondary school that uses the respective language exclusively. German is the main medium of education at the secondary level in 'New Belgium'. In the North Tyrol almost 70 per cent of the pupils attend secondary schools where German is the medium of instruction for almost all subjects, and is also the language of administration and all daily activities. In Finland, at the lower level Swedish is the medium of instruction, and the upper level schools are also monolingual Swedish schools (Ostern, 1997). In Italy, the Slovene-medium secondary schools in the provinces of Goriza and Trieste cater for about 2000 pupils (Tosi, 2001).

In Austria it is legally possible to use Slovene as a medium of instruction at the general secondary level, but it tends only to be taught as a subject and competes with English as a foreign language. Where demand is low there is a tendency to mix children by age and ability at the secondary and academy level, and results in the creation of a single Slovene-medium school in Klagenfurt. Children from regions with a high density of Slovene speakers have to board. Parents resent being separated from their children and are deterred from choosing their preferred option (Busch, 1998).

Irish and Luxembourgish receive less provision at the secondary level than at the primary level. In Ireland, while it is used as a medium for several subjects, the general tendency is for Irish to give way to English at the secondary level, where it tends to be taught as a subject. Luxembourgish is compulsory for all students, but tends not to be used as a medium of instruction, being taught as a subject within the general curriculum (O'Murchu, 2001; European Parliament, 2002).

Elsewhere, state languages do not fare so well. In Alsace, German is provided only as a subject for either three or five hours a week (Van Der Schaaf and Morgan, 2001; European Parliament, 2002). Dutch is taught only as a subject in France, and then only at the discretion of the individual teacher. One Austrian school teaches Croat, Hungarian and German, the first two always in combination with the third! Another secondary school in Burgenland offers German and Croatian tuition in all subjects, and one other school offers Croatian as an optional core subject and bilingual tuition in several other subjects (Baumgartner, 2001).

There are also anomalies. Greek students pursue their secondary education for nine years, compared with six years for the Turkish group in Greece. Entry to the two Turkish-medium schools is by competition, depriving many pupils of opportunity. Recently about 25 per cent of applicants succeeded with the entry examination. Now access is available to all, but only 1149 pupils were enrolled in these schools in 2001–2. However, about 15 per cent of the children of this minority language group chose to attend mainstream Greek public secondary schools where religion alone is taught through the medium of Turkish (Tsitselikis and Mavrommatis, 2003). The two *Ierospou-*

dastiria or Islamic seminars in operation since 1999 accepted female students for the first time in 2000–1.

Gains for some extraterritorial state languages derive from heightened prestige and struggle. Such education is viewed as of relevance almost exclusively to the language group rather than to the population as a whole. A considerable sacrifice is demanded of those who seek such education. Boarding is often obligatory and involves both social and financial sacrifice. In this respect it is still treated as a non-normative concession to the language group.

Similar variation in provision pertains to the other language groups. In the Netherlands, 5 per cent of Frisian pupils receive an hour a week of Frisian during the first two years of the secondary stage (Renkema, Ytsma and Willemsma, 1996). North Frisian is a medium of instruction in one school in Germany, but in the other schools of the region provision is limited (Walker, 1997). The Ladin language in Italy is taught for two hours a week at the lower secondary level (Van der Schaaf and Verra, 2001; Carrozza, 1992). There is no provision at the upper level. Very little reference to Friulian is found at the secondary level. In France there is only a provision as a subject for the Catalan, Corsican and Occitan language groups, often at the discretion of the individual teacher. About 30 per cent of the pupils in five urban centres receive three hours a week of Occitan as an option at the lower and upper levels of the secondary schools. In two schools the language is used as a medium for some subjects, amounting to a total of eight hours a week (European Parliament, 2002). In Corsica almost 8000 pupils now subscribe to the statutory commitment (Fusina, 2000). Catalan in Aragon is taught for two hours a week on a voluntary basis (Martinez, 2004), as is Asturian (Gonzalez Riano, 2002), and the Tornedal Finns in Sweden (Lainio, 2001). Aranese is a compulsory subject within secondary education. During the first level all students receive part of their education through the medium of Aranese. At the higher level it is obligatory as a subject, but is rarely used as a medium of learning (European Parliament, 2002).

France has a single Basque-medium secondary school catering for about 350 pupils, and uses Basque for 12 hours a week and French for the remaining 15 hours of instruction. Elsewhere, Basque is taught as an optional subject in some institutions. (Stuijt et al., 1998). A similar provision applies to Breton. *Diwan* boarding schools exist where two-thirds of the teaching is through the medium of Breton. There are also 'bilingual' schools where Breton is used for 12 hours a week, and French for the remaining 15 hours, reducing to six hours of Breton at the higher level of the secondary cycle (Ar Mogn and Stuijt, 1998). Six per cent of the pupils in the French Catalan region receive one hour a week of Catalan at the lower level, and a further 4 per cent are taught the Catalan language and culture for four hours a week (European Parliament, 2002). There are two Irish-medium secondary schools in Northern Ireland, supplemented by community-based summer schools which are held in the Republic. The main drawback is the shortage of teaching materials (Willemsma and MacPoilin, 2001). Gaelic-medium education at the secondary level is found only in Glasgow and Inverness (Robertson, 2001; European Parliament, 2002).

For other groups provision is better. Within Catalonia, Catalan is the primary and obligatory language of instruction for about three-quarters of secondary pupils (Areny and Van Der Schaaf, 2000). In Valencia, Catalan is the main language of instruction in certain schools, and is an obligatory subject within the Catalan-speaking areas of the region. In the Balearic Islands about half of the pupils receive their secondary education entirely or partly through the medium of Catalan (European Parliament, 2002). In Galicia, Galician is obligatory in secondary level education, and all pupils should reach an equal level of competence in Spanish and Galician. At the first level, almost 90 per cent of the pupils receive at least part of their education in Galician. At the higher level a minority of the students study entirely through the medium of Galician, and a further minority mainly in the language. There are complaints about the non-observance of the legal requirement (Costas, 2001; European Parliament, 2002). All secondary level pupils have some exposure to Basque in the Autonomous Community. Almost a third of the secondary level pupils attend what are effectively Basque-medium schools. In Navarre provision is much more limited, even in the north of the region where most of the Basque speakers live (Gardner, 2000; European Parliament, 2002).

In Wales the goal of provision is to make Welsh-medium education at both primary and secondary levels within reach of every household in Wales. Of the 227 secondary schools in Wales, 48 teach all or most subject entirely or partly through the medium of Welsh; a further 18 teach entirely through the medium of Welsh and 153 teach Welsh as a second language. Three schools do not have any Welsh language provision (Williams and Morris, 2000).

The Sami High School in Kautokcinio, Norway, is a boarding school that caters for all of the Sami language groups from the three northern Scandinavian countries. The Sorbian language group in Germany has a single middle school and two lyceums which provide Sorbian-medium education for about 1400 pupils (Hemminga, 2001; Ela, 2000).

3.5 Vocational and higher education

At the tertiary level, provision for minority language groups declines. State, Celtic, Germanic and Romance languages are taught in the universities. Credit transfer makes it possible for members of minority language groups to seek university education in states and regions other than their own. An alternative to studying language and culture within modern language departments involves creating centres of studies which pertain to the language group rather than the language, and several subjects can be studied through the medium of the minority language. In Corsica about a third of the students are exposed to Corsican at this level (Fusina, 2000). A similar situation applies to the Sami groups in Norway, Sweden and Finland where the Sami High school in Kautokeinio, Norway, serves all of the Sami groups for teacher training and specialist subjects and research.

Provision at the primary or secondary level demands an element of pedagogic training. Sometimes this lies outside of the region as in the case of the Germans in Belgium, or within a more general institution which caters for teacher training as in the case for Luxembourgish and the various language groups in Austria. The Slovene language group in Austria has its own primary teachers' training centre in Klagenfurt (Busch, 1998). In the Spanish regions the rapid transition to minority language teaching led to retraining existing teachers. In Val d'Aran fewer than 40 per cent of the teachers were from the area, and only half of these were literate in the language. Retraining and facilitating return migration has resulted in 80 per cent of the teachers having the competence to teach the language (European Parliament, 2002).

Minority languages achieve significance when used as a medium of education across a range of subjects at the tertiary level so that the languages are absorbed into the higher levels of labour-market activity. Both the status and prestige necessary for motivational aspects of language production and reproduction are enhanced. Ireland has one university which provides some Irish-medium education, and in Wales the same role is distributed across the constituent colleges of the University of Wales, but is limited primarily to the arts and the social sciences, as well as teacher training. The Basques have the same level of provision, but the intention is to offer Basque-medium streams alongside the existing Spanish-medium ones. *Sabhal Mor Ostaig*, the Gaelic College in Skye, now part of the University of the Highlands and Islands, has run full-time Scottish Vocational Education Council (SCOTVEC) courses through the medium of Gaelic in management and business studies, computer studies and television training since 1984. There are also bilingual courses at Lewes Castle College (Stornoway) in office practice and media training.

In Galicia, supply falls behind demand, and. only about 10 per cent of the students receive all of their classes and a further 18.5 per cent part of their education through the medium of Galician (Turell, 2001). The situation is similar for the Catalan speakers in Valencia, but is somewhat better in the Balearic Islands. In Catalonia a third of the student population at the technical level receive their education in Catalan. The main universities in Barcelona have a very high level of competence among their students, and overall in Catalonia almost two-thirds of university classes at the tertiary level are taught in Catalan (Areny and Van Der Schaaf, 2000; European Parliament, 2002).

Among the extraterritorial state language groups the Swedes in Finland have the best provision. Full provision is available at the University of Abo, and further provision exists at the Swedish Business Management School and the School for Social Studies and Welfare at Helsinki University. Other institutions teach bilingually (Ostern, 1997). However, it is much more common for students from these groups to seek higher education in states where the relevant language is the state language.

4 Conclusion

Only under very special circumstances will a minority language group whose language does not play a role in the labour market survive. Only when devolved governance has significant power *vis à vis* education policy, where the numbers are considerable and where the labour market incorporates the minority language are we likely to see any real development in minority language education, allowing education to have a relevance for both language production and reproduction. Educational policy will involve immersion education at pre-school level, leading to primary level provision and a coherent awareness of the relevance of secondary education for the regional labour market that operates, at least partly, by reference to the minority language.

Rather than recognising the value of diversity for the economy, most states develop outmoded policies associated with state homogeneity or policies from a time when minority language educational provision was imposed on them following the two World Wars. Others have failed to be sufficiently self-confident to engage with a positive conception of diversity. Minority language provision is either missing, or merely serves as a concession to supporting a reproduction function that engages with civil society rather than the labour market. Minority languages pertain to emotion rather than reason. It betrays a limited ability to conceive of the relationship between language and reason other than by the arguments of the nineteenth century where reason was linked to syntax.

Where policy supporting the use of minority languages in education is developed, implementation is often missing, usually as a consequence of normative practice. It denies the autonomy of individual schools, and even of individual teachers. It is difficult to develop coherent policy under such circumstances. Positive policies often link with a failure to deliver the level of provision guaranteed by the state, which lacks the commitment to remedy such situations.

The object 'language' is constructed in different ways by different states, particularly in terms of how it pertains to the emotional or the rational. For many, pre-school and primary education pertains to socialising the child into the practices and normative structures of society, largely an emotional experience. The link between education and work places a premium on the rational at the secondary level, and is further enhanced at the tertiary level. There are states which do not give stateless languages any status, ignoring them entirely in their educational systems. Others limit the use of minority languages to pre-school and/or primary education. Those that accept the relevance of minority languages across the broad range of education are few, but are much closer to the normative construction of the relationship between language and education, this accounting for the tendency for these cases to involve extraterritorial state languages.

4
Reproduction: Family, Community and Household Media Use

1 Introduction

Civil society can refer to sociopolitical institutions, including the rule of law, limited and accountable public authority, economic markets, social pluralism and a public sphere. Others limit it to 'non-governmental civil society', or even to associations and the public sphere. Whatever the conception, the family and the community both belong to the 'public sphere'. The meta-narrative of liberal democracy sees civil society as having a relative autonomy from the state, a moral conscience that resists the progress of an authoritarian state. Alexander (1998:97) refers to civil society as 'a sphere of solidarity in which abstract universalism and particularist visions of community are tensely intertwined. It is both a normative and a real concept'. Modernism counterposes rationality and emotion, and democracy constructs the state as the rational basis for eliminating the remnants of feudalism, leaving a danger that civil society is constructed as the domain of the emotional.

Within democracy the individual is conceptualised as a rational, autonomous subject who is engaged rather than passive, who relates to other community members by reference to conscience and honour rather than greed and self-interest. The contrary, involving the emotive, the passionate and the irrational, incapable of forging the open, trusting social relationships which democracy insists upon, is often allocated to the family and the community. Amoral familialism, suspicion and paternalism are the characteristics of some accounts of civil society. The subjects must be repressed for the sake of civil society and for their own good. Irrationality and the absence of trust creates institutions that are arbitrary rather than rule-regulated, emphasising power rather than law, hierarchy rather than equality. Such communities tend to be exclusive rather than inclusive, promoting personal loyalty over impersonal and contractual obligation. Community organisations are organised by factions rather than social groups responsive to community needs. The premise of difference, constructed out of the rational/emotional dichotomy, leads to the construction of ideal types and a typological construction of associated traits. The practices of Sociology and Political Science relate to this premise as stabilised meta-discourses. If the minority language is constructed as an object which pertains to the emotional, then so also will the family and the community that pertains to the language group.

This distinction is not 'real', but is the product of how the discourse constructs the meanings. The normative discursive formation represents the individual by reference to those features that emphasise social order, preserving the interests of the state. Whatever is not normative cannot be democratic, and cannot by extension be rational! If language and community are constructed in the same way, the subject positions associated with these objects will similarly appear as symbolically negative *vis à vis* the normative. Taking in charge the normative subject position rather than that of this discursive formation is open for all bilinguals. This is the essence of Foucault's (1991) understanding of governmentality, and how we are 'governed' through, and by means of, our 'freedom'. It involves two poles of governance. The first consists in the forms of rule whereby various authorities govern populations, while the second is embodied in the technologies of the self through which individuals work on themselves in shaping their subjectivity. His work raises the question of the relevance of the distinction between state and civil society, in that modern governance links the public and private so that any particular practice or policy will not operate exclusively in one or other of these domains.

Early sociologists constructed society to replace a politics of pity constructed around the conception of domestic grandeur (Boltanski and Thevenot, 1991; Boltanski, 1993) to be an integral part of democracy. There was a single society for each state and this society was the basis of a normative order of which the state was a part. Society was conceived of as the legal State, a collection of institutions which functioned according to the principles of universalist and individualist rights. Each individual, was a rational being, conscious of her rights and obligations, who would submit to laws which respected her legitimate interests, and the liberty of her private life. The solidarity of society, of the social body, was maintained in good health by the effective functioning of its organs. This classical model was formed by the interaction of rationalisation, moral individualism, and the functionalism of institutions. The individual could not be truly human without participating in collective life, and in contributing to the functioning of society. The two supports of modernity – rationalisation and moral individualism – were in turn supported by the force of the state, and its link to what is termed 'national rights'. The common good, the general interest, or the 'nation', was the basis for defining the good and the bad, the normal and the pathological, of inclusion and exclusion, replacing the sacredness of tradition.

This was the essence of Durkheim's '*conscience collective*', and his claim that 'social solidarity is nothing other than the spontaneous accord of individual interests, an accord where the contracts are a natural expression' (Durkheim, 1912). Both the 'I' and the 'me', and the 'us' and 'we', are different. Durkheim constructed a link between the collective body and the collective mind, and struggled with the relationship between the local and the global dimensions of identity. There were two collectives at work in society: psychic lives and social thought. One was 'diffused throughout the entire social body' and tended to be spontaneous and taken for granted, requiring little reflexivity. The other was 'localised in a specific organ', the 'organ of social thought' – the state, which he viewed as the brain of society. The biological analogy denies tension between these two forms of collective consciousness (Durkheim, 1979:89.) Nonetheless, the 'brain' is the biological basis for reason! The sociologist speaks from the place of the state.

Civil society, as Tocqueville's 'art of association', led to the social contract. It involved a range of voluntary associations as the sphere of interest and choice, the essence of liberal democracy. It persists with the value of self-determining individuals, while opposing the coercive and compulsory nature of the state. The state had to be conceived of as a voluntary association of its citizens, the sum of the communities within its territory. While Locke refused to conceptualise the family as a voluntary association, most theorists argue that marriage is a voluntary social contract. Thus community and the family lie at the heart of the conception of civil society. Voluntary associations are meant to be the source of apprenticeship for the art of citizenship, where the virtues of civility are learnt. Society constitutes a quasi-nature, and both it and its economy have to be governed with respect for the laws of that nature, and also by reference to the autonomous capability of civil society to generate its own order and its own prosperity (Gordon, 1991). Unsurprisingly, for Foucault civil society becomes the correlate of a political technology of government.

The nineteenth-century disciplinary discourses constructed the family and the community as objects linked to the state, and since the two institutions constitute the language group, it also must have the same relationship with the state. Yet sections of this discourse have tended to view an inherent tension between the two objects (Gramsci, 1978). Hegel's (1971:280–3) view of the state as the highest form of social rationality which reconciled how social custom sanctioned the social bonds and particularist behaviour of individuals in civil society, with the goal of the best interests of the whole, has consolidated the centrality of the state in Western thought. It leads to a focus upon normative order and how minority language groups constitute a social order which deviates from the normative of the state.

Civil society involves the moral equality of humans, a 'natural' equality of every individual, regardless of society, carrying similar status and a sense of space in which every individual makes her decisions and acts without constraint. This leads to the idea of personal autonomy, a decision of rights and ultimately, the separation of a private sphere from a public sphere, the sphere of civil society as distinct from that of the state. In civil society individuals can exercise choice according to conscience and are protected by rights. One form of pluralism involves a vision of social groups or cultures, each defined by and expressing its own values. The other form is a vision of individuals choosing to pursue different values within a framework of law which protects individual freedom while setting limits to such freedom (Siedentrop, 2000:201). Nothing in the pluralist vision of groups or cultures as flourishing protects individual choice. Evolutionism and social Darwinism have contaminated the entire sense of equal moral standing, relegating some social groups to the perimeter of the normative order.

2 The family

'Good government' originally applied to the household or other sub-political organisations, and was applied to politics in the modern period. As governmentality focused upon populations, the family disappeared as a model of government and became an element within the population and an instrument in its governance (Foucault, 1991:98–101). Governing people according to principles of freedom accommodates individualisation and socialisation. The individual exercises self-control as a mastery of the self, and this was linked to the social imperative (Rose, 1995). The individual enacted the responsibilities her liberty consisted of, the associated practices being based on normality, rationality and sensibility. Language was a feature of these practices. This moral self-regulation was scrutinised and judged by oneself and others in the community and the family. It is the basis of a normative order. This civil morality was linked to religious morality, and religious institutions were at the heart of the scrutiny and judgement. The private authority of the family was wedded with its public duty. The emotional nature of the family had to be harnessed for public benefit, and the governance of the family embedded in the governance of the state. Compulsory state education limited the family as a private, legally inviolable sphere under the sovereign control of the head of household. The activity of children was policed to insure school attendance.

Schooling brought family members into the world of reason, ensuring that family cultural practices coincided with the new normative order. It was particularly pernicious by reference to minority language groups. The family became an object of scrutiny, subject to external comment about the normative nature of its social practice, including language use. The state assumes the power to protect children from their parents. The right to remove children from the family influenced children's use of language for their own 'good'. Religious institutions also played a role. The 'private' ethic of 'good' language as the language of the state was linked with the 'public' ethic of social order and 'linguistic' hygiene. The autonomy of the family was retained, and, in the name of social and organic solidarity, parents used a language with their children which they themselves had scarcely mastered. The principle of the interdependence of the individuals of any society overrode the state of dependence associated with 'natural associations' such as the family (Donzelot, 1991). The state is divorced from social relations and stands outside of them, assuming responsibility for progress.

Family reproduction and language reproduction involve the socialisation function and the concern of the state with how the family can generate structures which are contrary to its existence within democracy. The entry of the media into the household plays a fundamental role as a socialising agent. A lack of synchronisation between family and media by reference to language production/reproduction is crucial.

As the point of reference for the individual, the social relates to the sense of self. Each identity exists by reference to some 'Other', and involves how the individual interpolates with the discourse responsible for constructing and constituting social groups:

> every human being normally learns in early childhood a language which has been spoken by others before that individual child was born . . . the language one speaks, which forms an integral part of one's personality, is a social fact presupposing the existence of other human beings and . . . every human being, in order to become fully human, has to learn a pre-existing language . . . children acquire with their language aspects of the fund of knowledge of the society in which they grow and constantly mingle with the knowledge they may acquire through their own experience.
>
> (Elias, 1991:21, 37)

Ceasing to separate the individual from language clarifies that society is a feature of language. The language group is one of the social groups which the individual speaker cannot avoid being interpolated into. Whether or not the individual takes in charge the subject positions associated with membership of the language group, this is where identity is or is not constituted. It is the point of transformation of the individual into the subject.[1] Normally socialisation establishes the behavioral correlates of normativity, and language acquisition is a natural process of parent–children interaction, leading to intergenerational transmission. There is a difference between being a speaker and identifying with the language group. The family may generate competence, but not a language group identity. Negative identity involves rejecting intergenerational transmission and refusing to take in charge the subject position of a member of the language group.

Socialisation as normativity can lead to parental negative identity involving non-reproduction. The extent of language production in colingual societies is a measure of the struggle over normativity. In most societies the relationship between state and minority languages never stabilises to the extent of becoming a normative order. The discourses associated with the ideological forces which influence the language/s used in the home and the relationship between associated subjects and objects rarely stabilise. The family as an agency of language reproduction should be viewed in conjunction with other factors, especially the status that accrues to the language object within discourse, and language prestige.

The family is not always coterminous with the household. The role of the extended family in social and cultural reproduction persists, while the extended family is integrated into the economic structure. The extended family can also continue to carry emotive and other practical functions. It is difficult to divorce the family from its subordination and contribution to the economic system.

3 Language group endogamy

The reliance of capitalism on the circulation of capital for the creation of wealth integrates local economies into a higher level order which stimulates the further circulation of capital and the associated circulation of labour. This intensification of migration and emigration separates extended family members from the localised rituals that symbolically sustain the extended family. It also influences patterns of exogamy and endogamy. Patrilocal or matrilocal residence patterns disintegrate, and the link between family and locality is ruptured. All that remains is an emotive link to the sense of a family locality. Autochthony links language, the individual and the region, and sustains the relationship between time, person and place implicit in kinship constellations.

Language groups are social and autochthonous groups, demonstrating an intricate link between language, culture and locality through the intertwining of space and society. The family has the capacity to relate its own reproduction to the reproduction of language within a confined spatial context. The state transcends this link, making language the basis for physical survival as the language of economic and legal-administrative structuring. State languages cannot be avoided. Minority language groups are obliged to consolidate the link to their territory in ways which lack the integrative functions that is an inherent feature of the state. The family is crucial to minority language production and reproduction.

Language group endogamy, is conceived of in terms of space, with different localities forging cross-locational links. The spiralist nature of career structures makes language group endogamy more difficult for the geographically mobile classes. This link between residence, class endogamy, language group endogamy and space relates to how economic forces structure society in specific ways. Economic restructuring intensifies the relationship between the migration of capital and the migration of people and influences the incidence of language group endogamy.

Minority language groups have a restricted territorial context within existing states, being constituted by reference to the spatial and social boundaries that link place with the 'us' and 'them,' of identity. This limits the extent of the spatial. However, cross-frontier language groups may operate across state boundaries with members of other language groups who share the same language. Territorial endogamy is a precursor of language group endogamy unless it involves return migration. The weak internal integration of peripheral regional economies involves external control of much of that economy. The few locally controlled economic activities tend to involve the family enterprise, influencing the control of the language group over the regional economy and the relevance of the family for language reproduction.

Few states gather information about the language competence within minority language groups, but some empirical observations that guide more general statements about language group endogamy can be made. Without social factors which influence selectivity, the incidence of endogamy depends upon language density, and territorial variation in language density results in variation of language group endogamy. Thus language group endogamy figures are generalised estimates, and average figures for the entire population can be misleading. Sources used to derive the figures include the language-use surveys, census data where available, the Euromosaic language group reports (LGR) and specific studies. A high incidence of language group endogamy does not guarantee a high level of language reproduction, but does present the conditions whereby the family can serve as the agency of reproduction. Language group exogamy can link with geographical endogamy under specific circumstances. Also, where language group exogamy is evident, it does not mean that intergenerational transmission or reproduction is not evident.

Two factors influence the relationship between language group endogamy and reproduction – the willingness of the family to use the minority language and the impact of in-migration upon marriage patterns. This relates to the significance of the minority language in economic restructuring and of the autochthonous region in the European economic restructuring process.

The contents of the following evaluation of endogamy and use is summarised in Table 4.1.

3.1 High incidence of language use and language group endogamy

Where family minority language use and language group endogamy are high, the conditions for reproduction are favourable. High family use indicates a desire to reproduce the language within a context which is quite different from that of courtship and the decision to marry. The use value of

Table 4.1 Language group endogamy and family language use

	Language group endogamy	
	High	**Low**
High family use	Turkish, Friulian, Ladin, Occitan/Italy, Albanese, Galician, Asturian, Aranese, Mirandese, Catalan, Basque, Frisian, Catalan/Valencia, German/Italy, Catalan/Mallorca, Luxembourgish, German/Belgium, Swedish/Finland	Breton, Occitan, Vlach, Sardinian, Arvanite, Sami/Finland, Sami/ Sweden, Tornedalen, Alsacian
Low family use	Basque/France, Welsh, Slovene/Austria, Slovene/Italy, Danish/Germany, Gaelic, German/Denamrk, Irish, Croat/Austria, Sorbian	Cornish, Irish/ N. Ireland, N. Frisian, E. Frisian, Portugese/Spain, Catalan/Italy, Catalan/France, Slovak/Austria, Czech/Austria, Corsican, Hungarian/Austria, Dutch/France, Franco-Provencal

the minority language will be evident, even within exogamous marriages. Where endogamy is higher than use, the desire to resort to the family as an agency of minority language reproduction is weak. High endogamy is found in peripheral regions subject to limited economic change. For this to be accompanied by high family use depends upon a high status for the language, a status that may or may not accrue from language prestige.

As a language group which is also a religious group, Turks in Greece display the highest incidence of language group endogamy and use of the language in the family. The language group boundary is reinforced by religion, giving a high degree of social closure that is intensified by an antagonism between the two states. The separation of schooling and community institutions limits social interaction across the language groups (European Parliament, 2002:81; Aarbakke, 2001).

Older members of the Macedonian language group in Greece are largely monolingual, those aged between 20 and 40 bilingual, and the young use

Greek and Macedonian. Language group endogamy exceeds 80 per cent, and the language is widely used within the family, many of which are three-generation families (European Parliament, 2002; Kostopoulos, 2000; LGR Turkish/Greece).

Parts of northern Italy have experienced limited economic growth. The Friulian region is still highly dependent upon tourism and agriculture. Friulian is widely used within the family and links through to community use, and the incidence of language group endogamy is also high (Picco, 2001). In north-western Italy most of the permanent residents belong to the Occitan language group. This high language density contributes to the high language group endogamy. The language is used widely within the family, despite the continuing decline in the number of speakers (Bauer, 1999; LGR Franco Provencal/Italy). The Ladin speakers occupy a similar Alpine region where they control an economy consisting primarily of tourist and agricultural activity. Language use in the family and language group endogamy are high (Kattenbusch, 1996; LGR Ladin/Italy).

The 49 localities in Italy where the Albanese language group is located are devoid of industrial activity. They feature high language group endogamy and strong use in the family. The territorial fragmentation and the existence of three distinct language varieties hinder operating as a coherent community. As many as 80 per cent of the inhabitants speak the language, out-migration is common on account of the relative deprivation and high level of unemployment, and yet this has not affected the high incidence of language group endogamy. The use of the language within the family remains strong, notwithstanding that the younger generation tends to use Italian within their peer groups (Carrozza, 1992; LGR Albanese/Italy).

In Spain, Galician and Asturian display a close linguistic proximity to the state language, influencing language use in the family and in both regions language group endogamy is high (Bauske, 1998). In Asturias much of the population believe that Asturian is a form of Spanish and would not distinguish between them! In Galicia, between 70 per cent and 80 per cent of marriages are endogamous by reference to language, but with an urban/rural difference. Like Asturias it is a region which has experienced little in-migration in recent years. Over 70 per cent of those aged 16–25 who speak the language have learnt it in the family (Rei-Doval, 2001).

Val d'Aran, in Catalonia has an economy devoted mainly to tourism and increasingly less to agriculture. Over 50 per cent of the population speaks Aranese, spatial endogamy is high, with language group endogamy also high. About three-quarters of those who speak the language, use it in the home. The Catalan-speaking part of Aragon has also experienced limited economic restructuring, and both language group endogamy and language use in the family is high (European Parliament, 2002; LGR Catalan/Aragon).

The Mirandese of Portugal is a small language group which has an endogamy index of about 70 per cent, and a high reported use of the language in the family. The 15 000 speakers live in 32 villages in the Duoro Department where they control the agricultural sector. During the 1960s and 1970s there was strong out-migration to the industrial centres, but little in-migration and the region has experienced a population decline (Fereira, 1999).

In such areas out-migration is far more prominent than in-migration. Consequently, marriage tends to involve geographical and language group endogamy. The indigenous population tends to control the means of production within the region. They are small farmers or the owners of small companies in the local retail and limited manufacturing sector. Public sector employment is also high.

The same degree of language group endogamy is rare within the high density industrial regions of Europe, where geographical mobility is common. It requires a high density of minority language speakers and a large number of speakers for that particular language. It also requires either a role for the minority language in the economy or a highly specific in-migration pattern, as well as a political will.

In Catalonia, Catalan endogamy exceeds 65 per cent, and the family language use is even higher (Farras, Torres and Xavier Vila, 2000; LGR Catalan/ Spain). In the Valencian urban centres Catalan language group endogamy tends to be low, and family use is variable. Families politicised by reference to language use the language. In rural areas both language group endogamy and family use are high (LGR Catalan/Valencia, Marin, 1996). In the Balearic Islands spatial endogamy is about 90 per cent and about 80 per cent of families with the competence use Catalan in the home (Govern Balear, 1988; Moll, 1994; LGR Majorquin). The recent in-migration has resulted in almost a third of the residents being born outside of the Balearic Islands, but has not had a proportional effect upon language group endogamy. The social boundary between the local and the in-migrating population is reinforced by language and culture.

With only 24 per cent of the population speaking Basque the endogamy index of over 70 per cent in the Autonomous Community suggests a selective process of marriage that relates to the highly politicised environment and the polarisation between the indigenous population and the 29 per cent of the population born outside of the Autonomous Community. Also, 61 per cent of Basque speakers use the language exclusively with their children, a further 13 per cent using both languages equally with their children, and the remaining 27 per cent using more Spanish than Basque with their children (Basque Regional Government, 1996; LGR Basque/Spain).

The German-language group in Italy, and the Swedish-language group in Finland control most of the means of production in small industrialised regions. Among the German-language group, 90 per cent of marriages are between German speakers and there is a high use of German in the family. There is positive integration between the motivation to reproduce the language through the family and the relevance of the language outside of the family (Egger and Mclean, 2001; LGR German/Italy). The situation is similar for the Swedish-language group in Finland. The rate of endogamy is high in the core areas, but declines in the bilingual areas. High language prestige and status and widespread institutional use reinforce family practice (Modeen, 1995; LGR Swedish/Finland).

In Luxembourg the status of being a state language carries significant support for the use of Luxembourgish within the family. Despite in-migration, language group endogamy remains at about 70 per cent (Fehlen et al., n.d; LGR Luxembourgish). Similarly, the German-language group along the German-Belgium border displays high endogamy and use rates. The earlier tendency for parents to favour French because of their children's employment prospects has been reversed. This is supported by employment opportunities in Germany and the strong support for the language outside of the family (Lenoble-Pinson, 1997; LGR German/Belgium).

Language group endogamy among the Frisians exceeds 65 per cent in the rural areas (Gorter and Jonkma, 1995; LGR Frisian/Netherlands). It is somewhat less in the urban centres, but again fairly high. Most of the 40 000 or so in-migrants who entered the area during the 1970s located in the urban centres. When both parents speak the language, almost all of the families use Frisian for interaction, and 68 per cent of them do when only one parent speaks the language. The close linguistic proximity between Frisian and Dutch makes learning Frisian easy for in-migrants.

The language group may not exert overt pressure upon young people to marry within the language group, but there remains a desire to reproduce the language. Thus some groups such as the Catalans and Basques display a higher rate of language use in the family than would be expected from the rate of language group endogamy, for example, and reproduce the language even when both parents do not speak the language. Yet the same groups show a decline in language group endogamy as a consequence of recent in-migration.

3.2 High incidence of language group endogamy and low incidence of family language use

These language groups are undergoing a very rapid process of intergenerational rejection of the language. The older generation will invariably almost all speak the language and will have been brought up in homes using the language. In contrast, the younger generation, despite a high degree of competence among the parents, have been raised in homes where the minority language is absent. Marriage patterns involve geographical endogamy, but not language group endogamy.

Most of the groups in this category are in France and Greece. In 1950 as many as 75 per cent of the population used Breton whereas today that percentage has declined to 17 per cent. In a 1990 survey only 21 per cent of those interviewed claimed competence, 72.5 per cent of whom said their children knew no Breton, and 70 per cent claimed that their parents spoke the language (Broudic, 2000). Over a third of the older population use the language daily, but only 3.5 per cent of the younger population have sufficient competence to use the language. Language group endogamy is high among the older generation. Among the younger generation geographical endogamy is high, but language group endogamy is low (LGR Breton).

Similarly, fewer than 10 per cent of families use Occitan, and then mainly among the older population. Again geographical endogamy is high, but language group endogamy among the younger families is rare. The decline in competence has been extremely rapid. The change cannot be accounted for by in-migration and economic restructuring (Berthoumieus and Willemsma 1997; LGR Occitan/France).

Most of the older generation in Sardinia speak Sardinian, and the degree of language group endogamy is high, but declines among the younger generations. The varieties of Sardinian make mutual comprehension difficult leading to the use of Italian as a lingua franca. Since the 1970s, the subservient role of women has been equated with the social and familial context which focuses upon the use of Sardinian leading to a rejection of Sardinian. This change is more marked in the urban areas (Rindler Schjerve, 1996; LGR Sardinian).

Among the Arvanite or Albanian language group of Greece the older population has a broad competence whereas the knowledge of the grammar and lexical resources among the younger population is limited. The young only use Arvanitik within strongly marked contexts involving older members of the extended family. They view the language as inadequate for the modern world and their future economic activities. The young are strongly opposed to the idea that their children should learn Albanian and put pressure on their parents not to use the language (Tsisipis, 1998; LGR Aravanite/Greece).

The Vlachs or Aroumanians are divided across four states, which influences their transhumant pastoral practices and communication across the different language groups. In Greece they have lost much of their land and their flocks, and have moved to the urban centres. The disarticulation of their social and kinship networks has resulted in rapid assimilation. The women have relinquished a world where they had limited exposure to education, experienced early marriage and physical restriction to the world of the home. The young have only a passive knowledge of the language, whereas their grandparents have a wide degree of competence. The situation in the rural areas is moving in the same direction. The rate of language group endogamy has rapidly declined to below 50 per cent (Kahl, 1999; LGR Vlach/Greece).

The small size of the Sami language groups means that exogamy is pronounced, especially among the Inari and Skjolt (Hirvonen, 1995). There is some family use of the languages within concentrated communities, but the younger generation use Finnish within the family. The declining link between the extended family and the exploitation of economic resources has been accompanied by a reduction in the use of Sami languages as the means of consolidating kinship networks. Some rituals which link the languages to reindeer herding persist, but these can be accommodated using Finnish interspersed with Sami terminology. The situation is similar among the Sami in Sweden. A change in the *corral* system of reindeer herding and the associated division of labour leaves the women unemployed and they move to Swedish urban centres. This accelerates the process of language group exogamy. Among the Russian Sami endogamy remains high. Long periods of absence of the males in pursuing their economic activities mean that it is the women who tend to determine the language used in the home (LGR Sami/Finland/Sweden).

Intergenerational rejection of the minority language also exists among the Finnish-speaking Tornedalians in Sweden and the German-language group in France. During the 1960s Swedish became the home language for many Tornedalians, most of whom were not literate in the language. Only the educated and militant middle classes resist this development. Regional endogamy remains high, but language group exogamy is also high (LGR Finnish/Sweden). In France the use of Alsacian with the young has been extremely limited since the end of the Second World War, leading to a significant transition over three generations. The rate of language group endogamy has declined (Hudlett, 2000; LGR German/France).

These language groups have chosen not to reproduce their languages. This is mainly as a consequence of the state discourse which has equated the use of the language with an outmoded atavism. Policy development for the minority language and its relevance for the economic activity that is a feature of reproducing the language within the family is missing.

3.3 Language group endogamy low and family use high

A quarter of a million people live in Iparalde, 80 per cent of them in the district of Lapurdi, where over a third of the population are mainly third-generation in-migrants. In the other two districts, over 80 per cent of the population is indigenous to the region. Spatial endogamy is high within the entire region. Within Lapurdi a third of the population has a knowledge of Basque, compared with more than two-thirds of the population in the other two Departments. Among those over 65 years of age, 42 per cent have a knowledge of Basque, whereas this declines to 35 per cent for those aged 16–24, most of the ability deriving from the family and the community. When both parents speak the language, 74 per cent have Basque as their first language, 13 per cent claim both languages as their 'first language', while 12 per cent have French as their first language. When only the mother speaks Basque, 10 per cent have Basque as their first language, 17 per cent have an equal knowledge of both languages, and 73 per cent have French as their first language. When only the father speaks Basque, the respective figures are 3 per cent, 14 per cent and 84 per cent. Only 2 per cent of children from families where neither parent speaks Basque have a knowledge of the language (Basque Regional Government, 1996; LGR Basque/France).

In Wales in 1991 there were 39 820 families where one parent spoke Welsh and 42 870 families where both spoke Welsh. In 1981 only 58 per cent of the families where one parent spoke the language reproduced the language, compared with 93 per cent when both spoke the language. When only the mother speaks Welsh, 58 per cent of daughters and 48 per cent of sons learn the language, and the figures are only slightly lower when only the father speaks Welsh. The rate of exogamy increased between 1981 and 1991, but so also did the numbers of children from exogamous marriages who learnt the language. This is a consequence of the increased prestige of the language, and the enhanced access to education through the medium of Welsh. Even amongst those families where neither parent spoke Welsh, 13 per cent of the children spoke the language. Exogamy is increasing, but so is language use within the family (Williams and Morris, 2000).

The Slovene language group in Austria has a high rate of endogamy within the core area, but in the urban centres this rate declines. While 50 000 claim to understand the language, 33 000 speak it regularly. South of Klagenfurt and Vilach the density of speakers is high, as is the rate of endogamy. Among this core group there is a high rate of use within the family which plays a prominent role in reproduction. The endogamy rate is about 50 per cent, but there is also a fairly high language reproduction rate, even within exogamous families. Members of the Slovene language group in Italy number about 85 000. The economy has increasingly focused upon the service sector leading to in-migration. Language group endogamy is about 50 per cent, and the use of the language in the family is high (Busch, 1998; Ogris and Domej, 1998; Reiterer, 1996; LGR Slovene/Austria).

Among the Danish in Germany the language is used with children within both endogamous and exogamous marriages. About half of the marriages are endogamous by language group. Among the German language group in Denmark, most families use German. The rate of language group exogamy is high and increasing, partly as a consequence of the small size of the language group which comprises about 6 per cent of the regional population (Christiansen and Teebken, 2001; LGR German/Denmark).

About 40 per cent of the 66 000 Scots Gaelic language group live in high language density areas in the Western Isles. A third of the families are endogamous by language group, and about half of the speakers live in families where everyone speaks the language. The rate of endogamy is higher in the core areas. In families where both parents speak Gaelic, three-quarters of the children also speak the language, whereas only 13 per cent of the children in families where only one parent speaks the language also speak Gaelic (UK Census of Population, 1991).

In Ireland, some of the *Gaeltacht* communities have a language density in excess of 90 per cent, and the average for all *Gaeltacht* locations is 76 per cent. Two-thirds of the speakers use the language daily. Over 80 per cent of the children of natives of the *Gaeltacht* who never left the region speak the language, and household use of the language is equally high. These figures decline to 50 per cent for returned natives, and to 35 per cent for strangers, or those who have married into the region (O'Riagain, 1997; LGR Irish).

The Croat language group in Austria numbers about 25000 or about 10 per cent of the population in the region. Within the rural area, in contrast to the urban areas, endogamy is high and use in the family is strong. Overall the endogamy index is less than 50 per cent (Austrian Centre for Ethnic Groups, 1996; LGR Croat/Austria).

The Sorbian language group consists of the Catholic population of Upper Lusace, and their Protestant counterparts in both Upper and Lower Lusace. For the entire population the rate of language group endogamy is 25 per cent, but this figure is considerably higher among the rural population, and especially among the Catholic population in these rural areas. Similarly, almost all of the Catholic families in Upper Lusace use the language with their children, but the rate is much lower among the remainder of the language group (Hemminga, 2001; LGR Sorbian/Germany).

Language groups which have this relationship between marriage patterns and language use patterns have a propensity for the families to reproduce the language, even though not everyone in the family speaks it. This is easier where the two languages are linguistically similar, and when the language has a role within the economic order and/or a highly politicised construction of the language as an object.

3.4 Incidence of low language group endogamy and low family use

When the size of the language group is small and its territory loosely defined, the likelihood that language group exogamy increases is considerable. It takes considerable organisation and determination to retain language group endogamy, and even this is unlikely to succeed. Language use in the family is also likely to be limited.

The Cornish speakers are few in number and few families use Cornish exclusively. Endogamy is rare. The Irish language group in Northern Ireland is a larger group and it is also a religious group. However, fewer than 10 per cent of those who claim competence can sustain conversations in Irish, and the use of the language in the family is extremely limited. Endogamy as a religious group is high, but not as a language group. The symbolic relationship between religion and language as markers of a distinctive social group means that even where the one partner does not speak the language, support for its family use is high.

The 10000 members of the North Frisian language group constitute about 6 per cent of the regional population. The rate of endogamy and the use in the family have been declining slowly during the past three decades. The same decline has been much more rapid among the East Frisian who number fewer than 2000 and constitute 17 per cent of the population in the locality (LGR Frisian/Germany). The same description applies to the Portuguese language group in Spain, which numbers less than 4000 members. Endogamy is low and family use is declining rapidly (Luna, 2001; LGR Portuguese/Spain).

Of the 14 000 Catalan speakers in Italy, 88 per cent retain it as their principal language throughout their life. Yet by the end of the 1970s only 24 per cent of the parents used Catalan with their children, and only 13 per cent of the children used it with one another. An additional 13 per cent of the parents used both languages with their children. Of those over 50 years of age 60 per cent used Catalan with their parents, compared with only 15.5 per cent of those under 30 years of age. By 1992 the percentage of parents who use Catalan with one another had fallen from 40 per cent to 18 per cent, and the percentage of parents who always used Catalan with their children had declined from 19 per cent to 3 per cent. At the end of the 1970s, only 39 per cent of marriages were between partners from the region. Language group endogamy was 5 per cent (LGR Catalan/Italy).

Language group endogamy for the Catalan language group in France is about 50 per cent, and most members have learnt Catalan in the home. The language group numbers in excess of 150 000, also has a fairly high density in the region, with almost half of the region's population speaking the language, and a third being fluent speakers. Two-thirds of the speakers claim to use the language daily (Becat, 2000; LGR Catalan/France).

The Slovaks and Czechs in Austria are small language groups living mainly in, or close to, Vienna. Their reproduction relies on highly formalised social networks associated with institutional support. Links with the former Czechoslovakia are tentative, and the extent of language group endogamy is weak. Language use within the family is significant among members of both language groups, but much of this use pertains to the extended family within an urban environment. This is supported by the relationship between social networks and economic interests.

The Hungarian language group in Austria has a broader spatial distribution and involves both rural and urban contexts. The group numbers about 7000 speakers, and constitutes less than 2 per cent of the regional population. The region has the highest incidence of unemployment, and the lowest per capita income in Austria leading to the out-migration of young people, mainly to Vienna and Graz. Language group endogamy is limited to the rural areas, but the high proportion of the group which is of retirement age contributes to the use of the language in the extended family. The loss of control of the agricultural economy by the language group has also been a factor in recent years (LGR Hungarian/Austria).

High in-migration and the tendency for the indigenous population to migrate to the mainland in search of work, means that half of the population of Corsica is born outside of the island. The population is almost evenly divided between urban and rural residents, most of the in-migrants residing in the urban centres. Labour markets are segmented, and there is a distinctive social boundary between those involved in the respective segments. The marginalisation of the rural, indigenous economy means that language serves as a marker of that marginalisation. Language group endogamy is low and use in the family is also low among the urban population that speaks Corsican. This is less true in the rural areas. Over 50 per cent of the population have a knowledge of the language and 10 per cent speak the language as their first language (Fusina, 2000; LGR Corsican).

The Dutch language group in the north of France has a relatively small proportion of the regional population and does not display a high language density. Policy support is weak and language group endogamy is low. Industrial decline has led to heavy out-migration. Fewer than 5 per cent of the young use Dutch frequently with their parents, whereas for more than half of their parents it was the main language of the home. Only 11 per cent of the young report a high degree of competence, while 72 per cent claim that they never speak Dutch (Marteel, 2000; LGR Dutch/France).

The population of Val d'Aosta is 188 000, a third of whom are in-migrants, and many others live there only for part of the year. The permanent population is divided between that of Val d'Aosta which numbers 109 000, and that of Turin which has a population of 79 000. In the former the Franco-Provencal language group is in the majority and 5 per cent speak French, whereas in the later it constitutes only a third of the population. Language group endogamy is about 50 per cent, and the reported use of the language in the family is considerable (Telmon, 1992). It contrasts with the Greek speakers living in two localities of southern Italy who constitute a very weak language group. It would appear that intergenerational transmission ceased during the 1950s (LGR Franco-Provencal/Italy).

These language groups are subject to different circumstances which can account for the low incidence of language group endogamy and use of the language in the family. The small size of the language groups, especially in locations of high population density can combine with rapid in-migration over a relatively short period of time, especially where the in-migrating population seizes control of the more dynamic aspects of the regional economy. Even so, reproduction can operate if the language is integrated into the wider context of society and its economy. It is the marginalisation of a language which plays the most significant role in the inability of the family to play a role in language reproduction.

3.5 Conclusion

Variation in the ability of the family to serve as the agency of language reproduction is evident. Substantial in-migration and the absence of a language function outside the family leads to a decline in family use. In the absence of the language from the labour market the pressures of economic life upon family behaviour leads to the family abandoning the language in favour of the language which does give employment and social mobility. Conversely, where language prestige is high families do reproduce the language, even where structural forces influence language group endogamy.

4 Community

Democracy involves social relationships based on trust and openness. Any incompatibility between the function of the family and the community is discussed by reference to pathology. Sociology has followed this line of argument in developing its conception of community.[2] The current return to the nineteenth-century beginnings of neo-liberalism and its link to democracy involves transferring responsibility and accountability from the state to the individual and the community as an antidote to how welfarism has created a dependent relationship between the individual as citizen and the paternalistic state.

Since the eighteenth century ideas about normativity and social order have involved community (Williams, 1992a:8–14). It has been conceptualised as the consequence of localised face-to-face interaction that conditions and sustains identity. Its demise has been a central feature of the evolutionist claim for the increasing individualism of society associated with industrialisation, urbanisation, evolution and social progress This is the basis of a series of dichotomies, including Toennies's *Gemeinschaft* and *Geselschaft*, Durkheim's mechanical and organic solidarity, and Weber's substantive and formal rationality. Collective consciousness informs community and yields to the individualism of modern society through progress leading to liberal democracy being conceived of by reference to individualism and a rejection of communitarianism (Seidentop, 2000)

Contrasting reason and nature prompted the relationship between community and the state. Reason was constructed as the basis for the essential unity of humanity. Rousseau claimed that in a state of nature, society was based upon integrating moral principles. Community became the resting place of social order. Later Condorcet argued in favour of a relationship between reason, progress and evolution, claiming that society was becoming so complex that if the moral imperative was to persist, then social order had to be vested in a superior entity – the state. The normalising, rationalising and 'pastoral' projects of nineteenth-century liberalism were failing to escape the effects of industrialisation and urbanisation on social fragmentation, individualisation and social order (Donzelot, 1984). Opposition between community and the state thereafter was restricted to the writings of anarchists such as Kropotkin and Stirner.[3] The Romanticism associated with the conservative discourse of Chataubriand, Maistre, Haller and Bonald *inter alia* linked with the evolutionary thrust in polarising two forms of social order, one constructed as the mechanical solidarity of modernity as progress and the other as an organic solidarity of an atavistic tradition.

This led to the creation of three hierarchical spatial levels. The first involves the discourse, the effects of which constructs the state. The individual is constructed as a 'citizen', located within the territorial space of the state, and pertaining to the 'us' of the state that contrasts with the 'them' of the citizens of other states. Internally it has ruptured the relationship between time and place. This is partly the effects of the discourse of capitalism which insists on the free mobility of labour in order to reduce the cost of labour in securing profit. Second, 'Regions' have emerged as the replacement for kinship territories. It is axiomatic that any region is part of a larger, often preconstructed, unmarked entity, which tends to be the state. The 'us' that is constructed out of regional boundaries is subordinate to the 'us' of the state. Third, the community becomes a local object which tends to lack the strict spatial and legal definition of the state and the region, and how it emphasises and marks the 'us' of inclusion. The community is amorphous, but always inclusive by reference to the state.

The discourse of democracy has sought to deny how a community is simultaneously defined in a competing discourse as pertaining to some other existing or potential state than the one which legally defines it. It involves extraterritorial language groups, and also autochthonous groups whose being combines the territorial referent of language with aspirations for statehood. In the former case, community and region become synonymous, constructing the space that defines 'us', not by reference to the inclusion of the existing state wherein they are located, but to the neighbouring state which also contests, or has contested, that region as territory. The second case involves a contesting discourse which defines the region as a community defined by language and history such that the inclusive 'we' contrasts with the 'them' of the remainder of the state within which they are located. This 'we' is constructed in such a way that it unites time, person and place in the form of a justification for the existence of an unfulfilled object creation where the community becomes a state. Where the 'us' of the citizen is sustained by the legal discourse that confirms the state boundary, the 'us' of the aspiring state is confirmed by history and how the prior discourse leaves traces in the contemporary construction of subjects and objects.

Ethnicity involves part society, part culture (Williams, 1998), occupying part of the state territory. Since there is only one society for each state, each ethnic group has to be part of that society. State activity integrates all of the state's population into a common citizenry constructed out of cultural commonality. Groups constructed out of cultural difference are incorporated into that culture as part of, but marginal to, the normative order and are treated with suspicion. Since modernity and progress would insure universal homogeneity, such groups were constructed as involving an atavistic tradition. The ethnic community, whose borders of inclusion and exclusion were marked by cultural attributes, most significantly language, became a specific kind of community. Language groups become ethnic groups. The struggle of autochthonous language groups is a struggle over normativity.

Important here is the distinction between an identity constructed out of inclusion as opposed to exclusion. The relationship between language as an object that confirms the identity of subjects as pertaining to a common 'we' through shared understanding, and the space occupied by these subjects as a territory, is exemplified in the concept of autochthony. This becomes a speech community by exclusion – the 'them' of the excluded is not defined by territory, but by the inability to be incorporated into the 'us' of the language group as a speech community. In contrast, the 'us' of the region is an inclusive identity determined by space and including everyone who lives within that space. LP, as an activity sanctioned and practised by the state, is an attempt to find the discursive context within which the 'us' of the state, responsible for social policy, overlaps with the 'us' of the language group.

Because the modern state has sought to create its territory as a uniform, culturally homogeneous social space, autochthony does not pertain to the local space, but to the wider space of the region. The emergence of capitalism and its expropriation by the state has changed this construction of community, incorporating the relationship between person and place into itself, while levelling time to 'now'. This is a feature of modernism and of the concern with normativity and social order, that which became Sociology, but which emerged in the eighteenth century as an explicit, applied political science in search of an alternative to the prevailing political order.

Because of how the normative order that pertains to the state is constructed, and how the minority language group becomes deviant from the normative, many language groups are constructed so that the only place that they can speak from is one which constructs their practices as defensive. The evolutionist thesis which sustains the state as 'progressive' constructs the minority language group as atavistic, and the only subject place which the minority language group can occupy is based on defence against this construction. The related subjects and identities are constructed so that the outcome is a kind of collective survival involving networks of solidarity.

The institutions which also serve to construct community as something more than an identity constitute a form of social organisation built around the subjects, who engage with them as minority language speakers, and the institutions themselves as related objects. Institutions become a central feature of the discourse on community. They assume an identity of their own, as symbolic objects, and become important agencies for producing and reproducing the minority language. The demise of the institution has profound implications for language as an object.

It is difficult to separate discussions of the family, the household and the community. They are different spatial constructs that have become mutually dependent. The relationship between autochthony and the reproduction of regional space and language reproduction as time deserves the same focus. Local communities are constructed through collective action, and are preserved through collective memory as specific sources of identity within which time, person and place are constituted in a particular way. Where institutions link the local with the regional and focus upon the use of the minority language, there may well be a degree of segmentation within the local community. This may involve polarisation around different constructions of 'us' and 'them' that may, or may not, bear reference to a sense of autochthony, or it may involve coexistence and an overlap of incorporation for the same individual as subject.

These relationships between different subjects and objects are stabilised within discourse, becoming a feature of institutionalisation. The extent to which the minority language is institutionalised as the means of communication within stabilised social practices within community institutions sets a normative order that transcends the individual community and, in so doing, establishes a language group across territory to the extent that its spatial terms of reference involves a variety of communities.

Gaffard and colleagues (1993) refer to the variation in the 'modes of living' within Europe, a variation constructed out of collective memory and how it influences behaviour and values; local modes of organisation including family organisation, and solidarity structures; and local collective dynamics which involve civic customs. Putnam (1993) controversially emphasises the difference between Northern and Southern Europe. Northern Europe is characterised by a plethora of societies, clubs, teams, daily press readers, engagement in public issues, a faith in public governance, solidarity, trust and co-operation. Southern Europe is characterised by hierarchically organised public life which defers public affairs to others, where involvement in social and cultural associations is minimal, where there is less deference to law, but where discipline and order are demanded for fear of lawlessness. Patron-client relationships prevail. The relationship between the state and civil society differs across Europe. It is this distinction which partly fuels the debate about the relationship between reason, community, civil society and the state within the orthodox discourse of democracy.

Historically, much of the social activity within the community has focused around religion, involving the institution as the focus of social interaction and physical integration of the individuals who are constituted as subjects through the institution. The religious discourse has a universal impact upon behaviour as a moral order. This explains the close historical relationship between the Church and the State. It is important to consider the extent to which religion has transcended space as a feature of normativity.

There is a difference between centralised and devolved religious institutional organisations. Devolved structures do not involve fragmentation since the discourse on the moral order as something that conditions social practice transcends organisational structures. In centralised organisational structures the relationship between the Church and the State has been of central importance prior to the advent of the modern state in that it involved the link between the King as Divine and the discourse that legitimised domestic grandeur (Boltanski and Thevenot, 1991). The demise of royalty as the order of power, and its replacement by the state, did not remove the link between Church and State. In the community, religion and education became the institutional focus where the influence of the state penetrated. The replacement of Latin by the various vernaculars within religion was a slow process, and at the end of the eighteenth century the argument about state languages being languages of reason penetrated religion. The Church in the community became an agency that sustained the linguistic homogenisation of the state.

There are also cases where the link between Church and State has remained intact, but where the Church sustains minority language use, and cases where the Church becomes a symbolic feature of resistance against the state. An overlap between language use and religious practice can assume an explicitly political signification. Church support can influence the ability of the language group to reproduce itself. There can be a fundamental tension over the relationship between language use in religion, and the obligation of the clergy to their constituents. Centralised policy may be opposed by regional ecclesiastical administration. As a decentralised form of community organization, non-conformism can give each community its administrative autonomy.

Politics and religion are bound by morality. Establishing community mores minimises the idea that everything has to be organised and guided by law (Tocqueville, 1998). Transferring responsibility and accountability from the central institution to the individual and the community through self-guiding mores reduces the importance of the central authority. This is a debate about the nature of civil society and its relationship to the state. How this is practised by community and religion in Europe helps explain the differences identified above (Gaffard et al., 1993). The difference between the centralised organisation of the Catholic Church and the Greek Orthodox Church on the one hand, and the Protestant sects on the other is also indicative of how the relationship between community and the state is conducted. It involves distinctive ways of understanding the relevance of self-guiding mores within the respective religious philosophies, as Weber's work on protestant sects and voluntary associations in civil society testifies (Weber, 1978). How membership linked to individual decision, and the idea of individual responsibility within society was a manifestation of Weber's concern with the meaning an action has for the individual subject, and involved treating *being* as existing outside of language. It contrasts with the paternalistic orientation and universal membership of state Churches that claim to represent the community within a moral order which transcends the spiritual and the civic. The clergy influence the selection of community leaders and determine the nature of moral responsibility. Communities that have institutionalised the language in religious institutions at the community level during the nineteenth century will have developed a strong institutional base for that community.

Secularisation is obliging communities to develop alternative structures of community organisation that can produce and reproduce the language. The language of social practice within the community is not simply a matter of individual choice, but is associated with sustaining social practice as stabilised discourses that are constantly modified. Institutionalising this social practice involves a close integration between institutions and the normative order.

Minority language groups are defined not merely by language, but by a non-normative culture. Many of the group's institutions are linked to these cultural activities and tend to be denigrated as 'traditional', to the extent that developing community around them can be counter-productive. For many language groups popular music has been the means of entering the world of the 'modern' through their language. The Super Furry Animals and Catatonia began by singing in Welsh, Joan Manüel Serat is renowned for his commitment to the Catalan cause. A focus upon youth and popular culture in itself is insufficient and there is a need to target the broad range of activities labelled as 'cultural', but which pertain to society in its entirety. Sports involve such activities. There are language groups that have their own associations, such as the Slovenes in Austria. Others have their own sports that are exclusive to them. These become a focus around which much of the community of speakers are integrated. However, within the universal sports, how the various sports federations are structured hinders the development of anything more than the token use of the minority language.

The following discusses the role of religion as an organisational principle, and the existence of other institutions within the community which play a positive role by reference to the minority language. It considers how language groups have accommodated secularisation in confronting the issue of community language use. The typology around which the discussion is structured is presented in Table 4.2.

4.1 Religious support and institutional support high

Some language groups are also religious groups marked by a religious affiliation that is different from that of the wider society. This makes sustaining the language easier, since the social closure exerted by language is sustained by a religious orientation which conditions much of social life. All members of the Turkish language group in Greece are Muslims. All services are conducted in Turkish. These rights are protected, both by Greek law and by the Treaty of Lausanne. Much of the informal social activity within the community revolves around the Mosque and the Turkish language school (Tsitselikis and Mavrommatis, 2003).

Table 4.2 Religious and institutional support

	Religious support	
	High	**Low**
High institutional support	Turkish, Ladin, Welsh, Danish/Germany, Slovene/Austria, Catalan, Basque, Catalan/Valencia, German/Italy, Catalan/Majorca, Slovene/Italy, Luxembourgish, German/Belgium, Swedish/Finland	Galician, Aranes, Catalan/France, Frisian, Catalan/Aragon, Mirandes, Macedonian, Franco-Provencal/Italy
Low institutional support	Basque/France, Gaelic, Irish, German/Denmark, Albanese, Croat/Austria, Catalan/Italy, Hungarian/Austria, Alsatian, Tornedalen	Cornish, Irish/N. Ireland, N. Frisian, E. Frisian, Portugese/Spain, Breton, Slovak/Austria, Friulian, Czech/Austria, Corsican, Dutch/France, Sorbain, Macedonian, Sami/Finland, Asturian, Sami/Sweden, Arvanite, Occitan/France, Aroumanian

Where the religious organisation operates in a language which differs from that of the state there is an overlap between religious and linguistic closure. The Catholic Church in Spain and Italy and the Greek Orthodox Church have been particularly centralist in their organisation and lack of tolerance of linguistic diversity. Where these Churches have sustained the minority language groups has been as a result of a protracted struggle on the part of both the clergy and the parishioners. This centralism has been less evident in the Protestant sects.

In the Autonomous Community 71 per cent of Basque speakers use Basque with the priest, the same figure as for family use (Aixpurua, 1995). There is concern that the inability of the clergy to speak Basque hinders religious-based community activities in the Basque language. The use of the language varies in accordance with the density of speakers within the social network of the individual and the institutional context where the formal community activities occur. The political militancy, and the significance of the language for national identity, involves numerous Basque-language secular institutions. A concerted effort is being made to insure that leisure activities for the young, many through the Church, are conducted through the medium of Basque (Gardner, 2000). The conscious integration of Basque into formal activities is not evident in Navarre where the use of the language in the community is less, even if the incidence of use in the family is similar.

The Catalan language groups in the Balearic Islands, Catalonia and Valencia have used the Catholic Church as a focus of mobilisation, leading to tension between the central and regional Church authorities. Almost all of the priests of the Catholic parishes speak the language and use either of the two languages. In the smaller villages Catalan language masses are often missing, while in Barcelona more than half of the masses are conducted in Catalan. Rites of passage are conducted in the language desired by the family. However, much community activity is separate from any influence by the Church. Such a large language group has all of the amenities of any state language (Farras, Torres and Xavier Vila, 2000).

In the Balearic Islands and Valencia about half of the religious services are conducted in Catalan and most of the clergy use the language with their parishioners (Moll, 1994; LGR Majorquin). In Valencia the Church did play a role in the Castilianisation of the general population. Much of the priest-hood and the congregation in Valencia view the integration of Catalan into normative religious practice as essential (Generalitat Valencia, 1992).

Integrating a minority language into religious institutions when the organisational structures of some religions involve a single institution representing the entire population means that activities offered in the minority language must be segregated from those offered in the state language. Such accommodation can become a feature of the struggle over normativity within the broader community.

Eighteenth-century Nonconformism argued that it was easier and cheaper to reach the monoglot through the medium of Welsh than by teaching her English. The autonomy of the chapels, and integration of Welsh speakers into non conformism, led to the almost exclusive use of Welsh. Parallel English-medium institutions were established when English became the language of progress in the nineteenth century. Nonconformism has played a positive role in promoting Welsh, representing a radical opposition to the landed gentry who were closely linked with the Church of England. Class, national, political and religious opposition were integrated. Secularisation has reduced the effectiveness of religion in community affairs. Thirty years ago membership of one or other of the chapels was closely linked to employment prospects and social control at the community level. The ability of the language group to establish secular institutions that use the language at both national and community level has been fairly successful. The tendency for school activities to overlap with Welsh language cultural activity integrates community-based action (Williams and Morris, 2000).

The use of minority languages in devolved Protestant chapels is also evident among the German language groups in Italy and Belgium, the Ladin language group in Italy and the Danish language group in Germany. In Alto Adige all of the clergy speak German and both Italian and German are used in the services. Almost two-thirds of the language group attend Church (Egger and McLean, 2001; LGR German/Italy). For the Danish language group in Germany, Danish is the language of Church activities that include cultural activities as semi-religious voluntary activities. These activities do not pertain to any 'traditional' culture, but to the organisation of activities that parallel those that are common within German society. The degree of secularisation is relatively high (Christiansen and Teebken, 2001; LGR Danish/Germany). The German language group in eastern Belgium is served by a Church whose officials all speak German (Jennings, 1991; Lenoble-Pinson, 1997; LGR German/Belgium). The Church articulates with other aspects of community life and also with a German language education system which has a strongly coherent social organisation as a consequence. In the Province of Bolzano all the priests speak Ladin, participation is high and half of the services are conducted in Ladin. However, the language is rarely used in the other valleys. Throughout the Ladin region many of the community-based social activities linked to the Church are conducted in Ladin and secular voluntary associations also use the language (Kattenbusch, 1996; LGR Ladin).

In Finland the Lutheran State Church operates with parallel systems for each language group. Separate parish structures exist for the Swedish language group which has close to 300000 members, giving the basis for a strong institutional structure. Their social life runs parallel to that of the Finnish language group and operates almost entirely through the medium of Swedish (Ostern, 1997; LGR Swedish/Finland).

The Church of the Slovene language groups in Italy and Austria is important in the production and reproduction of Slovene. Half of the Slovene language group in Italy attend the Catholic Church regularly, and most Church activities are conducted in Slovene. The administrative structure of the Church includes the provision of Slovene-speaking Bishops at Gorizia and Triest (Carrozza, 1992; LGR Slovene/Italy). Like the Czech language group in Austria, the Slovene language group was divided by political ideological differences after the Second World War, leading to the duplication of a number of functions within the community and the emergence of parallel institutions. The distinction between culture and politics is often blurred, and political institutions have cultural wings. One faction is firmly aligned with the Catholic Church which has its particular Carinthian tradition and a strongly nationalist aspiration. Religious participation is high, with 25 per cent of the 95 per cent of the population that is Catholic attending weekly. The Slovene Bishopric in Carinthia has a high degree of autonomy, partly because language and religion are so closely linked. In about 80 per cent of the parishes, both German and Slovene are used side by side, whereas in the remaining 20 per cent there is a tendency to separate the two languages. Masses are conducted in both languages within the same service, whereas singing activities are confined to Slovene. Singing is a core activity, and both the secular and the religious factions have their respective choirs and musical institutions. Theatre is also important. The priesthood insists that Carinthia constitutes a cultural area with its own literary culture and tradition expressed through the medium of Slovene. This conception flows over into the Church. Community activity is focused upon preserving this culture while making it relevant for the 'modern' world. The institutional structure is strong, and many of the associated social networks are closed, displaying a high degree of multiplexity (Busch, 1998; Reiterer, 1996; LGR Slovene/Austria).

As a widely used state language Luxembourgish has a significant role within the community. About a third of the language group is active in religious institutions. Virtually all of the clergy are fluent in the language which is the main medium used for religious purposes. This links with the informal activities and the voluntary associations at community level, most of which involve the use of the language (European Parliament, 2002; LGR Luxembourgish).

4.2 Religious support weak, institutional support strong

These language groups have not been able to break the centrism and state language use of Church activities. Secularisation is not harmful for language production and reproduction since the language groups have developed social alternatives to those which focus upon the Church-focused activities.

Hostility to the use of Galician in the formal activities of the Catholic Church in Spain has persisted beyond the Franco regime. Yet 55 per cent of the priests, especially the young, claim that Galician was the easiest and most relevant language to use in the liturgy and parish life, and 90 per cent of the clergy speak Galician. Over 80 per cent of the language group have come under the influence of the Church, and more than 60 per cent still attend. The formal aspect of Church services are in Castilian, but the situation is slowly changing. Social religious activities use more Galician than is found in the religious rituals. Outside the Church there is a high level of activity associated with theatre, music and sport that use Galician as an alternative community sphere, activities which parallel those in the wider Spanish society (Rei Doval, 2001; LGR Galician).

In French Catalonia only about 10 per cent of the clergy have a knowledge of Catalan and few services or rites of passage involve the language. Historically the Church has occupied an ambiguous position, having played a role in preserving some features of the Catalan language within the Church, while simultaneously being actively involved in insisting that learning and catechism should ignore the language. The local authorities help support some activities, and there is considerable support from Spanish Catalonia. Use within the community remains high, but the contexts of use remain limited by the prevalence of French (Becat, 2000; LGR Catalan/ France).

The centralism of the Catholic Church is evident in Aragon and Catalan has not been widely used in religious services since 1870. Most Catalan speakers attend the Catholic church regularly, and most of the clergy have a knowledge of the language. Couples wishing to be married in the Catalan language are obliged to do so outside the region. Outside of the family the use of Catalan tends to be informal and formal community activities are mainly conducted in Castilian. A transition from the prohibition of the Franco period to one where Catalan became the normative expression in the community has not occurred. Use in the community remains high across all age groups, but is increasingly restricted to social networks rather than formal activity and voluntary associations (Nagore Lain, 1998; LGR Catalan/Aragon).

In Val d'Aran only the archbishop speaks Occitan, and most of the masses are conducted in Catalan. Rites of passage in Occitan are possible if the family requests it. There is less Church hostility towards the minority language than elsewhere in Spain. Occitan is the language of most community activities in the villages and in Viehla (Gargallo, 1999; LGR Aranese).

The centralism of the Church is also problematic in Portugal, but the priesthood is recruited from among the local population so that 90 per cent of the priesthood has a knowledge of Mirandais in the region. The language is rarely used in the formal activities of the Church. In the informal activities on the other hand, Mirandais is widely used by the priesthood which plays a considerable role in the social life of the community (LGR Mirandais).

There are three autochthonous regions where the Church refuses to use the regional language. In Greece the Macedonian language group receives little support from the Church, but despite the strong persecution which the language group has experienced at the hands of the Greek state there is considerable use of the language in community activities (Friedman, 1997). In Holland few of the clergy who serve the Frisian language group have a knowledge of Frisian (LGR Frisian/Netherlands). The same is true of the priests who serve the Franco-Provencal language group in Italy. These languages are absent from religious institutional activities. Outside of this context the use of both languages is sustained in community activities, especially outside of the main towns.

4.3 Religious support strong, institutional support weak

These language groups receive considerable support within the religious sphere, but have little other institutional support. This must be seen in terms of the importance of religion for the language group members and the general regional community, and the extent to which different regions of Europe develop formal institutional contexts for community activity. In contrast to Northern Europe, in Southern Europe the Church dominates many of the voluntary associations and it is only the informal social networks which lie outside of its influence. This picture differs notably from that in Northern Europe.

The Croat language group in Austria has strong links with the Catholic Church, as many as 35 000 parishioners indicating a desire for Croat language Church services (Austrian Centre for Ethnic Groups, 1996; LGR Croat/ Austria). The Church supports Croatian language publications and bilingual services, but refrains from taking a militant stance or a proactive role in organising Croatian language community activity. Much of the social life of the speakers revolves around limited activities in the formal associations associated with cultural activity or in informal social networks within their respective communities. Community activities in the rural areas are increasingly conducted in German at the expense of Croat. Also in Austria, the three main religious bodies among the Hungarian language group – the Catholic Church, the Augsburg Evangelical Church and the Swiss Reformed Church, all use the Hungarian language. They also support secular cultural activities, most of which are 'traditional' cultural activities distinctive to the population. Yet the use of Hungarian within voluntary associations is in decline (ibid; LGR Hungarian/Austria).

In Italy, Italian is used as a lingua franca between the different Albanese speech communities. The Church is one of the few integrating forces other than the print media, which tends to have a relatively small circulation. It is difficult to develop a coherent system of voluntary organisations which transcend the different communities. Religious participation is strong, and most community activities revolve around the Church (LGR Albanese/Italy). Also in Italy the Church in Alghero has been pro-Catalan since the Middle Ages. Despite the introduction of Castilian as the official language in the seventeenth century, the clergy used Latin as the written language, and delivered services in Catalan. The current bishop continues this policy. However, only seven of the 18 priests derive from the area, and only four deliver the mass in Catalan. Nonetheless, many of the social activities of the Church are supportive (Carrozza, 1992; LGR Catalan/Italy).

Among the Basques in France about a third of the language group attend church regularly. Most of the clergy speak the language which is used in half of the Church services. Families can choose to use the language for rites of passage. The use of Basque in the wider community is considerably less than it is in the Autonomous Basque Community, and the voluntary associations tend to be weak (Basque Regional Government, 1996; LGR Basque/France). Similarly, among the German speakers of Alsace, 60 per cent of the Catholic clergy and 80 per cent of the Protestant clergy speak German. About half of the Church services use German and the rites of passage are readily available in German. Among the Lutherans, German has always been the language of the Church which has played an active role in sustaining the language group. The Catholic Church is less positive in its support. Outside of the

Church there is a degree of social activity which revolves around the use of German, but this is far less than the influence of the Church (European Parliament, 2002; Hudlett, 2000; LGR German/France).

The rate of religious participation among the German language group in Denmark is also low, even if it is higher than for the general Danish population. The religious officers use both German and Danish and integrate organisationally with their equivalent in Germany. About 75 per cent of the priesthood have a knowledge of German. The Danish National Church has opened special religious offices for the language group in four local towns, while in the rural area along the border co-operation with German churches is close. It is the Church which is the main integrating force for the language group, and secular voluntary associations are weak (Christiansen and Teebken, 2001; LGR German/Denmark).

Religion in the Gaelic communities in Scotland is the responsibility of the Church of Scotland, the Free Church of Scotland and the Free Presbyterians. All of these have had a Gaelic language mission. In the Western Isles of Scotland almost all clergy speak Gaelic, regardless of denomination, and over three-quarters of the population attend church regularly. Almost two-thirds of the services are in Gaelic. Such Gaelic language services are still held in Skye, but elsewhere on the west coast they are sporadic. The extent to which voluntary associations using Gaelic flourish depends upon location, and outside of the Western Isles they are few and far between (Robertson, 2001).

The Catholic Church in both the Republic of Ireland and in Northern Ireland have supported the language group and its attempts to reproduce the language. The Church is a prime focal point for community integration. Masses are held in Irish in the *Gaeltacht*, and also to a much lesser extent elsewhere. Outside the *Gaeltacht*, services are not community focused and Irish speakers from a wider area use the facilities. Almost all of the clergy have a knowledge of Irish, but few are fluent speakers (O'Riagain, 1997; LGR Irish).

Finally, the Finnish language group in the Tornedalen region of Sweden has relied heavily upon the clergy in sustaining the language. Sermons and masses continue to involve a use of the language and the Swedish religious authorities pay an extra subvention to clergy who can operate bilingually. Given the rapid decline in the use of the language in the family, religion remains one of the few contexts where the language is used (LGR Finnish/ Sweden).

4.4 Religious support and institutional support weak

Most language groups in this cluster lack both religious and community support for the respective languages. Community plays a minor role in the production and reproduction processes. If this role is relegated to the family and formal education, a coherent social role for minority language-based activity is limited. Language use is constrained and it is difficult to provide a public rationale for the use of the language. This occurs where the Church conforms with the centrist orientation of the polity and where the state places pressure on communities not to use the minority language.

The Greek Orthodox Church prioritises religious similarity over any diversity associated with language and culture. Three language groups in Greece – Macedonian, Arvanite and Aroumanian – do not receive any support from the Church for the use of the respective languages. Greek becomes the language of all Church-related activities. The goal of the Greek authorities has been to eliminate all trace of the languages (Kostopoulos. 2000). Public officials working in the respective regions could have no knowledge of the language of that region and any public officials from these regions were deployed outside of that region. Language group exogamy was also encouraged. During the 1930s minority language use could be punished with imprisonment, and during the 1950s speakers were publicly and collectively lectured against using their mother tongue. This prevents the different language groups from developing voluntary associations that use the minority language (Tsitsipis, 1998; Kahl, 1999).

While this degree of denigration and persecution has not been evident elsewhere in recent years, many of the other language groups have been dissuaded from developing community structures that use the minority language. In Brittany few of the clergy are young, and they generally have no knowledge of Breton. Few Church activities are conducted in Breton. The Celtic literary tradition, much of it oral, which has focused upon the lives of the Saints is being lost. The universalist principles of the state prevail. Two-thirds of Breton children attend Catholic schools, and the link between the State and the Church in the lives of the people is strong. Any community role in the reproduction of Breton is weak. Community activities in Brittany increasingly focus upon Breton culture to the exclusion of the language, allowing everyone, regardless of language competence to be involved. This has led to a revival of Breton dance and music, but not of the language (Broudic, 2000; LGR Breton).[4]

The role of the Occitan language in community affairs is even less than in Brittany. Few of the priests speak Occitan, and it is rarely heard in church. Community activities using the language are often limited to 'folkloristic' activities, unrelated to social practice and focusing upon their importance for tourism (Berthoumieus and Willemsma, 1997; LGR Occitan/France). Similarly, all of the Church activities in the region of Spain occupied by the Portuguese language group are conducted entirely in Castilian (Luna, 2001; LGR Portuguese/Spain).

A priesthood that speaks the minority language does not guarantee a wide use of that language in religious affairs. Among the Friulian the percentage attending church is high, and almost three-quarters of the priests speak the language, and have played a prominent role in the regional language movement. Apart from recent use in the liturgy, the services have rarely been conducted in the language and the rites of passage are invariably conducted in Italian. Community use of Friulian is increasingly linked to social networks rather than voluntary associations (Picco, 2001). The same is true in Sardinia where, even though 90 per cent of the priests speak Sardinian, the language is rarely used in the Church. All ceremonies are conducted in Italian. Community use of Sardinian within formal settings is rare (Rindler Schjerve, 1997; LGR Sardinian).

Most Czech language group activities in Austria which use the language are secular. Their voluntary associations involve Czech choral and theatrical events, often supported by the Czech embassy, and sport. They are voluntary leisure activities among a dispersed city population which is integrated into the normative aspects of Austrian social life. The Slovaks have a single clergy responsible for the religious activities of the language group (Austrian Centre for Ethnic Groups, 1996).

About 20 per cent of the clergy who serve the Dutch language group in France can speak the language, but it is rarely used either in the Church or in the voluntary associations (Marteel, 2000; LGR Dutch/France). Among the Griko language group communities in Italy few priests have a knowledge of the language and it is rarely used in religious ceremonies. Some are demanding the use of the language in the orthodox form of the religion, but it has not been used in the Church for 400 years. The ageing population who use the language cannot sustain its formal use in the community (LGR Griko/Italy).

Only 10 per cent of the Catholic clergy who serve the East and North Frisians can use the language and it is little used in Church services. Community use of the language among both Frisian language groups is limited (Hollander and Steensen, 1991; LGR Frisian/Germany).

In the past Protestants in Northern Ireland embraced Irish, but today it is emblematic of Irish nationalism which is anathema to most Protestants. The degree of Irish competence among the Catholic population is limited, but the Church does play a significant role in supporting Irish-medium education and cultural activities. Support is strong, but the limited ability means that few community activities focus upon the use of Irish (Willemsma and MacPoilin, 2001).

About 30 per cent of the Sorbian language group are Catholics, 70 per cent being practising Catholics. In Upper Lusace about three-quarters of the clergy speak Sorbian, whereas in Lower Lusace only three of the Evangelical clergy speak the language. This is reflected in the use of Sorbian in religious activities. The use of Sorbian in community affairs varies across communities. It is strongest where the Catholic Church plays a prominent role in the community (Hollander and Steensen, 1991; LGR Sorbian).

The Sami relationship with Christianity has not been a happy one. Conversion actively began in the seventeenth century, leading to a form of syncretism. The revivalism of the nineteenth involved a degree of Messianism. Since the Middle Ages the Skolt and Kola Sami have belonged to the Eastern Orthodox Church, whereas the other language groups belong to the Roman Catholic and Evangelical Lutheran Churches. Marriage structures have been influenced by this distribution. These institutions use the state language for their respective practices, and the current attempts to develop voluntary associations which use the various Sami languages are struggling on account of the number of languages involved across such a small population. Religion has failed to provide an integrating role (Aikio, Aikio-Puoskari and Helander, 1996).

The necessity for community to be a self-defining, rational process seems to be missing among the Asturian language group. Asturian is only used in informal community activities, and community activities are unrelated to a sense of conscious language promotion, and language group activities are set apart from the broader social activities within the community (Bauske, 1998; European Parliament, 2002).

4.5 Conclusion

Religion has had an ambiguous role by reference to linguistic diversity in Europe. The Catholic Church rarely provides a service through the medium of the minority languages, the exceptions being the result of the efforts of regional clergy recruited from among the local population. A clergy which fails to use the language in the Church services can play a prominent role in secular activities that do use the language in the community. This link between Church and community partly explains the limited degree of voluntary activity within the communities in Southern Europe.

It is the Greek Orthodox Church which has been most intransigent by reference to operating a policy that accommodates linguistic diversity. The Church is prominent in the Greek nationalist movement, and the goal of the Greek state, since its inception, has been to establish a monolingual state. The clergy have played a part in limiting the use of minority languages in community affairs.

The devolved nature of religious administration among the Protestant sects leads to minority languages being accommodated in their activities. Even the Protestant State Churches have ceded regional autonomy and decision-making functions by reference to language use, which means that the language and administration of religious activity is a matter for the local community. They have also played a central role as the moral authority in community affairs, so that if the minority language is used it has an air of authority that otherwise would be missing.

5 Media in the household

How the family links to the wider community which constitutes the language group writ large is mediated by the media. In penetrating all families

Table 4.3 Availability of print and broadcasting media

	Broadcasting media	
	High	Low
High print media	Welsh, Catalan, Basque, German/Italy, German/France, German/Belgium, Swedish/Finland, Galician, Irish	Corsican, Sorbian
Low print media	Basque/France, Gaelic, Frisian, Catalan/Valencia, Catalan/Majorca, Aranese, Basque/Navarre, Catalan/France, Breton, Friulian, Ladin, Slovene/Italy, Slovene/Austria, Sami/Sweden, Sami/Finland, Luxembourgish	Cornish, Irish/N. Ireland, N. Frisian, E. Frisian, Portuguese/Spain, Griko, Slovak/Austria, Czech/Austria, Dutch/France, Mirandais, Macedonian, Sami/Finland, Asturian, Sami/Sweden, Arvanite, Occitan/France, Aroumanian, Hungary/Austria, Danish/Germany, Croat/Austria, German/Denmark, Turkish, Franco-Provencal, Sardinian, Occitan/Italy, Albanese, Catalan/ Aragon

by reference to a specific language, it conditions their view of the world, especially by reference to aspects of life that are specific to the use of that particular language. It transcends individual communities and plays an important role in integrating the language group as a social force, as a self-conscious solidaristic community. Only through consensus and self-awareness can a social group engage with the 'political' in the quest for social justice. The difference in how the 'national' media and the minority language media construct their subjects by reference to universal and particularist principles involves the relationship between the individual, the community and the media *vis à vis* diversity and pluralism The media operates as an 'integrator for democracy', uniting everyone regardless of social standing into a single community of citizens. It is both universalist and individualist in that not only does it address everyone, but it also addresses each person as an individual in their own home, in relation to their own problems, thereby integrating the family into citizenship (Rose, 1995:224). The voluntary nature of the use of the media places it in the realm of civil society, even though this is contentious for many. Below, access to the media is categorised in terms of the print and broadcasting media. Again the typology is presented in Table 4.3.

5.1 Broadcasting and print media widely accessible

There are nine language groups which have a wide access to both forms of media that derive from their territory. Some of these groups have benefited from both forms of media for several decades, whereas others have only recently gained access to the entire range of media activities.

Irish language radio broadcasting began in 1926, but Radio na Gaeltachta only came into existence in 1970. It is estimated to have an audience of 30 000, mainly in the *Gaeltacht*. Demand led to establishing a comparable Irish language television service in 1996. The *Irish Times* devotes about 10 per cent of its print space to Irish, and there are two weekly newspapers and one monthly entirely in Irish. Their circulation is small (O'Murchu, 2001).

Radio broadcasting in Welsh began in 1923, and television broadcasting in Welsh in 1958. A Welsh language television channel, S4C, was established in 1981. It broadcasts four hours daily during peak hours and runs a complete digital, Welsh language service. The BBC provides a complete radio service in Welsh. The print media is less prolific. In the nineteenth century numerous Welsh language newspapers reached most of the Welsh-speaking public. Now there is no daily Welsh language newspaper, even though one daily newspaper includes some Welsh. There are two weekly journals and numerous periodicals, but readership is not large. However, a series of Welsh language community newspapers have a joint readership in excess of 200 000 (Williams and Morris, 2000).

The end of the Franco era led to the reintroduction of minority language media in Spain. Catalan media broadcasting began in 1964 and has multiplied since. Currently, almost 1400 hours of transmission occurs in Catalan. TV3 and Canal 33 broadcast entirely in Catalan, reaching almost 3 million viewers. As many as 192 municipal radio stations in Catalonia broadcast almost entirely through the medium of Catalan. There are numerous daily and periodical print media entirely in Catalan that have a considerable circulation. These receive subventions from the regional government. Yet sales are less than those of their Castilian language equivalents (Busquet and Sort, 1999).

In Galicia, whereas 87 per cent of the population speaks Galician, only 46 per cent read it, but this level of literacy can sustain a viable print media. The linguistic proximity of Spanish and Galician means that much of the media service in Galician can be universally understood. Galician language broadcasting began in 1974 and CRTVG was established in 1985. One of its television services, TVG, has 24 hours daily production which is broadcast globally. In 1997, 8070 hours or 73 per cent of all its transmission was through its own production. Radio Gallega which broadcasts exclusively in

Galician has an audience of 152000 listeners, RNE1 which broadcasts almost nine hours daily in Galician has 185000 listeners and RNE5 which broadcasts 41 hours a week in the language has a further 32000 listeners. There are similar figures for private radio outlets, but there is no daily print media that appears exclusively in Galician. The greatest percentage of content in the dailies is 30 per cent. The circulation of Galician language periodicals is low (Ledo Andion, 1999).

There is only one daily Basque language daily newspaper, having a readership of 17000. Three other dailies provide some print in Basque. There are three main journals which appear weekly or monthly in Basque, but with limited circulation. Local Basque language papers on the other hand have a circulation of about 250000. There are two Basque language radio stations which reach an audience of about 100000 and a further two private radio stations with an audience of 25000. The Basque language television channel has an audience in excess of 200000 (European Parliament, 2002; LGR Basque/Spain).

The German language group in Italy not only has access to German language broadcasts from Austria and Germany, but has its own media services. It has a daily newspaper with a circulation of 40000, two other bilingual newspapers and several journals. There is also a German language radio station and RAI provides a German language radio service. This is in addition to private radio stations. Television transmission in German is less, consisting of about 15 hours a week (Pircher, Huber and Taschler, 2002; LGR German/Italy).

Similarly, the German language group in Belgium has access to the media in neighbouring Germany, and its own daily newspaper and a variety of journals. It has its own radio station which broadcasts exclusively in German as well as the provision of a television service (Lenoble-Pinson, 1997; Jennings, 1991; LGR German/Belgium).

The German speakers in Alsace have the daily newspaper *DNA* which publishes 75 per cent of its material in German, and has a circulation of 55000, whereas *Alsace* has half of its print space in German and has a circulation of 20000. Two other newspapers and two journals use less German. Radio France Alsace provides six hours of daily broadcasting in German, and there is a limited German language service on FR3 Alsace. Several private radio stations also broadcast in German. Extraterritorial television broadcasting in the language is readily available (Hudlett, 2000; Van der Schaaf and Morgon, 2001; LGR German/France).

The Swedish language group in Finland has a radio service of 19 hours a day from a single national radio station as well as various private stations. It also receives 845 hours of Swedish language television broadcasting each year through the Swedish programme unit of FST. This is in addition to 200 hours of sports news which are transmitted bilingually each year. The language group has its own daily newspaper which sells across Finland, various newspapers which publish several times a week, and a variety of periodicals which cover a range of interests (Liebkind, Broo and Finnas, 1995; Ostern, 1997; LGR Swedish/Finland).

5.2 Broadcasting media prominent, print media less prominent

A larger cluster of language groups have access to both forms of media, but not to the extent that they can play a predominant role in media-related activities. None of the groups have a comprehensive print media service in the relevant language, but the broadcasting media service is stronger and more exhaustive than their access to the print media.

The Gaelic language group in Scotland is served by Radio nan Gaidheal and, more recently, a Gaelic language television service, and two independent radio broadcasters transmit some programmes in Gaelic. The television service amounts to 300 hours annually; broadcasting on Radio nan Gaidheal amounts to 35 hours a week and is available throughout Scotland. Publishing is supported through the Scottish Arts Council which refuses to distinguish between High Culture and popular culture, and tends to treat all culture as Scottish. There are no daily or weekly papers entirely in Gaelic, but various newspapers incorporate articles in Gaelic. There are also several state-supported Gaelic language magazines and periodicals (Robertson, 2001; LGR Gaelic).

There are three daily newspapers which devote about 5 per cent of their space to Frisian language articles and several periodicals with limited circulation which appear in the language. A single radio station broadcasts about 70 hours weekly in the language and two hours a day of Frisian language programming appear on television (Gorter and Jonkma, 1996; Renkema, Ytsma and Willemsma, 1996).

An autonomous television service in Valencia was created in 1989 and about two-thirds of the programming on TVV is in Catalan. Barcelona's TV3 can be received but not everywhere. Canal 9 is a public radio station that broadcasts entirely in Catalan and there are also Catalan language services on the various municipal and local radio stations. There is no Catalan language daily newspaper, but there are several Catalan language periodicals with a limited circulation, and several bilingual publications covering a range of ages and interests (European Parliament, 2002, Marin, 1996; LGR Catalan/Valencia).

In the Balearic Islands financial support is available for Catalan language media activities. Until recently there was an English language daily newspaper serving the islands but none in Catalan! There are several Catalan language periodicals with limited circulation and others have some Catalan content. Radio 4 used to broadcast entirely in Catalan, but now the only such service is via local radio stations. Several stations provide a partial service. Public television in Catalan is limited to about 10 hours a week, but private stations provide considerably more.

The main Catalan media language service derives from Barcelona (LGR Majorca).

The Aranese language group receives considerably less media support than does Catalan. In Val d'Aran there is no print media that produces entirely in Aranese and only one daily that has some articles in the language. Catalonia Radio broadcasts seven hours a week in Aranaese, while the Municipal Radio broadcasts nine hours a week in the language. Televisio de Cataluña transmits only 15 minutes weekly in the language (LGR Aranese).

In Navarre, Basque speakers benefit from the services provided in the Autonomous Community. The regional government in Navarre does provide subventions for Basque language publications. Yet there is no Basque language daily newspaper and the various periodicals have a limited circulation. There are two main Basque language radio stations, but again the audience is limited (Basque Regional Government, 1996).

There are three Basque language journals with limited circulation and a further three which publish some material in Basque in Iparalde. There is no Basque language daily newspaper in the region. State radio broadcasts an hour daily in Basque, but there are four private radio stations which between them broadcast 147 hours in the language each week. State television service provides three hours a year in Basque! About a quarter of the language group can receive the service from the Autonomous Community in Spain and do use it (LGR Basque/France).

In recent years, in addition to the state services, the state has devolved responsibility for broadcasting to the regional authorities and has deregulated broadcasting, prompting private provision to become more readily available. This opens up space for minority language services. The extent to which this happens depends upon the political organisation of each state and the nature of devolution in this structure. A comparison of the preceding cases with cases from France is instructive.

The Catalan language group in France has one limited-circulation Catalan language weekly journal which is owned in Catalonia but printed in Perpignan. There are also several specialist Catalan language magazines in the region. The regional extension of the state radio service, RF Rousillon, broadcasts a few hours weekly in Catalan whereas a private radio station broadcasts 168 hours weekly. Televison broadcasting in Catalan is limited (LGR Catalan/France).

Breton language television programmes amounted to no more than 25 hours a year, but the opening of a private service led to a service of 17 hours a day. Local radio produces about 64 hours a week in Breton across all of the radio stations. The print media in Breton is extremely limited, consisting of periodicals which reach a limited audience (Ledo Andion, 1997).

Two regional daily newspapers use a limited amount of Friulian in their publications and there are several journals which will publish the occasional article in the language. RAI 3 broadcasts a cultural radio programme each week and the private radio station Onde Furlane broadcasts 70–80 hours weekly in Friulian. Also Tele Friuli televises one evening a week in the language (LGR Friuli). The situation is similar by reference to the Ladin language group in the Alto Adige region. A journal entirely in Ladin is published once a week with a circulation of 3000 copies. RAI broadcasts four and a half hours a week in Ladin while a private radio station broadcasts a further four hours weekly in the language. Television broadcasting is minimal (Van der Schaaf and Verra, 2001; LGR Ladin).

There are three Slovene language publishing houses in Italy publishing books and monthly journals which have a considerable circulation. They also produce three important weeklies and a range of less important journals. The press caters to specific interests as well as to the language group as a whole. The group also has access to a complete Slovene language radio service, but television broadcasting in the language is limited. This is very similar to the service for the Slovene speakers in Austria. The group has its own publishing houses funded by the Austrian and Slovene states. There are no daily newspapers, but the periodicals are widely read. Radio broadcasting amounts to 50 minutes daily and television to 30 minutes a week. Audiences are high (Reiterer, 1996).

Luxembourgish is very much the poor relative of both German and French in the media. The daily press in Luxembourg uses some Luxembourgish, but far less than the use of German and French. There is a single journal devoted exclusively to the language. A complete Luxembourg language radio service is available on more than one station. Television broadcasting in the language is limited to two hours daily and four hours on Sunday (Fehlen et al., n.d; LGR Luxembourgish).

Given the limited population of the various Sami language groups, the media has presented a particular challenge, involving a Nordic service which broadcasts from Norway. There are also initiatives within Sweden and Finland. The central private radio station located in Norway uses all Sami languages during the seven hours of daily broadcasting. Television satellite broadcasting also derives from Norway. Print media is limited to a monthly periodical which is widely distributed (Aikio, Aikio-Puoskari and Helander, 1994).

5.3 Print media prominent, broadcasting media less so

There are only two language groups in this category. The Sorbian language group in Germany has a daily newspaper entirely in Sorbian and a weekly, half of which appears in Sorbian. This is in addition to a range of other periodicals. Publicly financed radio services give about 30 hours of transmission weekly. In comparison, television broadcasting in Sorbian is extremely limited (LGR Sorbian). The other language group is Corsican in France which has a daily newspaper with limited circulation, and several periodicals written entirely in Corsican. It also benefits from a large use of Corsican on the radio, but has only 40 minutes weekly on television (Fusina, 1999; LGR Corsican).

5.4 Both print media and broadcasting media weak or absent

Since broadcasting has tended to be developed through the state, with the 'national' press pursuing a 'national' and international agenda, those states with centrist policies are least likely to promote minority language media. Small language groups are unlikely to have the resources for developing private services. These groups are small populations and are located in Greece, Italy and France, states that do not have a very effective devolution of media services.

The language groups with limited populations include North Frisian which has no stand-alone media organs. The language is used to a limited extent in German newspapers, radio and television. East Frisian is served to an even lesser extent. In the UK five minutes a week of Cornish is broadcast on the BBC's regional service, Radio Cornwall. *An Gannas*, a general interest paper with a circulation of 200–300 is published monthly, and a literary publication *An Dherwen* which has a circulation of 50 appears three or four times a year. The Irish language group in Northern Ireland has access to both radio and television services from western Scotland and the Republic of Ireland, but little in the way of its own media services.

In Spain the Portuguese language group has a single publicly financed bilingual journal with limited circulation. Radio and television broadcasting from Portugal can be received by the language group. However, the variety spoken differs considerably from the Portuguese standard (LGR Portuguese/ Spain). The Mirandais language group in Portugal has no media provision in its language.

The Danish language group in Germany has a single periodical, most of which appears in Danish. It also has a radio service of 30 minutes weekly. It can also access the Danish language service in Denmark (LGR Danish/Germany). The German language group in Denmark has its own German language journal, but no radio or television service other than what they receive from Germany. This implies that the two language groups are conceived of as extensions of the respective states (Chistiansen and Teebken, 2001).

In Austria the Croat language group has a number of low-circulation journals, but no daily newspaper. It also receives 42 minutes of Croat language radio broadcasting and 30 minutes weekly on television (LGR Croat/ Austria). The situation is similar for the Czech group by reference to the print media, but it has no radio or television service other than that directly from the Czech Republic, which is not universally accessible. The Hungarian language group has monthly periodicals, 25 minutes of radio weekly and less than two hours of television annually, while the Slovak language group has a minimal amount of print media and relies on trans-frontier reception for access to broadcasting (Austrian Centre for Ethnic Groups, 1996; LGR Hungarian/Austria).

In Greece there is no use of Macedonian, Arvanite or Aroumanian within the mass media, but the Macedonian language group does benefit from Skopje TV, but it can only be received in Florina, but both Radio Skopje and Radio Sofia can be received universally (European Parliament, 2002). The same is true of the Turkish language group in Greece which, despite attempts to blank out terrestrial transmission, receives Turkish radio and television programmes. Printed material emanating from Turkey is intercepted and confiscated at the border. As a consequence of the Treaty of Lausanne, the language group does produce three periodicals and it receives two hours of radio broadcasts daily via one of the public service broadcasters (Aarbakke, 2001; LGR Turkish/Greece).

The French state has recently introduced a minimal minority language radio and television service, and regional authorities can authorise financial support for the print media. The Flemish language group in France has no Flemish language daily newspaper, whereas three regional reviews do produce materials about the language group in French. There is a single periodical produced in standard Dutch published in Belgium for the community. While there is no television service, about 10 per cent of the radio service of a single radio station is produced in Dutch (Marteel, 2000; LGR Dutch/France). The only use of the Occitan language in daily press amounts to a single page each week, and the regional government does not provide a publication subsidy. Yet there are about 20 limited circulation periodicals published in Occitan. None of the public radio stations broadcast in Occitan, but there is limited use on private radio. The use of Occitan on television is limited to about 30 hours annually (Berthoumieux and Willemsma, 1997; LGR Occitan/France).

The Greek language group in Italy has two periodicals with limited circulation which include the language. There is no radio or television provision. The Franco-Provencal group has periodicals, again with limited circulation. The radio station RAI broadcasts 15 minutes daily in the language. Similarly, RAI TRE televises a further 15 minutes daily in France-Provencal. Sardinian is only used in a limited number of journals. Some private radio stations use a little of the language, and regional television makes the occasional use of the language (LGR Franco-Provencal/Italy). There are several journals which use the Occitan language, but their circulation is small. These do receive support from the regional government. The language is rarely used on television or radio. The Catalan speakers in Sardinia have some content within regional journals and a limited number of radio programmes. Local television broadcasts 10 per cent of its programmes in Catalan, consisting of five hours a day of emission (LGR Catalan/Italy). The Albanese language group has very limited representation on radio and none in television. The print media using the language consists of a limited number of periodicals which use the Catalan together with Italian.

The exception to this pattern is the Catalan language group in Aragon. It is viewed as a language group that is marginal to the existence of the region, and it is also viewed as pertaining to another region, benefiting from the media provision there. The regional authorities do not offer any grant aid to Catalan language publication. There are two daily newspapers which have 15 per cent of their content in Catalan, and some of the Municipal radio stations have some content in Catalan (Nagore Lain, 1999).

5.5 Conclusion

A small number of stateless languages with a fairly large membership located in Spain and the UK and the main extraterritorial language groups have managed to generate a broad media service. Other stateless languages within the same states have been reasonably successful, and some of the extraterritorial language groups which benefit from international treaties have also managed to secure a role in the media. There remain almost as many language groups which have a minimal mass-media service.

Many of the extraterritorial language groups benefit from the services provided by the states where that language is the normative language, and this exposes the television viewer to the oral and even written standard of the language, while generating confidence in the use of the language. However, transmission does not reflect any sense of the language group as a spatial and social entity which transcends the individual community. If anything, it leads to further integration with the transnational source and culture, and contradicts the view of the language group as a social group with its own culture which may not necessarily have much to do with the culture of the state where the language is normative.

6 Conclusion

The community can play a role by reference to both minority language production and reproduction, and where this occurs the family also plays a predominant role in language reproduction. A handful of language groups have a high degree of language endogamy and/or language use within the family, and also have the community organisational structure which uses the minority language in a range of contexts. They also have access to the mass media which allows the language group to develop a sense of coherence and direction which transcends the local context of the community. The language group has the capacity to become a group for itself and can organise on a wide front, mobilising the language group around a common, defined set of interests.

Discussions of civil society have viewed the individual as constructed out of a sense of moral or 'natural' equality. The belief in the moral equality of humans was central to both the medieval Natural Law and the Social Contract which preceded the idea of civil society and social liberalism. It leads to the legal order being based on the rights and duties of individuals. Personal autonomy, human rights and contract take a central position. By insisting on the role of fundamental human rights, this discourse separates private sphere from public sphere, civil society from the state. In civil society individuals can exercise choice according to conscience and are protected by rights, but equal treatment which extends to the right to use one's mother tongue has not been accommodated in how some European states have developed their sense of democracy. The idea of civil society as the local level at which the individual engages with the assembly in sharing public power is also missing. The current thrust which seeks to narrow the gap between civil society and the state by integrating individuals into the community also ignores issues of pluralism, diversity and personal autonomy. The notion of citizenship often appears to involve a suffocating insistence on the priority of the state over the citizen and civil society.

Siedentop (2000:124) argues that certain 'virtues' are necessary for effective leadership within democratic society – sensitivity to needs and expectations, the ability to identify morally and socially acceptable avenues of change, and the ability to mobilise consent through educating public opinion. Where these are absent, their place will be taken by the media, and there is a primary role for the media in creating the pluralism and diversity that are central to democratic society. The media constitutes one means whereby society sees itself, while also informing it about the polity that governs it. The existence of a vivid media relevant to minority language groups is an indication of any society's commitment to pluralism.

This discourse of democracy can construct both the family and language as related objects which overlap, and which are anathema to the construction of a democracy which is conveyed as 'freedom'. On the other hand there are competing discourses on democracy that have direct relevance for the extent to which the family reproduces the language or rejects it in favour of the single language of both democracy and reason. How diversity and pluralism are accommodated in the discourse of democracy is crucial. Where they are accommodated, bilingualism and multiculturalism are also evident. However, their appearance will always be in a subordinate position to the need to bring all institutions in line with the centrality of the state by reference to social order. Political scientists persist with this model of democracy in the name of freedom, despite the evident link between the meta-discourse of Political Science and state interests. The assumptions of this discourse are being questioned, albeit it is rarely by reference to the discourse of democracy, which seems to carry its own ideological momentum.

The integration of the orthodox democratic discourse into capitalism makes it difficult to discuss the family in terms of production/reproduction in isolation. The role which the family plays in sustaining a healthy workforce relates to what has been said above about the family and democracy. The construction of the relationship between the family and society involves the family being the object which forms the individual social subject. If economic efficiency derives from rationalism, as the economic discourse claims, then this formation must be undertaken by a rational agency. It leads to the claim that the family must be transformed through the influence of the state. The allegiance of families to what are constructed as outmoded institutions – the extended family, the emotive community and so on – must be broken and allegiance must be to the state. The family not only plays a role in producing rational, economic individuals, but also good citizens!

5
Language Prestige

1 Introduction

The relationship between economic organisation, space and time is not unrelated to person and how the subject is constructed within the different discourses that integrate language and economy. The central motivating force for the production and reproduction of minority language groups is the relevance of the minority language for social mobility – language prestige. Once a language is incorporated into the activities of the labour market, it becomes an object which has a particular signification for the individual within a society which is constituted through the relationship of individuals to the economic order. It involves how democracy constructs the individual as a free agent in the quest for the good life.

Foucault claims that:

> It was through the science of government that the notion of economy came to be recentred onto that different plane of reality which we characterise today as 'economic' . . . and thanks to the isolation of that area of reality that we call the economy, that the problem of government finally came to be thought, reflected and calculated outside of the juridical framework of sovereignty.

(1991:91)

Modelling government on the family was replaced with its modelling on the notion of economy. Governance focused upon welfare, and the relationship between the family and the economy realigned itself. A new space was opened for the government to intervene in the economy on behalf of the population. Political economy was born. The individual is constituted as a free, independent, enquiring individual who selects from among alternative courses of action on the basis of reason. Economic behaviour is the most important feature of this rational behaviour. The speakers of a language which has relevance for the labour market are constructed as economic actors by reference to some aspects of the economy, labour-market incorporation not necessarily being across the entire range of economic activities. The state's control of its economy and the associated labour market insures that almost all economic activities include the state language. The market is a unifying practice that links with how the state constitutes the state language as a totalitarian unity. The increasing globalisation of the economy means that certain languages, most particularly English, will tend to prevail for some economic activities, regardless of the language of the state. Such international languages are constructed as objects differently from the state languages and they pertain to the economic order in particular ways. This may be mirrored by the relationship between state languages and regional languages.

Achieving the good life by citizens is a central tenet of the discourse on democracy. The good life is measured by reference to economic growth and benefit, and how the individual can achieve social mobility. The meta-discourse of economics is heavily focused upon the centrality of reason as the prerequisite for optimal economic behaviour. Democracy and the economic order relate through dependent societies relying on external state intervention, or some other source, so that claimed rights are more communitarian than individual and involve a tendency to resist an imposed politics of modernisation (Touraine, 1994:3). Since they fail to defend personal liberty:

> It is a mistake to say that this tension does not have anti-democratic effects and that democracy has no place in a society divided between the authoritarian intervention of the state and communitarian defence, and where the state constantly risks removing the language of the community and thereby becoming totalitarian.
>
> (ibid: 30; my translation)

Thus democracy can only exist within the richer countries of the world which dominate the markets and the global economy. Democracy is not an attribute of economic modernisation – or some stage in an evolutionary conditioned history constructed as a market – and instrumental rationality. This has particular significance for the relationship between private liberty and social integration within democracy. Even economists are challenging the significance of instrumental action within the meta-discourse of Economics (Williams and Morris, 2000:209–53). It brings democracy in line with the conception of endogamous or indigenous sustainable development.

Minority languages have been constructed by reference to the third estate and hereditary factors. The combination of the economic conditions of life and hereditary privileges was what democratic society was obliged to eliminate. How the sociopolitical discourse links the family, education and economy leads to its insistence upon abandoning non-state languages in developing rationality, individual freedom and opportunity through social mobility. The family had an obligation for private improvement and responsibility associated with social mobility within the economic order. In contrast to how the sociological meta-discourse viewed the subject in terms of objective situations that determined collective and individual behaviour, Touraine (1989:185) argues that situations do not determine action, but rather, 'action brings to light relations of domination and subordination which lack a visible juridical or political expression.' Social movements replace the concept of social class.

Social mobility is central to democracy, in that democratic systems give the individual the means to achieve the good life that must, at least in theory, be achievable by everyone. Either equality or equality of opportunity lies at the heart of discourses on liberal democracy. The social mobility is linked with education and the ability to conform with both the reward system of the normative order and the way it is sanctioned by the state in developing its labour market. Minority languages have been conceived of as lying outside of the rational principles of any normative orientation to economic rationality.

The sociological meta-discourse constructs social structure by reference to the economy as a determining force, which leads to viewing social structure independently of the individuals who occupy social positions. This is compounded by the tendency to separate the language from the social, something that derives from how Sociology has constructed language as an object separate from the subjects that speak it. The study of language and society are treated as separate variables, one correlating with the other. This determines the relationship between language and the economy.

Marx's *Das Capital* is less a work about material things than it is about individuals and how they are constituted as social beings in being the bearers or occupiers of social roles. The production of objects is the critical activity in social development. How the economy operates as a mode of production relies on relations of production which set the parameters for social relations:

> My view is that each particular mode of production, and the relations of production corresponding to it at each given moment, in short 'the economic structure of society', is the real foundation, on which arises a legal and political superstructure and to which correspond definite forms of 'social consciousness', and that 'the mode of production of material life conditions the general process of social, political and intellectual life'.
>
> (Marx, 1976:175n)

This is characteristic of its time, and has been rightly criticised as such (Carrithers, Collins and Lukes, 1985:298–9 *inter alia*). However, it is the economic determinism that links economic order to social order rather than the details of the structure that derives from Marx's account that is criticised. For Marx, individuals, in using the economic concepts of everyday life, enter into social relations or roles 'independent of their will'. From these relations the individuality of the subject is constructed. This conception of social relations builds upon Bonald's model of society that is functional to communication (Macherey, 1992:31), and draws upon commodities as objects and their owners as individuals who posses a 'will'. The individual might or might not perform the actions and use the concepts from which, over time, social relations are constructed and maintained. On the other hand, the individual may be a 'bearer' or 'personification' of roles and relations which they enter independent of their will. The economy generates specific subject places occupied by individuals in relations to specific objects. There is a distinction between the subject and the individual.

Until recently the state has closed its labour market through regulation and the normative structure of society plays an important role in this. The state is itself the effects of a discourse which has emphasised universality and rationality, creating a single language of reason that is common to the entire population. The relationship between the individual and the state is such that the state represents the individual. The needs of capitalism are informed by a normativity which insures that the free flow of labour is assisted by recourse to a single language which is also the language of reason. The construction of language as an object rests upon this normative order.

Capitalism is not a uniform system, but rests upon the relations of production. Integrating the labour market through language is only one part of the picture. Internal social differentiation also relates to language and discourse. The absence of class varieties of minority languages derives from their exclusion from the world of production where the relations of production are constituted (Williams, 1987a). Conversely, state languages contain class varieties as forms that express the relations of production and class position in society. However, social class is not the only dimension of inequality, but involves inequalities premised upon age, gender, race and language group.

Education and language are important for the labour market. Most minority languages have been excluded from the state's educational processes. Increasing language prestige, by incorporating minority languages in employment involves two parallel processes – a struggle over language and a struggle in language (ibid.). When a language has relevance for social mobility, it has relevance for achieving the good life and becomes a feature of democracy. Language prestige becomes the motivational force for language production and reproduction. In the struggle over language, establishing the significance of the minority language for work has been undertaken on the basis of justice, arguing too that bilingualism affords enhanced intelligence and, more recently, by empirically demonstrating that multilingual workers receive better remuneration than their monolingual counterparts (Grin, 1999). Another argument involves the relationship between the social construction of meaning and innovation; poststructuralism argues that meaning is conditioned by discursive form and how it constitutes its subjects and objects. Members of language groups have limited margins of deviation from 'the traditional regulating conventions governing speech behaviour in a group' (Elias 1991:62). The mixing of discursive forms associated with different languages leads to a melange of meaning which is the very basis of innovation.

Autochthonous minority language groups pertain only to a fraction of the state territory. The meta-discourse of Economics involves principles related to the regulatory capacity of the state, constructing a single labour market regulated by the state, and occupied by the citizen as subject and economic actor within that market. Regional and local markets refer only to the concept of labour-market segmentation. Some (Denney, Borland and Fevre, 1992), have found it extremely offensive to inhibit the operation of the single state labour market, treating it as a form of 'racism' that affords advantage to its promoters.

This linking of labour-market segmentation and claims of racism is not fortuitous. Establishing any Race Relations Act must ensure an open labour market that guarantees the free mobility of labour since whatever limits the mobility of labour acts to exclude certain individuals from a portion of the labour market. When language segments the labour market and limits mobility into occupational and geographical positions, with language being a marker of distinction between 'peoples', accusations of 'racism' appear. Such claims become less valid with the appearance of the Single European labour market. It heralds how 'ethnic' groups succeed in cornering private-sector niches (Bonacich, 1972; Saxenian, 1999).

The liberalisation of the relationship between language and public services leads to promoting a language for public-sector employment. Neo-liberalism emphasises replacing the public sector with the voluntary sector, and the parallel valuation of an entrepreneurial private sector. Where at least part of public-sector employment involves the minority language, the visibility of minority language speakers in the public sector, together with their relative absence from the private sector, can lead to the claim that members of the language group lack a sense of entrepreneurialism. This is the converse of the 'racism' argument, linking this deficiency to language and culture, resulting in the 'blaming of the victim', and to the calling for the removal of minority language and culture from any economic relevance. The neo-liberal insistence upon the importance of diversity, meeting the needs and expectations of the public, and reconstructing and reconstituting language as a skill dissolves these arguments.

Most European minority language groups are located in the periphery. Peripheralism involves how discourse constructs and orders economic space. It can refer to the periphery of each state, involving the relationship between economic process, the spatial organisation of the economy, and state regulation. It can also involve how the mobility of capital ignores state boundaries. The process of economic activity involves expansion from the core to the periphery, with the core controlling much of the economy of the periphery. Functions that transcend economic sectors have percolated from the core into the service centres of the periphery, and this process determines the language used in these activities. This has wrongly been interpreted in terms of rural-urban differences, the atavistic nature of 'rural society' being responsible for the limited use of minority languages in urban centres.

Economic restructuring involves the relationship between the state, economy and space, and has a profound influence upon the relationship between the spatially restricted language group and its significance for the labour market. Given the relationship between the single labour market, a mobile labour force, the state and a single language of reason, the implications for minority language groups should be evident. The effects of discourse upon economic practice are considerable.

2 Minority languages and language prestige

The integration of the minority language into education at the post-primary level is a prerequisite of any substantial labour-market impact. The greater and broader the nature of this provision, the stronger the relationship between education and language prestige. Educational policy depends upon the extent of devolution. The relationship between the 'territory' of the language group, the associated labour market and language prestige will not necessarily be uniform. If the segmentation pertains to particular economic sectors and these sectors are spatially dispersed, then the link between language and the labour market will also have a particular spatial configuration. Language prestige is the main motivational basis for language production and reproduction (Williams, Roberts and Isaac, 1978). It involves a different construction of minority languages as objects from those existing in Europe thus far. It involves a struggle over normativity and new-use contexts for minority languages. It is hardly surprising that few minority language groups have achieved relevance in the regional labour market.

2.1 The Sami

The struggle of the different Sami language groups lies both within and outside of capitalism, involving the coexistence of modes of production where one mode dominates (Wolpe, 1979). While capitalism has not displaced the kinship mode of production, it does have the force of having the entire legislative power of the modern state behind it. The Sami are seeking to safeguard the community rights of usufruct of the kinship mode of production over the individual ownership of natural resources of capitalism.

The rights associated with hunting, fishing, gathering and reindeer herding are collective rather than individual rights, and this discourse on the economy pertains to collective rather than individual subjects. These activities are treated as subsistence activities that supplement any alternative income, while also keeping them aloof from welfarism. Within the kinship mode of production the individual must show membership of the collectivity, through descent and kinship affiliation, in order to have the right of usufruct of the resources.

Capitalism transforms subsistence activities into commercial activities and challenges rights of usufruct. This deprives the Sami of their resources, and the value-added profit accrues outside of the region. It also upsets the delicate balance between resource reproduction and market demand, or between nature and resource exploitation. This was the basis of the Sami Environmental Programme ratified at the Thirteenth Sami Conference in 1996 (Myntti, 1997).

Defining 'Sami' by reference to language will not protect these resource rights, since anyone can learn a language. Also, since the state has individualised land rights, and broken the relationship between kinship groups and territory, residence qualification offers no protection, except for reindeer herding where the animals follow fixed tracks known only to the herd and the owner. An EU directive has excluded reindeer herding in the region from the general principles of deregulation. The increasing degree of exogamy also precludes kinship as a defining criterion of group membership. Since the state recognises the Sami by reference to language and culture, an overlap of the rights to natural resources and the official identity is necessary. The favoured solution involves a mixture of descent, self-identity and language. Self-identity is meaningless in that it is capable of manipulation. Hunting rights are by land ownership, but since the state owns two-thirds of the forest land, this is less of an issue than might otherwise be the case. Fishing rights are by tradition, allowing the landless to retain such rights. Here, 'tradition' can only mean 'descent', but is in danger of running counter to any legislation that aims to exclude racism.

This is a struggle over how the Sami are constructed, both as a collective and an individual subject. The Sami construct themselves as a social and language group, involving the past relationship between kinship groups and resources. The individual identity is subordinate to the collective identity. In contrast, the state seeks to integrate the Sami into mainstream society, constructing them as individuals, subject to the same legal structures as the remainder of society. While the state will not deny the existence of the Sami as a social group, it will seek to make such a construction compliant with the broader normative order.

If the terms and conditions of the kinship mode of production guarantee exclusive access to raw materials that enter the capitalist market, considerable benefit will accrue to the Sami. They will control these resources on their terms in the region, while still in competition with the wider capitalist market by reference to the value of these products. The struggle currently revolves around these issues. If language becomes part of the definition, then value will also accrue to knowing the language. If it is not part of the ascription then, while the Sami will survive, they will not necessarily survive as a language group.

2.2 Labour market exclusion

Given the relationship between post-primary education and the labour market, language groups with little significance at this level of education will have low language prestige. Only minority language primary teachers open the labour market to the language, while highly localised employment in small enterprises may involve the use of the minority language. However, language prestige refers to social mobility rather than employment. Furthermore, motivation relies on this mobility being seen as an upward mobility that is facilitated by a knowledge of the particular language.

Legalisation has recently allowed the use of some minority languages within the public sector. In contrast to the earlier legislation in Austria which was based on 'rights', the more recent legislation pertains to a neo-liberal conception of public services, involving enabling and empowering the individual. The relationship between legitimation and institutionalisation changes. In Wales the Welsh Language Board, a body responsible for implementing the 1993 Language Act, serves as a language policing force which seeks to guarantee the relationship between legitimation and institutionalisation. While it can insure that the structures are in place for the individual to be empowered to use the language, it cannot guarantee that individual behaviour will be modified to the extent that the service will be used. Empowerment can be counter-productive. Yet empowerment will influence the relationship between language and public sector employment. In legislating this use of the minority language within the labour market the state is, simultaneously, silencing the claim of racist practices in employment. The symbolic impact of legitimation extends beyond opening a segment of the labour market to the minority language and its speakers. The language is reconstituted as an object, one that allows the speakers as subjects to operate as economic agents.

Public sector use of minority languages includes their use within the legal structure. This rests on the importance allocated to equal access to the legal system for all citizens, a central principle of the democratic discourse. An adequate translation service is a minimum obligation, but will extend as far as is necessary to insure that access leading to justice is seen to apply. It must not prejudice the relationship between the state, its official language(s) and the legal system. Again, it does have an impact upon the relevance of the minority language for the labour market.

Legislating for the use of minority languages within the public sector is not necessarily repeated by reference to the private sector, for fear of upsetting firms which may relocate. Privatising the public utilities and shifting welfarism from the public to the voluntary sector reduces the extent of public-sector employment. Private-sector action is voluntary and tends to focus upon symbolic display of the language. Two studies, one in Galicia (Rei Doval and Ramallo 1995) and the other in Catalonia, (Generalitat de Cataluña, n.d.) show that advertising in the minority language influences the willingness of minority language speakers to buy the product being advertised. In the Basque country and in Catalonia there has been a coherent attempt to persuade firms in the private sector to increase the use of the respective minority languages. One Basque language university focuses explicitly upon the needs of business in the region. By 1998, 14 large enterprises, most of them in the Alto Deba area, participated in the initiative which seeks to insure the use of Basque for work. In Galicia many enterprises already use Galician in the workplace and there is support for extending such use (Bouzada and Lorenzo Suarez, 1997). In Catalonia the regional government is entering into agreements with the larger private sector employers within the region by reference to extending the use of Catalan in work (Generalitat de Cataluña, n.d.).

The drive to enable the use of the respective languages in the public sector is in addition to the local and regional government employment, where policies promote the use of the language in many administrative procedures. This is often accompanied by legislation. Some bodies will treat this obligation as a form of tokenism, and there is a long way to go before even the public bodies subject to such legislation resort to using the minority language across all of their daily operations.

Even the official language planning agency established by the Generalitat in Valencia has done little to improve the situation. Local administration ranges from the complete use of Catalan to no use of the language. Nonetheless, there is considerable use in the public sector, even if it is not universal. Catalan is rarely a requirement for employment in Valencia unless there is direct public contact involved in the work. Legitimation does not always lead to the institutionalisation of the minority language in daily practice (Marin, 1996; LGR Catalan/Valencia).

In the Balearic Islands the Normalisation Law seeks to extend the use of Catalan in the public sector, but no attempt is made by either central or regional government to ensure that public officials can use the language. Rarely is such a knowledge seen to give any candidate an advantage in the competition for employment. The situation is better at the municipal level, but use is largely determined by the party in power in each locality. However, there are some professions, most notably the teaching profession, medicine and commerce, where Catalan is quite widely used for work (LGR Majorca).

The various autochthonous language groups have tended to control the agricultural sector, this having implications for other sectors. In the Austrian region of Carinthia the Slovene language group has an extensive network of banks and credit and the oldest commodity co-operatives in Austria, founded in 1872 (Reiterer, 1996). It has 30 branches in Carinthia and a balance of 430 m Euro and a turnover of 21 m Euro. It operates at three levels: the local level where there are seven banks with 17 branches which overlap with the activities of the co-operatives and warehouses; the regional level through the bank's centre in Klagenfurt; and the state and international level through membership of the Vienna-based Raiffeisen Group. The zadruga markets, or commodity co-operatives, were created to service the agricultural sector, but have subsequently diversified. The bank offers credit to Slovenian language group entrepreneurs against Slovene bank guarantees. The structure belongs to the language group and employs its members. Slovene is the language of work for the 300 or so employees, while the bank uses whichever language its customers prefer. A knowledge of Slovene is mandatory for its employees. It sponsors Slovene language cultural and sporting activity. It has recently extended into community development activities through an institution which represents over 70 companies which employ 2000 workers. All members must be Slovene speakers (LGR Slovene/Austria).

This, together with the use which the language commands in the public sector through legislation, is responsible for employing an estimated 4000 people out of a total number of 40000 speakers, of whom perhaps 16000 might be in employment. This may be too small within the regional labour market to influence people to learn the language for the sake of employment. Neither is the situation helped by the difference between legislation and institutionalisation in the public sector. Educational should integrate with this relatively large impact of the language upon the local labour market, but this is hindered by regional educational planning.

The 18000 or so Ladin speakers in Italy have succeeded in controlling certain economic resources, mainly in agriculture and tourism, thereby increasing the prestige of the language (Tosi, 2001). This control of the means of production is important. Indeed, 70 per cent of the local SMEs are involved in the tourist sector. Within the province of Bolzano the statute of autonomy insures that a knowledge of Ladin is obligatory for certain positions, and is an advantage for others. All public officials are obliged to be fluent in three languages – Ladin, German and Italian (Aufschnaiter, 1994; LGR Ladin).

The German language group in Italy is similarly privileged. As the official language within the region, German guarantees employment in public administration, education and the media. With the German language group consisting of about 70 per cent of the population, the need for a proportionality in employment guarantees their predominance in employment. The private sector is controlled by the German language group and operates through the medium of German (ibid.; LGR German/Italy)).

The only context within which Slovene is formally accepted within public administration in Italy is in the law courts, and that only in Gorizia and Trieste. Within regional government Slovene is neither used nor forbidden. It is only local administration that recognises the language, but even here use is minimal. However, there is a presence of the language in the media, education and in some private-sector enterprises.

In the early 1970s Irish language ability was essential to enter the Irish civil service. Since this requirement has been abolished, the prestige of the language has declined considerably. There are certain spheres of employment where a knowledge of the language is either essential or desirable, but they tend to be in the *Gaeltacht* and, to an extent, in Dublin (O'Riagain and Tovey, 1998).

In Luxembourg on the other hand, where two-thirds of the population are mother tongue speakers and three-quarters of the population speaks the language, and most of the non-speakers are immigrants who are obliged to learn the language, the situation is stronger. A competence in Luxembourgish is regarded as essential in the service sector. The language is only used in oral communication between central administration and the public. The legal requirement to use any of the three languages with the public has led to a strong institutionalisation of the use of Luexembourgish. Yet there are variations across the different services in the public sector. There is an advantage in being trilingual, even though theoretically any institution could use different personnel with different language abilities for different functions (European Parliament, 2002; LGR Luxembourgish).

In Finland, the Sami region relies upon public-sector employment. Unemployment among the Sami is as high as 33 per cent, this and the low activity rate of 40 per cent means that the sector plays a strong role in their lives. Almost a quarter of the employed work in the service sector and almost a quarter in the retail and construction activities. The males are heavily involved in subsistence activities and it is the women who tend to be employed in the public sector. Increasingly, political pressure has been exerted by the Sami to insure the use of the language wherever possible and this has served to gain a certain hold on many public sector jobs. In Sweden little official use is made of the Sami language by the local authorities, and most of the employment which the language benefits from derives from the need to translate Swedish documentation into Northern Sami (Aikio and Hyrvarinen, 1995).

In Aland, and in many of the bilingual areas of Finland, virtually all employment carries a Swedish language qualification. Use in the public sector is considerable and any enterprise owned by members of the language groups tends to use the language in work. The breadth of economic activity using the language means that social mobility involving Swedish can extend across occupational sectors (Ostern, 1997; LGR Swedish/Finland).

Among the German speakers in eastern Belgium the use of German in public-sector employment is ratified by law and integrates with educational use. Deregulation means that this language group can also access the labour market in Germany (Jennings, 1991, Lenoble-Pinson, 1997; LGR German/ Belgium). In Federal Germany itself the only minority language group of any size, the Sorbian speakers, have little opportunity to use their language in employment other than in teaching and Sorbian language institutions, and it has a relatively low prestige (Hemmings, 2001; LGR Sorbian).

The Slovene language groups in both Austria and Italy, and the Croat, Czech. Slovak, Slovene and Hungarian language groups in Austria have benefited from the integration of the new member states with the EU. The banking sector was among the first to link with the new political-economic context. Extraterritorial state language groups such as the Danes in Germany, Germans in Denmark and Italy have also benefited from European integration. Some border extraterritorial language groups, such as the Alsacians who work for the large Mercedes factory on the German side of the frontier, take advantage of their language ability in entering the labour market of the neighbouring state. The Turkish language group in Greece cannot avail themselves of the same advantages while Turkey remains outside of the EU. Within Greece, no guarantee is given *vis à vis* the use of Turkish in local administration. It is claimed that those of the language group who seek public-sector employment are discriminated against, a claim that tends to be supported by the absence of Turkish speakers in public positions, even where they constitute a majority of the population (European Parliament, 2002; LGR Turkish/Greece).

3 The media sector

In the preceding chapter I commented on the use of the media in the household. Minority language broadcasting also provides employment in a highly visible, highly skilled and relatively well-paid sector that is important in the regional economy. It involves small production companies, the main financing arms of the sector, and it has the technical capacity to link with the major players on a global basis. While they retain regulatory power, the states must sanction and often finance such developments. Apart from Brittany, the main developments have been in Spain and the British Isles, where they have spawned broad multimedia activities.

Analogue broadcasting set limitations on what states were willing to provide and minority language services became part of general service provision, leading to complaints from those who did not have a minority language competence. The minority language group argued for a separate service. Such issues were peripheral to language prestige which relied on the use of the minority language as a skill, regardless of the transmission structure.

Given a limited potential audience, the private sector will rarely encompass such a service without state intervention. Low-cost broadband narrowcasting will change this. To date it has been an important part of the arguments concerning provision. It applies less to Catalan, which has a substantial population of about ten million and is capable of supporting private-sector involvement, than it does to Welsh for example. Deregulation will expand this provision still further.

The one hour a week of Catalan broadcast by TVE's regional service in 1964. doubled in 1967. The changes after 1976 led to bilingual broadcasting with a reach that encompassed the Balearic Islands, Catalonia and Valencia. The Statute of Autonomy led to further growth to 65 hours a month in 1979–80. In 1983 TVE Cataluña became the second most important programme production centre for RTVE in Spain. By 1992 TVE Cataluña was providing more than 2000 hours of programming per year, more than half of it for regional broadcasting. Five years later they were producing more than 2000 hours of programmes for the region alone, of which 1387 hours were in Catalan (Busquet and Sort, 1999).

Over the years the Catalan broadcasting sector has gained enormously in skills and experience (European Parliament, 2002). TV3 broadcasts entirely in Catalan and relies heavily on regional production. By 1998 CCRTV, created in 1983 and operating almost entirely in Catalan, had a budget of ∈216 m. A further income of ∈84 m is generated by advertising revenue. The broadcasting channel, Televisio de Cataluña (TVC) was initiated in 1984, and has 29.1 per cent of the audience and a staff of 1500 employees. There is a limited amount of Catalan language broadcasting on the private channels (European Parliament, 2002).

In 1989 the Ens Public de Radiotelevisio Valenciana (EPRTV), operating on Canal 9, was created in Valencia, offering a bilingual service that is also available in the Balearic Islands and southern Catalonia. This was partly a reaction to the encroachment of TV3 into Valencian territory. A second channel – Noticias 9, which broadcasts mainly in Catalan was also created (Xambo, 1996). The relevance of Catalan in the regional labour market was enhanced.

Once convergence is established and web-based broadcasting becomes a reality, local television achieves salience. Local television services started in Catalonia in 1980, and there are 116 such stations in operation. The most important of these is Barcelona Televisio (BTV) which belongs to the Town Council of Barcelona and broadcasts entirely in Catalan. There is a similar initiative in Palma de Majorca, covering the entire island of Majorca.

In 1985 CRTVG the regional broadcasting authority for Galicia was established. Two commercial agencies with Galician language advertising were established, one for radio – Radio Gallega – and TVG which broadcast entirely through the medium of Galician. The programming objectives were expressed as follows:

increasing TVG's own programme production and in so doing, aiming at programming based on Galician themes and authors, of universal value, to assist the dissemination of such productions in other markets and to bring a return on investment in the field as well as projecting the image of Galicia abroad.

(Ledo Andion, 1999:5)

A broader context was expressed by Barreiro Rivas, vice-president of the Xunta:

TVG was not born to establish an industrial fabric around the audio-visual sector, but merely to replicate the type of public broadcasting service common to any television under the control of state governments in Europe ever since the onset of this medium. The idea was to find a way of providing the territory with sociopolitical and cultural structuration, with special attention to the normalisation and widespread use of the Galician language and its culture.

(ibid:5)

The development of a relevant labour force and the impact upon the prestige of the language was an inevitable consequence of this political objective.

The teletext service is the most extensive such service in Spain, again generating considerable employment. An educational component foresees multimedia learning platforms. In 1989 TYVE in Galicia undertook the professional training of public-sector employees to increase their oral and literary competence in Galician, leading to public-sector institutions increasing their internal use of the language, and greater numbers accessing the regional labour market through the medium of Galician. In 1995 TVG began broadcasting for Galicia TV, a satellite channel with global coverage which accommodates the more than two million extraterritorial Galician-speaking population. It broadcasts 24 hours a day, including 17 hours of principally Galician language original programming, primarily using TBG's programming grid. In 1995 the sector was expanded and integrated with other aspects of language mobilisation. Almost €6 m was provided for promoting Galician film, a sum expected to generate a return of €30 m. The Galician language is prominent in all the associated developments.

TVG broadcast over 8000 hours using its own production facilities in 1997, with a further 2970 hours of purchased production. It currently holds second place in Spain to the Basque regional broadcaster ETB. Almost €10 m are spent on external production, much of it on dubbing. It has the goal of making half of the advertising available in Galician. In 1996, 64 hours of advertising was broadcast in the language and 221 hours in Spanish (ibid.).

A model of a single commissioning agency supplied by multiple independent producers was created in most of these regions. Within Galicia there are about 100 small production companies. CRTVG's Annual Report for 1999 states:

Twelve billion pesetas [∈72.12 m] or 80 per cent of the budget, reverts to the Galician economy and 4 billion pesetas [∈24 m] directly into private initiatives in the Galician audio-visual sector . . . Next year will be important for the audio-visual sector in Galicia since strong capital investment is to be made and close to 500 jobs created in the overall sector. Industrially and culturally speaking, audio-visuals and telecommunications are the strategic aim of the European Union in facing the challenges of the next century.

This is an issue discussed in the concluding chapter.

Telefis na Gaeltachta, established in 1996, has spawned a number of small production companies, most of which are located close to the TnaG broadcasting station in the Connemara Gaeltacht. Ireland has invested much of its Objective 1 development money in the new media and multimedia activities. The clustering of media and multimedia firms include many which use only Irish.

Not all of the operations involve the minority language, but concerted efforts are made to ensure that the various operators can use the relevant languages. In Wales the integrative aspects of minority language television production involve encouraging new companies to undertake those functions previously drawn in from outside the region and the language group. The minority language becomes the language for the relations of production and associated skills are developed by reference to the minority language. The language is used for work rather than being used in work.

4 Conclusion

Most European minority languages have little or no relevance for the regional labour market: all of the minority language groups in Greece; Albanian, Griko, Sardo and Croat in Italy; Mirandese in Portugal and Portuguese in Spain; Cornish in the UK; Czech and Slovak in Austria; Tornedalen in Sweden *inter alia*. Family enterprises and locally owned enterprises may operate the relations of production and the link between production and the local market in the regional language. However, for language to have value for social mobility requires a far broader economic context. Some languages may have enhanced relevance within the broader Single Labour Market of the EU. The trans-regional relevance of extraterritorial state languages gives a degree of prestige to other languages, most notably German, Danish, and even Basque and Catalan.

The extraterritorial languages in Austria, Swedish in Finland and, to an extent, Sami, Luxembourgish, Catalan, Basque, Galician and Welsh have benefited from legislation involving the use of the minority language in the public sector. Some have also benefited from media-sector activities. This has given them confidence about the group's ability to produce and reproduce the respective languages. The enhanced prestige of the language motivates parents to give their children every advantage in entering the labour market, whether or not they speak the language themselves. Parents seeking social mobility for their children within local and regional labour markets are most likely to take advantage of such opportunities (Williams, Roberts and Isaac, 1978). The educational facilities to access those occupations that bear relevance to the prestige of the minority language must be universally available if accusations about labour-market segmentation and exclusivity are to be avoided. Language does segment the labour market, and it is the responsibility of educational policy to ensure that there is an equality of opportunity for everyone.

How the discourse of democracy characterises 'development' as a politically driven escape from the traditional authority of a pre-modern form does no favours for minority language groups. It has led to many of the European states resisting the entry of minority languages into economic activity, and can result in a commitment to a questionable rationalisation displacing the freedom of the individual. The European Union is replacing the state as the source of economic regulation. It promotes geographical mobility, but is reluctant to interfere in the internal labour markets of the individual states. It restructures rural and peripheral economies through the structural funds and, indirectly, it influences the relationship between minority languages and regional labour markets. Minority languages may be introduced into economic activity, but they may not be used in the relations of production. The language object may extend its meaning, but this will not necessarily have an impact upon the constitution of the speaking subject within the associated practices. It is this concern with language as social practice that is the focus of the next chapter.

6
Institutionalisation of Language Use

1 Introduction

The membership of any language group, viewed as a social group, revolves around the use of the language as social practice within the group's activities. Unlike state language groups, this is not possible across the range of contexts within the autochthonous territory. The relationship between state, minority and international languages rarely permits the institutionalisation of more than one language across all contexts, largely because not everyone is bi- or multilingual. Language use is segmented as a feature of the normative context. The struggle over language is a struggle to institutionalise language use across as many possible contexts as possible, making use normative for the speakers of that language.

Institutionalisation is not a rational process, but the process wherein discourse is stabilised. Language use as social practice involves the subject positions that open up for the individual to occupy or to reject in relation to particular objects, and the associated place which allows certain things to be said and prevents others from being said. Language is the central object, and the subject is the individual as the minority language speaker, both are constructed in different ways within different discursive formations. Each use context constitutes a discursive formation, and the totality represents the order of discourse (Foucault, 1972:45). This totality as it pertains to the language group determines the propensity of language groups to be reproduced. The interpolation of the individual is the outcome of the relationship between competing discourses and prior discourses which may well construct subjects and objects in different ways (Williams, 1999a). There is a direct relationship between legitimation and institutionalisation. The state is evident in legitimation, having a direct impact on LP and standardisation, the main thrust of Bourdieu's (1982) work[1] on the relationship between legitimation and the relationship between social groups (O'Riagain, 1997).

The 18 language-use surveys of the Euromosaic study,[2] and other similar studies are used to develop configurational statements for each case. The full

150

analytic capacity of the surveys is left aside for the purpose of this chapter. For these groups, the data is matched against other evidence.

2 Family

Most cases demonstrate a high incidence of geographical and language group endogamy, and a high degree of family use. This is true of Welsh, Catalan in Aragon and Majorca, Galician in Galicia, Slovene and German in Italy, Turkish in Greece, Friulian, Ladin and Franco-Provencal. The respondents tend to have married partners from the same region, the incidence of language group endogamy is in excess of 75 per cent, and minority language use within the family over the past three generations high and consistent.

In contrast, two generations ago Breton was the exclusive language of the family, whereas now the use of Breton within the family is rare. Yet geographical endogamy and language group endogamy are high. Three-quarters of the respondents and their partners claimed they spoke only Breton or a mixture of French and Breton with their parents. Yet only 11 per cent spoke Breton solely with their own children, and 14 per cent used both languages. Among the children, fewer than 2 per cent used only Breton to each other, while another 9 per cent claimed to use both languages. Many can speak Breton, but choose not to do so.

Almost 80 per cent of the grandparental generation, and 67 per cent of the parental generation were fluent in Occitan. Local endogamy was high, but only 39 per cent of the partners spoke the language. As many as 55 per cent claimed their parents use mainly Occitan and 41 per cent mainly French to each other. A quarter of the respondents used only Occitan with their partner, while 7 per cent used both languages together. Fewer than 5 per cent used only Occitan at meal times and 17 per cent used both French and Occitan. Only 1 per cent claimed to use Occitan exclusively with their children and 17 per cent used both languages. None of the children used Occitan exclusively, and only 1 per cent used both languages together.

There is a high degree of local endogamy among the Corsican respondents, but 17 per cent were born on the French mainland and 24 per cent had spent time living outside of Corsica. Almost 40 per cent of the partners learnt Corsican as their first language, and a further 30 per cent claimed to have learnt both Corsican and French as their first language. As many as 86 per cent of the respondents claimed that their partners were fluent in Corsican. Among the grandparents of the respondents, over 30 per cent spoke little or no French and only two-thirds claimed fluency in French for their parents, compared with over 80 per cent who were fluent in Corsican. Over 71 per cent were raised in homes where Corsican was the family language.

Only 15 per cent of the respondents claim to use only Corsican with their partners, and a further 57 per cent use both Corsican and French. Similarly, just 6 per cent claim to use only Corsican with their children, while 63 per cent use both languages with them. This contrasts with their own childhood when 42 per cent spoke only Corsican with their parents and 30 per cent used both languages, while 37 per cent used Corsican only and 35 per cent used both languages with their siblings. Only 12 per cent claimed that their partners used solely Corsican with their children and a further 65 per cent of the partners used both languages with them. Only 2 per cent of the children used Corsican to each other, while 38 per cent used both French and Corsican.

Despite a high degree of regional endogamy only about a third of the partners had Danish as their first language in Germany. The linguistic proximity between Danish and German helps mutual comprehension. Only about a third claimed that Danish was the first language learnt and only about half of them used any Danish in the home. In the present generation, 27 per cent claim to use Danish with their children and a further 32 per cent use both languages with them. Fewer than half of the children use Danish with their siblings. As with the Welsh, Catalan and Basque language groups, agencies other than the family are also responsible for production and reproduction.

The Sorbian language group has a high degree of patrilocal endogamy. Among the grandparental generation those marrying into the group were quickly assimilated. Now however, the younger generation is rapidly assimilating into the German language group, using little Sorbian within the family.

Language group endogamy among the Sardinian language group is in excess of 80 per cent, but with only 14 per cent of the children using Sardinian to each other. Only 15 per cent of the respondents use solely Sardinian at home, while 55 per cent use some Sardinian in the home. Also, 9 per cent use only Sardinian with the children, and 31 per cent use both Sardinian and Italian. The language group has a large demographic base, but is quickly being eroded.

Local and language group endogamy are high but declining among the Gaelic speakers, with 75 per cent of the respondent's partners speaking Gaelic. However, 36 per cent claim not to use any Gaelic with their partner. Among the respondent's grandparents, 86 per cent spoke Gaelic and 84 per cent used Gaelic almost all of the time in the home. By the parental generation these figures are 90 per cent and 76 per cent. Currently 38 per cent of the partners use Gaelic almost exclusively with their children, 31 per cent only English and the remainder a mix of the two languages. Among the children, 17 per cent use Gaelic exclusively together, 52 per cent use only English together and the remainder a mix of the two languages. Within the home, Gaelic is the language at mealtime for 38 per cent of the families and English for 28 per cent of the families.

Local endogamy among the Irish speakers in Northern Ireland is high, but 12 per cent of the partners are from the Irish Republic. Only 17 per cent learnt Irish and English simultaneously as their first language. About 20 per cent of the respondents use both Irish and English in the family, but even here it is mainly English that is used. Fewer than 5 per cent of the families use Irish exclusively. Among the children, 10 per cent use primarily Irish together and a further 12 per cent use both languages.

The data on the use of the broadcasting media is presented in Table 6.1. Media provision for Occitan and Breton[3] was rare, but the use of French language media was also rare. Sardinian speakers also had limited access. Only 80 per cent of the Sorbian speakers had access to broadcasting in their language, and fewer than a third had access to the limited private provision in Friulian. A third of the Franco-Provencal speakers also claimed that they could not receive the limited service provided.

The border communities have access to service from neighbouring territories. The Catalans in Aragon use the Catalan language services more than they do the Spanish language services, whereas the reverse is true of the Majorcans. The Irish in Northern Ireland receive a service from the Republic. The Turkish language group in Greece receive both satellite television and radio broadcasts from Turkey. Their use of Greek language services is minimal.

The use of Corsican radio is considerable, but less than the use of French services. Gaelic speakers use the limited Gaelic language services more than the English. The Ladins use of the trilingual provision is spread across all three languages. The Danish speakers in Germany do not generally use the available broadcasting services, but those who do, use both language services.

The Welsh and Galician language groups have good media provision. In Italy only 71 per cent of the language group claimed access to the available television service in Slovene, whereas 59 per cent of those who did have access, used the service. The use of radio in either language was low. Over 70 per cent of the German language group in Italy do not use the Italian language radio service, and 53 per cent do not use the Italian language television service.

Educational exclusion limits the level of literacy in the respective languages. Occitan, Breton, Sardinian, Friulian, Catalan in Aragon, Galician and Franco-Provencal groups have very low incidences of written and reading competence (Table 6.2). Other groups – Danish in Germany, Welsh, Ladin, German and Slovene in Italy – have high levels of competence on both measures.

There is a correlation between the above figures and those for the consumption of print media (Table 6.3). Large language groups such as Occitan, Breton or Sardinian, have low readership figures, even though competence levels sustain a viable market. Only the Danish in Germany, and Germans

Table 6.1 Daily household use of minority language broadcasting media

	Radio				Television			
	0	0–1 hr	1–2 hrs	>2 hrs	0	0–1 hrs	1–2 hrs	>2 hrs
Occitan	0	0	0	0	0	0	0	0
Breton	<56%	>	39%	5%	<63%	>	34%	3%
Sardinian	84%	14%	2%	0%	73%	24%	2%	1%
Irish in N. Ireland	64%	34%	0%	2%	58%	42%	0%	0%
Gaelic	32%	36%	14%	18%	28%	51%	6%	15%
Danish in Germany	65%	25%	8%	2%	45%	49%	5%	0%
Corsican	45%	30%	23%	2%	24%	50%	20%	6%
Friulian	79%	8%	8%	5%	85%	7%	7%	1%
Sorbian	47%	43%	8%	2%	95%	5%	0%	0%
Catalan in Aragon	24%	35%	26%	3%	11%	28%	56%	5%
Catalan in Majorca	<90%	>	4%	6%	<69%	>	18%	13%
Welsh	40%	30%	11%	19%	10%	52%	26%	12%
Ladin	37%	36%	19%	8%	38%	29%	25%	8%
Galician	47%	30%	12%	11%	22%	51%	19%	8%
Franco-Provencal	78%	16%	6%	0%	56%	36%	8%	0%
German in Italy	54%	20%	17%	8%	45%	30%	17%	8%
Slovene in Italy	62%	25%	7%	6%	58%	32%	7%	3%
Turkish in Greece	16%	13%	21%	50%	16%	5%	18%	61%

Note There is no significance in the order of the language groups in this and subsequent tables.

Table 6.2 Reading and writing competence of respondents by language group

	Reading				Writing			
	Very good	Quite good	Little	None	Very good	Quite good	Little	None
Occitan	14%	28%	30%	29%	8%	11%	15%	66%
Breton	17%	22%	37%	24%	5%	12%	23%	59%
Sardinian	18%	24%	41%	17%	6%	8%	30%	56%
Irish in N. Ireland	24%	24%	46%	6%	22%	21%	46%	11%
Gaelic	43%	33%	22%	2%	32%	34%	25%	9%
Danish in Germany	74%	12%	10%	4%	67%	14%	13%	6%
Corsican	20%	34%	25%	21%	10%	19%	28%	43%
Friulian	24%	43%	26%	8%	9%	12%	38%	42%
Sorbian	58%	25%	9%	8%	42%	34%	15%	9%
Catalan in Aragon	13%	14%	26%	47%	8%	7%	11%	74%
Catalan in Majorca	60%	27%	12%	1%	23%	32%	33%	12%
Welsh	77%	15%	5%	3%	71%	17%	8%	4%
Ladin	74%	21%	4%	1%	59%	20%	15%	6%
Galician	16%	39%	36%	9%	11%	16%	38%	35%
Franco-Provencal	18%	32%	37%	14%	9%	7%	26%	58%
German in Italy	80%	15%	2%	3%	70%	21%	3%	6%
Slovene in Italy	86%	6%	6%	2%	79%	10%	5%	6%
Turkish in Greece	17%	78%	1%	4%	5%	14%	76%	5%

Table 6.3 Use of print media by language group

	Book reading				Journal reading			
	Often	Sometimes	Rarely	Never	Often	Sometimes	Rarely	Never
Occitan	N.a.	N.a.	N.a.	N.a.	N.a.	N.a.	N.a.	N.a.
Breton	4%	9%	12%	75%	6%	7%	7%	80%
Sardinian	2%	2%	22%	74%	1%	1%	12%	86%
Irish in N. Ireland	19%	20%	22%	39%	20%	22%	20%	38%
Gaelic	13%	25%	22%	40%	10%	17%	27%	46%
Danish in Germany	54%	20%	7%	19%	66%	13%	8%	13%
Corsican	7%	14%	17%	62%	9%	18%	17%	56%
Friulian	0%	7%	33%	60%	2%	6%	25%	67%
Sorbian	21%	29%	27%	23%	46%	20%	17%	18%
Catalan in Aragon	1%	4%	8%	87%	1%	3%	17%	79%
Catalan in Majorca	14%	15%	36%	33%	11%	18%	37%	32%
Welsh	17%	28%	25%	30%	32%	23%	13%	32%
Ladin	11%	17%	32%	40%	N.a.	N.a.	N.a.	N.a.
Galician	6%	13%	28%	53%	7%	6%	17%	70%
Franco-Provencal	3%	8%	26%	63%	6%	12%	29%	53%
German in Italy	70%	15%	9%	6%	49%	25%	16%	10%
Slovene in Italy	26%	16%	40%	17%	68%	11%	13%	9%
Turkish in Greece	11%	12%	31%	46%	15%	36%	28%	21%

and Slovenes in Italy have high figures for book readership. Such state language groups have their own daily newspapers. The Slovenes in Italy read newspapers and journals more than they do books.

Among the Occitan, Breton, Sardinian, Corsican, Friulian, Catalan in Aragon, Galician and Franco-Provencal, exposure to print media in their own language is very limited. Yet only the Catalan in Aragon have universally limited reading practices. Among the others newspapers and journal readership is higher than book readership, and reading in the state language is high. There are four exceptions. The Slovene and German groups in Italy, the Turkish group in Greece, and the Danish group in Germany read more in these languages than in the state languages. Among the Turkish speakers, three-quarters never read any Greek books, and almost half never read Greek language journals nor newspapers. The Franco-Provencal read mainly in Italian, but also read more French materials than literature written in Franco-Provencal. Among the Catalan in Majorca about half of the respondents never read books, but as many as 80 per cent read Spanish language newspapers and magazines regularly. The same pattern exists among the Friulians.

3 Community

The perceived change in language use in the community between childhood and present adulthood was high where there has also been a pronounced change in the incidence of the minority language use in the family. The figures in Table 6.4 pertain to the percentage of respondents who claimed that the relevant minority language was/is heard 'often' in the respective contexts.

Turkish speakers conceive the community as operating almost exclusively through the medium of Turkish, and has done so for some time. Whereas the extent of perceived use is lower among the Slovenes and Germans in Italy, the degree of change over time is not perceived as significant. The extent of community use is even lower among the Danes in Germany, but again there is no perceived change over time.

Political change in Spain has recontextualised language use. The use of Galician and Catalan in the Church has increased in Galicia and Majorca, but not in Aragon. This indicates the role played by the Church in the language movement. In Italy, the use of Ladin in the religious institutions has also increased. More detailed figures for participation in religious activities among the respondents is given in Table 6.5.

Use among the Occitan groups was restricted to informal interaction, but this is claimed to have all but disappeared. A perceived destabilisation of language use across all activities is evident among the Gaelic and Sardinian language groups, and to a lesser extent among the Corsican, Welsh, Franco-Provencal and Friulian language groups. The Irish in Northern Ireland report an increase in perceived language use from a low base.

Table 6.4 Perceived change in language use

	Past use				Present use			
	Street	Shop	Church	Societies	Street	Shop	Church	Societies
Occitan	73%	37%	18%	15%	26%	11%	5%	10%
Breton	96%	81%	73%	50%	67%	23%	14%	31%
Sardinian	86%	80%	43%	26%	60%	38%	10%	12%
Irish in N. Ireland	3%	2%	14%	14%	7%	2%	11%	21%
Gaelic	85%	81%	84%	63%	42%	35%	45%	25%
Danish in Germany	50%	45%	56%	60%	52%	47%	53%	57%
Corsican	93%	87%	85%	68%	78%	73%	51%	37%
Friulian	88%	84%	47%	57%	66%	58%	35%	36%
Sorbian	56%	44%	60%	57%	29%	21%	46%	39%
Catalan in Aragon	90%	91%	7%	55%	98%	98%	4%	66%
Catalan in Majorca	77%	76%	51%	59%	79%	77%	78%	65%
Welsh	78%	76%	86%	77%	70%	55%	80%	65%
Ladin	93%	93%	34%	76%	94%	93%	63%	82%
Galician	77%	53%	8%	50%	81%	72%	26%	54%
Franco-Provencal	90%	88%	59%	71%	70%	63%	42%	52%
German in Italy	82%	74%	79%	83%	73%	64%	74%	76%
Slovene in Italy	87%	73%	89%	86%	78%	66%	84%	82%
Turkish in Greece	97%	94%	99%	97%	96%	92%	98%	96%

Table 6.5 Participation in religious activity by language group

	Often	Sometimes	Rarely	Never	NA
Occitan	11%	25%	28%	36%	0%
Breton	22%	24%	31%	21%	1%
Sardinian	30%	27%	28%	15%	0%
Irish in N. Ireland	63%	15%	12%	10%	0%
Gaelic	63%	15%	12%	10%	0%
Danish in Germany	18%	16%	29%	31%	6%
Corsican	8%	21%	55%	16%	0%
Friulian	32%	28%	26%	13%	0%
Sorbian	45%	15%	16%	24%	0%
Catalan in Aragon	23%	16%	34%	22%	5%
Catalan in Majorca	22%	21%	40%	17%	0%
Welsh	32%	22%	21%	23%	0%
Ladin	82%	10%	4%	4%	0%
Galician	←	65%	→	33%	1%
Franco-Provencal	38%	31%	24%	7%	0%
German in Italy	43%	28%	18%	11%	0%
Slovenian in Italy	30%	18%	25%	22%	4%
Turkish in Greece	99%	1%	0%	0%	0%

The extent of minority language ability and use among neighbours and friends, in the local shops, sports and cultural activities was recorded (Table 6.6). The difference between ability and use is a measure of change in language use from a community activity to a social network activity. Occitan, Irish in Northern Ireland, Breton, Sardinian, Corsican, Friulian and Franco-Provencal all report a difference between the ability and use figures across all five contexts, that is, a destabilisation of the institutionalisation of language use. In other cases this is only proceeding in some contexts. The figures for shopping and for sports activities tend to be lower than those for friends and neighbours. This is true for most language groups. A low incidence of ability, and little difference between the incidence of ability and use, indicates that speakers seek out contexts of use, as among the Danish language group in Germany and the Sorbian language group. There are other cases where use is significantly higher than ability rates.

The use of minority languages in sporting activities is limited. Several language groups have their own sports associations and or specific activities – Gaelic sports in Ireland and the Danish sports federations in Germany. The Friulian, Franco-Provencal and Welsh indicate that the language is used in sport, but in competition with the state language. The Breton, Corsican, Sardinian, Gaelic and Occitan language groups do not have access to most sports in the minority language.

Hunting and fishing, often linked to the ecological movement, are important in southern Italy. Minority languages are widely used for these

Table 6.6 Extent of ability and use by context and language group

	Friends		Shops		Sport		Cult. Assns.		Neighbours	
	Ability	Use	Ability	Use	Ability	Use	Ability	Use	Ability	Use
Occitan	16%	7%	5%	1%	9%	2%	13%	7%	33%	10%
Breton	60%	29%	18%	7%	19%	14%	54%	24%	73%	42%
Sardinian	80%	30%	75%	22%	21%	21%	77%	15%	82%	36%
Irish in N. Ireland	25%	10%	25%	47%	9%	16%	20%	28%	34%	71%
Gaelic	41%	33%	28%	23%	18%	8%	35%	33%	66%	41%
Danish in Germany	48%	40%	35%	37%	24%	25%	24%	32%	36%	32%
Corsican	76%	50%	47%	24%	46%	22%	76%	50%	73%	43%
Friulian	84%	68%	79%	60%	72%	52%	48%	28%	88%	69%
Sorbian	45%	34%	18%	18%	15%	15%	48%	46%	40%	38%
Catalan in Aragon	88%	93%	93%	97%	71%	72%	72%	73%	73%	85%
Catalan in Majorca	86%	78%	85%	77%	78%	71%	85%	67%	82%	76%
Welsh	74%	69%	49%	48%	47%	42%	83%	75%	67%	67%
Ladin	95%	88%	94%	91%	94%	90%	95%	91%	99%	94%
Galician	82%	70%	87%	73%	73%	45%	78%	54%	88%	77%
Franco-Provencal	60%	49%	49%	39%	42%	34%	49%	29%	73%	57%
German in Italy	80%	74%	74%	68%	56%	66%	52%	58%	62%	63%
Slovene in Italy	66%	73%	70%	77%	57%	81%	59%	73%	77%	69%
Turkish in Greece	99%	94%	72%	32%	14%	39%	36%	26%	99%	93%

activities. Similar activities flow over into music and theatre. These constitute parallel activities where the minority language is used, rather than
mainstream activities that can function bilingually. Apart from these activities, the main contexts for language use in the community are the informal
activities associated with the bar, the café and the family.

Each respondent indicated whether or not they could use the minority
language with a range of 33 individuals and institutions which most
people use daily; and whether they did use the minority language where it
was possible (Table 6.7). The number of contexts within which the
majority of the respondents in any language group claim that they 'can and
do' use the minority language, 'can but don't' use that language and
'can't' use the language indicates the extent to which the structural aspects
of interaction incorporate the minority language, and the extent to which
the members of the language group adopt the opportunity to use the
minority language when it is possible.[4] A high 'Can't' figure indicates that
the issue is a structural issue rather than one that pertains to a negative
identity, whereas a high 'Can but don't' figure is indicative of a negative
identity.

For Catalan in Majorca, Galician, Ladin, and German and Slovene in
Italy contexts in which the minority language cannot be used are few. This
may be a measure of the linguistic proximity of the state and minority

Table 6.7 Language use with community *interlocuteurs*

	Can and do	Can but don't	Can't
Occitan	0 (9%)	0 (16%)	18 (75%)
Breton	2 (17.2%)	9 (42.1%)	14 (42.8%)
Sardinian	6 (24%)	3 (27%)	24 (49%)
Irish in N. Ireland	0 (5%)	0 (12%)	18 (83%)
Gaelic	2 (18%)	0 (13%)	29 (69%)
Danish in Germany	3 (19%)	0 (17%)	33 (64%)
Corsican	20 (49.8%)	1 (24.7%)	15 (33.3%)
Friulian	22 (49%)	0 (18%)	11 (33%)
Sorbian	3 (17%)	0 (7%)	33 (76%)
Catalan in Aragon	20 (56%)	2 (6%)	10 (38%)
Catalan in Majorca	32 (75%)	0 (15%)	0 (10%)
Welsh	13 (40%)	0 (9%)	20 (51%)
Ladin	28 (73%)	0 (6%)	5 (21%)
Galician	24 (77%)	0 (22%)	0 (1%)
Franco-Provencal	7 (31%)	0 (5%) ·	27 (64%)
German in Italy	29 (62%)	4 (22%)	0 (16%)
Slovene in Italy	14 (46%)	15 (30%)	2 (24%)
Turkish in Greece	4 (25%)	0 (1%)	27 (74%)

Note The percentages refer to the percentage of respondents, while the numbers refer to the
number of contexts.

Table 6.8   Incidence of language use by possibility of use and language group

Incidence	Can and do	Can but don't	Can't
High	Galician, Ladin, Catalan in Majorca	Breton, Irish in N. Ireland, Sardinian, Corsican, Galician, Slovene in Italy	Occitan, Gaelic, Sorbian, Turkish, Franco-Provencal, Danish in Germany, Irish in N. Ireland.
Medium	Corsican, Welsh, Friulian, Catalan in Aragon, Slovene in Italy, Franco-Provencal, Turkish in Greece, German in Italy	Friulian, Occitan, Gaelic, Danish in Germany, Catalan in Majorca	Breton, Sardinian, Corsican, Friulian, Welsh, Catalan in Aragon
Low	Occitan, Gaelic, Breton, Sardinian, Irish in N. Ireland, Sorbian, Danish in Germany	Franco-Provencal, Welsh, Sorbian, Turkish in Greece, Catalan in Aragon	Ladin, Galician, Catalan in Majorca, Slovene in Italy, German in Italy

languages. Where this prevails, and the opportunity is accepted, the use of the minority language is normative practice. Galicians and Sardinians do not tend to use their languages, even when the opportunity is available, indicating that their use is not normative practice. There are structural and identity problems to be confronted. Among the Sorbian, Occitan, Danish in Germany, Gaelic, Sardinian, Turkish in Greece, Irish in Northern Ireland and Franco-Provencal, there are numerous contexts where the language cannot be used. The language groups are organised by reference to the three parameters in the following matrix (Table 6.8).

Inability to use the minority language is indicative of the lack of structural integration of that language into areas of social activity. Where the respondents claim to be able to use the language and choose to do so indicates a desire and willingness to use the language in various contexts. This correspondence indicates those cases where policy can be effective – Franco-Provencal, Turkish in Greece, and Sorbian, and, to a lesser extent, Welsh and Catalan in Aragon. The Slovene language groups in Italy and the Galicians choose not to use their languages. Minority language practice may not be stabilised by reference to the state language, or the distance between legitimacy and institutionalisation may be considerable – practice is legitimised by the authorities, but language use is not only not institutionalised, but is hindered. The Galicians tend not to avail themselves of the opportunity to use Galician, but display a high incidence of the use of Galician across all contexts. This is explained by the relatively recent legitimisation of language use and the relatively slow process of institutionalisation. Other groups with a high incidence of use and a wide range of potential use contexts are Ladin and Catalan in Majorca.

The use of language in public-sector activities partly depends upon the extent of political decentralisation in that some functions, most notably taxation and the police, are centrally controlled and are less likely to involve recruitment of local or regional personnel. Among the Majorcans, the Galicians and the Catalan in Aragon, it is the institutions responsible for telephones, taxation and driving tests which afford the least opportunity to use a minority language which is widely used by the regional administration. Those groups which do not tend to use their languages within local administrative contexts are the Danish language group in Germany, the Slovene language group in Italy, the Turkish speakers in Greece, the Irish speakers in Northern Ireland and the Sorbian language group. For the Bretons, it is the one context within which they can use the regional language, even if only for oral interaction.

Large supermarkets often operate an impersonal service in the state language, whereas the smaller enterprises which they are replacing often use the minority language. For retail functions, such as the local travel agency, electrical goods and so on, members of the respective groups seek out outlets where they can use the minority language. Minority language groups operate through familiarity with other members of the language group, overcoming the official reticence to use the minority language in large institutions. Among religious groups, such as the Irish in Northern Ireland or the Turkish speakers in Greece, local knowledge involves the interactive nature of the contact rather than the written and other elements of language use.

Professionals tend to be the most socially and geographically mobile. Often it is with the professionals – doctors, dentists, opticians, lawyers – that it is least possible to use the regional language. However the Turkish language group in Greece, the Slovene and German groups in Italy, the Galicians, the Welsh and the Catalans in Majorca do have a professional class which derives from the language group and which operates within the region. Banking establishments also recognise the value of the regional language within a competitive sector.

For all language groups most minority language use is in informal interaction with friends and neighbours within the community, in the bar or the café, but it also involves the church or chapel or, sometimes, the local school. Not all of the interaction in such settings involves minority language use. The groups which have such exclusivity are rare or involve closely bounded groups such as the Irish speakers in Northern Ireland or the Turkish language group in Greece.

4 Education

Table 6.9 refers to the use of existing minority language education by the respondents. Five language groups have no educational provision in their

Table 6.9 Language of children's education

	Primary					Secondary				
	Min. Lang.	State Lang.	Both	No choice	No preference	Min. Lang.	State Lang.	Both	No choice	No preference
Occitan (N.a.)	0%	100%	0%			0%	100%	0%		
Breton (n = 176)	0%	100%	0%	51%	4%	0%	100%	0%	50%	1%
Sardinian (n = 128)	0%	100%	0%	81%	2%	0%	100%	0%	81%	3%
Irish in N. Ireland (n = 127)	4%	62%	34%	41%	9%	1%	38%	60%	45%	11%
Gaelic (n = 174)	8%	54%	38%	49%	3%	3%	44%	53%*	45%	4%
Danish in Germany (n = 152)	49%	26%	25%	–	–	47%	32%	21%	–	–
Corsican (n = 153)	16%	73%	11%	56%	12%	7%	71%	22%	51%	19%
Friulian (n = 173)	0%	100%	0%	–	–	0%	100%	0%	–	–
Sorbian (n = 180)	29%	24%	47%	6%	1%	14%	23%	63%	4%	2%

Catalan in Aragon (n = 159)	0%	98%	2%	–	–	0%	100%	0%	–	–
Catalan in Majorca (n = 184)	27%	52%	22%	41%	4%	15%	54%	31%	40%	7%
Welsh (n = 564)	64%	11%	25%	37%	3%	30%	13%	57%	33%	6%
Ladin (n = 141)	0%	19%	81%	85%	4%	0%	17%	83%	80%	7%
Galician (n = 172)	19%	52%	29%	–	–	15%	46%	39%	–	–
Franco Provencal (n = 123)	4%	88%	8%	–	–	4%	94%	2%	–	–
German in Italy (n = 105)	77%	10%	13%	–	–	75%	10%	15%	–	–
Slovene in Italy (n = 195)	63%	8%	29%	–	–	66%	7%	27%	–	–
Turkish in Greece (n = 257)	97%	2%	1%	–	–	6%	93%	2%	–	–

Note Only those respondents with children responded. The respective number of respondents is provided after the names of the language groups.

mother tongue – the Occitan and Breton groups in France, the Sardinian and Friulian groups in Italy, and the Catalan language group in Aragon. The Corsican language group in France and the Franco-Provencal speakers in Italy have a low level of use and provision. Children of the Irish group in Northern Ireland, Gaelic speakers in Scotland and the Sorbian, Ladin and Galician language groups receive a bilingual education. The 53 per cent of children receiving a 'bilingual' English/Gaelic secondary education actually involves little Gaelic. It is only the Welsh and the Catalan in Majorca language groups which receive more education in their languages than there is bilingual provision. In both cases there was no choice available, while there was a reduction of minority language provision and an increase in bilingual provision as the children moved from the primary to the secondary level.

There is also a tendency for provision, when it is available, to involve the arts rather than the science subjects (Table 6.10).

The Danish in Germany and German in Italy language groups have both arts and science subjects provided. There are schools which teach all subjects through the medium of the minority language within the different regions, but the experience of the pupils indicates that the pattern in Table 6.10 prevails.

Table 6.10 Language of educational provision by subject

	None	Arts only	Arts > Science	Arts and science
Occitan	X			
Breton	X			
Sardinian	X			
Irish in N. Ireland			X	
Gaelic			X	
Danish in Germany				X
Corsican		X		
Friulian	X			
Sorbian			X	
Catalan in Aragon	X			
Catalan in Majorca			X	
Welsh			X	
Ladin		X		
Galician			X	
Franco-Provencal		X		
German in Italy				X
Slovene in Italy	N.a.	N.a.	N.a.	N.a.
Turkish in Greece			X	

5 Work

Most of the respondents from all of the language groups were either self-employed, working for SMEs, or for larger public-sector institutions. Few worked for large private-sector enterprises (Table 6.11).

Language use at work depends upon the ability of work colleagues, and their willingness to reciprocate its use. Such use must be institutionalised across a workforce which has the competence to conform. The competence of colleagues among the Sardinian, Franco-Provencal and Gaelic language groups, for example, is high but use is much lower. The development of language policy may well be the prerogative of the company manager. This may well depend upon her place of origin (Table 6.12)

Among the Corsican and Sorbian language groups, more than a third of the company directors derive from outside of the region. Elsewhere, apart from the Occitan, Sardinian, Gaelic and Sorbian language groups, most company directors are from the region and also speak the minority language.

There is considerable difference between a legitimisation which does not prohibit using the minority language in work, a policy seeking to promote its use in work, and the integration of bilingualism into management and working relationships. A greater proportion of company directors than other colleagues speak Turkish and Franco-Provencal, because of the number of SMEs owned by members of the regional language groups and the small proportion of the respondents working for large enterprises not owned by members of the group. The proportion of minority language speakers among the company directors is lowest for those groups such as the Sardinians and Sorbians, where the external ownership of enterprises is highest.

The relationship between the minority language competence of the workforce and the use of that language in work, an indication of high instiutionalisation, is closest among the Welsh speakers, the Catalan speakers in Majorca, the Danish language group in Germany and the Galician speakers. The greatest difference between competence and use is found among the Corsican, Gaelic and Franco-Provencal language groups. The minority language is used more with colleagues who lack authority, suggesting that language and power are closely related. Among the Catalan in Majorca, the Turkish in Greece and the Welsh language group, the use of the language is greater than the estimated level of competence, suggesting either selective social relationships within work, or polarised contexts involving very high and very low use. There are also cases where the use with subordinates is less than with 'colleagues' and 'directors'.

Oral competence is more important for work than the literary context in all cases, but among the Welsh language group and the German language group in Italy the difference across the competencies is not significant (Table 6.14). The production of oral competence corresponds with literary competence produced in formal institutional contexts for such language groups.

Table 6.11 Size of enterprise and location of head office for which the respondents work

	Size of enterprise					Location of head office		
	2–4	5–24	25–50	51–250	250+	Local	Within region	Outside the region
Occitan Breton (n = 241)	38%	29%	11%	17%	5%	71%	20%	9%
Sardinian (n = 180)	36%	25%	18%	14%	7%	60%	10%	30%
Irish in N. Ireland (152)	23%	23%	32%	12%	10%	55%	32%	13%
Gaelic (n = 229)	34%	33%	17%	14%	2%	54%	32%	14%
Danish in Germany (n = 150)	15%	30%	19%	27%	9%	63%	19%	17%
Corsican (n = 194)	31%	39%	11%	10%	9%	55%	22%	23%
Friulian (n = 142)	32%	47%	8%	11%	2%	62%	21%	17%
Sorbian (n = 196)	18%	35%	29%	11%	7%	65%	19%	16%

Catalan in Aragon (n = 130)	56%	35%	2%	2%	5%	81%	8%	11%
Catalan in Majorca (n = 167)	33%	35%	12%	16%	4%	67%	21%	12%
Welsh (n = 570)	19%	28%	14%	15%	24%	75%	10%	15%
Ladin (n = 229)	34%	56%	7%	2%	1%	86%	4%	10%
Galician (n = 220)	23%	32%	14%	13%	18%	73%	13%	14%
Franco-Provencal (n = 169)	31%	41%	16%	8%	4%	53%	37%	10%
German in Italy (n = 128)	29%	52%	8%	7%	4%	85%	11%	4%
Slovene in Italy (n = 188)	32%	52%	8%	4%	3%	60%	26%	14%
Turkish in Greece (n = 245)	74%	15%	6%	0%	5%	64%	28%	8%

Note Only those in employment or retired from employment responded. This included self-employed. The numbers responding are given in Column 1. They apply to Tables 6.11–6.16.

Table 6.12 Director's place of origin and language ability

	Place of origin				Minority language ability		
	Local	Region	Country	Abroad	Fluent	Und/Bit	None
Occitan	82%	17%	1%	0%	33%	40%	27%
Breton	52%	31%	16%	1%	50%	20%	30%
Sardinian	44%	39%	14%	3%	43%	29%	28%
Irish in N. Ireland	77%	18%	2%	3%	49%	42%	9%
Gaelic	47%	35%	17%	1%	26%	4%	70%
Danish in Germany	62%→		36%	2%	66%	16%	18%
Corsican	57%	26%	17%	0%	61%	10%	29%
Friulian	40%→		58%	2%	72%	14%	14%
Sorbian	71%	12%	4%	13%	37%	21%	52%
Catalan in Aragon	78%	4%	15%	4%	68%	23%	9%
Catalan in Majorca	65%→		30%	5%	77%	16%	7%
Welsh					62%	16%	22%
Ladin	78%	14%	6%	2%	90%	1%	9%
Galician	71%	25%	0%	4%	63%	12%	25%
Franco-Provencal	64%	32%		4%	61%	9%	30%
German in Italy	56%	26%	16%	4%	95%	3%	2%
Slovene in Italy	72%	26%	2%	0%	70%	4%	26%
Turkish in Greece					75%	7%	18%

Table 6.13 Language ability and use of colleagues at work – percentage competence and use of minority language

	Ability				Use			
	Director	Colleague	Subordinate	Client	Director	Colleague	Subordinate	Client
Occitan	20%	23%	27%	34%	7%	11%	10%	12%
Breton	57%	47%	50%	53%		v6%	19%	20%
Sardinian	41%	60%	66%	86%	12%	19%	21%	16%
Irish in N. Ireland	30%	34%	11%	25%	29%	35%	11%	33%
Gaelic	76%	59%	66%	52%	24%	26%	19%	25%
Danish in Germany	60%	50%	51%	37%	56%	49%	34%	24%
Corsican	59%	43%	41%	26%	23%	32%	29%	25%
Friulian	76%	62%	65%	46%	37%	54%	47%	25%
Sorbian	29%	35%	37%	25%	29%	28%	21%	32%
Catalan in Aragon	72%	63%	?%	87%	N.a.	N.a.	N.a.	N.a.
Catalan in Majorca	82%	59%	58%	37%	76%	76%	69%	50%
Welsh	60%	62%	62%	41%	58%	65%	58%	37%
Ladin	91%	91%	85%	67%	85%	90%	83%	74%
Galician	61%	73%	66%	67%	61%	67%	57%	68%
Franco-Provencal	66%	45%	44%	39%	26%	23%	18%	11%
German in Italy	89%	72%	85%	62%	77%	66%	55%	43%
Slovene in Italy	81%	72%	51%	81%	57%	63%	44%	46%
Turkish in Greece	53%	37%	19%	85%	66%	80%	76%	39%

Among the German speakers in Italy and the Turkish speakers in Greece, competence in the four language dimensions is relevant in work, which is organised around the minority language as much as it is around the state language. Neither group of respondents claim that the entire workforce can speak the relevant language, nor that this language is the only language used in work. Other groups which have integrated the four competencies into work include Danish speakers in Germany, the Slovenes in Italy, and to a lesser extent, the Welsh, Galician, Ladin, Catalan in Majorca and Gaelic language groups.

Oral competence in work is most necessary among the Danish speakers in Germany, the Friulian, German and Slovene language groups in Italy, Catalan in Majorca and Turkish speakers in Greece (Table 6.14). Few of the Catalan group in Aragon claim any knowledge of Catalan is either essential or useful in work. The Irish speakers in Northern Ireland, the Sorbian language group, Sardinian speakers, Welsh speakers, and the Ladin and Franco-Provencal language groups claim a low use of their languages in work. The Welsh and Ladin speakers operate in a segmented labour market, a knowledge of the language being essential for some and irrelevant for others.

German speakers in Italy, the Welsh, the Sorbian, the Catalan in Majorca and the Slovene speakers in Italy work for employers that have positive language policies (Table 6.15). Recruitment is from among minority language speakers among the Danish language group in Germany, the German and Slovene language groups in Italy, the Welsh language group and, to a lesser extent, among the Sorbian speakers and the Catalan speakers in Majorca.

The minority language is widely used in the employer's administrative practices among the Danish in Germany, Catalan in Majorca, Welsh, Galician, German and Slovene in Italy and Turkish in Greece, the Turkish speakers in Greece and the German speakers in Italy. For the first four of these groups there is a distinction between the use of the minority language in administration and its complete absence, again indicative of a split labour market.

A consideration of the context of language use in work is provided in Table 6.16. Employers operate a language policy among the Welsh, Danish in Germany, German in Italy and Catalan in Majorca groups. Minority language use is high across all contexts among the Danish speakers in Germany, the Catalan speakers in Majorca and the German speakers in Italy. Elsewhere consistency is less across contexts and use is less for both personnel management and sales, but not for public relations. Public sensitivity has implications for the status and the prestige of the language.

Table 6.14 Percentage of respondents claiming relevance for different language competencies for work

	Understand			Speaking			Reading			Writing		
	Essential	Useful	Neither	Essential	Useful	Neither	Essential	Useful	Neither	Essential	Useful	Neither
Occitan												
Breton	23%	43%	32%	28%	41%	31%	9%	15%	76%	17%	7%	76%
Sardinian	25%	29%	46%	17%	32%	51%	3%	11%	86%	4%	6%	90%
Irish in N.Ireland	19%	20%	61%	21%	20%	59%	17%	17%	66%	18%	16%	66%
Gaelic	31%	38%	31%	28%	43%	29%	18%	25%	57%	23%	18%	59%
Danish in Germany	59%	23%	18%	58%	20%	21%	67%	16%	18%	66%	16%	18%
Corsican	23%	45%	22%	23%	45%	22%	10%	18%	72%	9%	16%	75%
Friulian	54%	28%	18%	50%	32%	18%	8%	11%	80%	8%	8%	84%
Sorbian	22%	18%	60%	26%	15%	59%	22%	15%	63%	26%	14%	60%
Catalan in Aragon	23%	66%	11%	8%	25%	67%	12%	9%	79%	2%	40%	58%
Catalan in Majorca	56%	30%	14%	49%	36%	15%	35%	32%	33%	30%	26%	44%
Welsh	33%	22%	45%	36%	20%	44%	32%	13%	55%	30%	13%	57%
Ladin	41%	16%	43%	40%	16%	44%	34%	17%	49%	35%	17%	48%
Galician	27%	59%	14%	28%	60%	12%	13%	54%	33%	14%	43%	43%
Franco-Provencal	21%	32%	47%	20%	33%	48%	3%	9%	88%	4%	7%	89%
German in Italy	91%	8%	1%	89%	11%	0%	86%	13%	1%	88%	10%	2%
Slovene in Italy	66%	23%	11%	65%	23%	12%	61%	19%	20%	61%	19%	20%
Turkish in Greece	69%	31%	0%	71%	29%	0%	71%	24%	5%	71%	21%	8%

Table 6.15 Employer's language policy, recruitment and language of administration

	Language policy		Relevance of language for recruitment			Language used in administration			
	Yes	No	Minority language	State lang.	Neither	Minority > State	Both	State > Minority	State only
Occitan	N.a.	N.a.	N.a.	N.a.	N.a.	1%	1%	8%	90%
Breton	16%	84%	92%	6%	2%	41%	15%	44%	N.a.
Sardinian	9%	91%	0%	2%	98%	1%	1%	3%	95%
Irish in N.Ireland	28%	72%	85%	5%	10%	10%	10%	5%	75%
Gaelic	10%	90%	17%	2%	81%	9%	15%	–	76%
Danish in Germany	50%	50%	53%	2%	45%	42%	12%	46%	0%
Corsican	12%	88%	8%	1%	91%	N.a.	N.a.	N.a.	N.a.
Friulian	18%	82%	4%	0%	96%	0%	1%	0%	99%
Sorbian	40%	60%	25%	1%	73%	23%	14%	63%	N.a.
Catalan in Aragon	2%	98%				63%	8%	29%	N.a.
Catalan in Majorca	37%	63%	23%	1%	76%	30%	11%	22%	39%
Welsh	63%	37%	43%	5%	52%	28%	26%	46%	N.a.
Ladin	42%	58%	50%	1%	49%	63%	6%	31%	N.a.
Galician	20%	80%	4%	1%	95%	43%	15%	40%	2%
Franco-Provencal	7%	93%	3%	8%	89%	5%	9%	7%	79%
German in Italy	68%	32%	52%	0%	48%	51%	30%	16%	3%
Slovene in Italy	41%	59%	59%	0%	41%	25%	13%	0%	61%
Turkish in Greece	N.a.	N.a.	N.a.	N.a.	N.a.	70%	0%	0%	30%

Table 6.16 Employer's use of minority languages at work

	As policy	Customer relations	Reception	Public relations	Personnel management	Sales	Company reps.
Occitan	N.a.	N.a.	N.a.	N.a.	N.a.	N.a.	N.a.
Breton	2%	2%	93%	0%	4%	7%	2%
Sardinian	1%	33%	11%	31%	16%	15%	N.a.
Irish in N.Ireland	9%	18%	11%	17%	12%	6%	3%
Gaelic	12%	12%	9%	6%	6%	3%	1%
Danish in Germany	63%	62%	65%	66%	N.a.	63%	64%
Corsican	4%	5%	25	6%	2%	6%	N.a.
Friulian	N.a.	5%	10%	16%	N.a.	6%	4%
Sorbian	40%	32%	25%	32%	20%	17%	17%
Catalan in Aragon	12%	4%	4%	3%	4%	4%	4%
Catalan in Majorca	40%	36%	35%	35%	31%	30%	22%
Welsh	54%	57%	58%	59%	36%	34%	33%
Ladin	38%	65%	52%	65%	26%	48%	50%
Galician	19%	86%	67%	87%	15%	85%	64%
Franco-Provencal	4%	5%	1%	4%	0%	0%	0%
German in Italy	39%	34%	35%	46%	N.a.	31%	31%
Slovene in Italy	12%	50%	43%	36%	7%	17%	10%
Turkish in Greece	N.a.	N.a.	N.a.	N.a.	N.a.	N.a.	N.a.

6 Attitudes and identity

The subject and the object have been constructed in a series of statements, and the respondent is asked to engage with this construction. This seeks to uncover how the respondents construct the object themselves by reference to a series of preconstructed conditions. Respondents were also asked to express their opinion concerning the interest of a variety of different bodies and individuals in the minority language (attitudinal scales in Table 6.19). Identity is not a psychological process involving expressions such as 'I feel Welsh therefore I am Welsh'. A high correlation between subjective identity towards the language or the language groups as objects, and language use is not expected. Language use as institutionalised practice involves more than a simplistic relationship between the self as subject and the language as an object.

The claim that identity associates with cultural rather than state dimensions, with ascription becoming dominant is explored in Table 6.17 (Tourraine, 1997). Most respondents across all language groups have a self-conception involving the language group territory. The exceptions involve 'Occitan', 'Danish' and Catalan' in Aragon. This territory can take a number of forms – as a 'nation', as a 'country' or merely as a 'region'. These are different objects carrying significant relationships to the unmarked objects that

Table 6.17 Spatio-political identities and language groups

	Language group territory	State	European
Occitan	48%	71%	47%
Breton	95%	80%	59%
Sardinian	94%	88%	69%
Irish in N.Ireland	87%	15%	32%
Gaelic	81%	9%	9%
Danish in Germany	56%	N.a.	50%
Corsican	88%	59%	28%
Friulian	75%	82%	64%
Sorbian	73%	32%	29%
Catalan in Aragon	19%	76%	60%
Catalan in Majorca	93%	73%	76%
Welsh	94%	40%	26%
Ladin	85%	31%	38%
Galician	97%	94%	67%
Franco-Provencal	89%	63%	53%
German in Italy	89%	46%	83%
Slovene in Italy*	70%	9%	16%
Turkish in Greece	80%	10%	10%

* Alternatives offered on a single question.

constitute the 'other' that confirms the object construction. The political conception is subject to variation. The meaning that is constructed out of the object within the question that is asked of each respondent is not necessarily the same. Language groups which relate to extraterritorial state languages may construct 'Danish', for example, as a legal identity or as a language group identity. The data does not allow us to resolve such differences.

For the Breton, Sardinian, Friulian, Galician language groups, and the Catalan speakers in Majorca, the subject position *vis à vis* language and state territory is not ambiguous. The language territory pertains to the state, that is, it is a region of the state. However, the language territory is perceived of as pertaining to, or potentially pertaining to, a different political status for the Turkish speakers in Greece, the Irish language group in Northern Ireland and the Gaelic speakers in Scotland. The Turkish and the Irish speakers, as extraterritorial groups, conceive of the territory as pertaining to the 'home' state. For the Gaelic speakers it involves secessionist nationalism in Scotland. The Corsican, Sorbian, Welsh and Ladin language groups, and the German speakers in Italy have a contested situation, with many respondents not identifying with the state and many who accommodate both identities. Some express a negative orientation towards the state and a positive European identity.

The data in Table 6.18 evaluates the estimated support given by a variety of institutions to the language, and, by implication, to the language group. The strongest support across all of the language groups emanates from the self, the family and the network of friends. State support is strongest among extraterritorial language groups that have treaties to support their activities. An exception is the Slovene group in Italy who have a low estimation of the state support they receive.

The Sorbian language group evaluation of the German state may derive from a new, devolved political system. Regional government scores higher than the central government, apart from the Turkish language group in Greece who benefit from state treaties rather than regional government. The difference in the evaluation of the respective government is small among the Irish in Northern Ireland, the Corsican speakers and the Catalan language group in Aragon.

Where there is a strong relationship between Church and State which does not recognise regional variation, as among the stateless language groups in France, Italy and Spain, estimation of religious institutional support is low. It is highest where the religious institution has been at the forefront of the language movement – Welsh, Catalan in Majorca, Ladin, German and Slovene in Italy, and Gaelic.

The degree of support from private business reflects the control which the language group has on the private sector within the region. It is low among the Gaelic speakers and the Sardinian language group. It is highest among

Table 6.18 Estimated degree of support for the minority language among agencies

	Central. govt.	Local/reg. govt.	Church	Private business	In-migrants	Friends	Family	Self
Occitan	1.77	4.61	2.00	3.43	2.48	3.91	5.08	5.98
Breton	1.95	4.10	6.82	3.96	4.10	2.74	5.32	5.46
Sardinian	1.63	4.56	2.74	2.51	5.04	5.54	5.82	6.25
Irish in N.Ireland	2.25	3.32	4.74	–	2.77	5.19	5.42	6.26
Gaelic	2.46	4.59	5.23	2.90	3.57	5.89	–	7.10
Danish in Germany	3.96	6.57	–	7.11	5.79	7.17	7.74	8.16
Corsican	2.32	3.96	3.09	3.55	3.34	6.95	7.23	7.40
Friulian	1.37	4.95	4.82	3.92	4.45	6.50	7.05	7.32
Sorbian	3.91	5.66	3.79	–	5.29	5.54	6.24	6.22
Catalan in Aragon	2.17	2.18	2.28	3.44	2.57	4.30	4.13	4.42
Catalan in Majorca	2.49	5.91	5.84	3.77	2.64	6.90	6.96	7.67
Welsh	2.12	5.49	6.97	–	3.95	7.26	7.66	8.08
Ladin	–	5.07	6.37	5.23	4.89	6.65	6.66	5.99
Galician	2.33	6.29	3.95	4.04	4.41	6.17	6.38	6.81
Franco-Provencal	3.39	6.40	3.63	4.91	3.24	6.71	7.44	7.74
German in Italy	3.88	6.28	6.99	6.94	4.47	7.11	7.67	7.46
Slovene in Italy	1.57	4.75	6.43	5.42	3.39	7.38	8.29	8.36
Turkish in Greece	3.78	2.61	4.70	5.63	–	8.13	8.22	7.61

Note Scale extends from a low of 1 to a high of 9.

Table 6.19 Attitude scales

	1	2	3	4	5	6	7	8	9	10	11
Occitan	2.20	2.37	1.86	4.27	1.87	3.10	2.57	3.28	4.09	2.73	3.10
Breton	3.63	4.07	1.87	2.89	3.40	1.74	3.64	2.52	2.47	2.78	2.45
Sardinian	3.12	2.47	3.80	1.89	1.91	1.68	4.18	2.83	1.86	2.45	1.91
Irish in N.Ireland	3.17	2.39	2.54	1.68	2.77	2.62	3.30	2.19	2.34	2.62	2.69
Gaelic	3.09	2.20	4.46	1.68	4.11	1.69	4.09	2.41	2.87	2.56	4.18
Danish in Germany	3.52	1.32	4.06	1.32	4.31	1.61	3.89	2.15	4.16	1.30	4.31
Corsican	3.57	3.33	4.56	1.69	3.37	2.04	4.49	2.26	2.11	2.71	4.21
Friulian	3.43	2.42	4.51	1.35	2.35	1.66	4.49	2.71	1.68	2.23	3.90
Sorbian	3.21	2.86	3.95	2.62	4.02	2.41	3.93	3.15	2.22	2.21	3.35
Catalan in Aragon	2.72	2.13	3.09	2.12	3.05	2.05	3.53	1.97	2.72	1.97	2.29
Catalan in Majorca	2.18	1.83	3.65	1.34	4.06	1.59	4.25	1.62	3.62	1.48	3.30
Welsh	2.89	2.17	3.68	1.88	3.95	1.73	4.36	2.01	3.45	2.33	3.44
Ladin	3.51	1.94	4.21	1.96	3.70	2.25	4.53	3.02	3.64	2.02	4.11
Galician	3.21	1.45	4.40	1.77	3.51	1.76	4.56	1.65	3.18	1.76	4.33
Franco-Provencal	3.85	1.52	4.21	2.96	3.36	3.14	4.05	3.01	2.04	2.56	4.15
German in Italy	3.54	1.70	4.30	1.80	2.67	1.59	4.59	1.97	4.00	1.73	4.58
Slovene in Italy	2.19	1.50	4.58	1.58	2.63	1.56	4.77	1.60	3.82	1.78	4.68
Turkish in	3.85	1.89	4.49	3.13	3.15	2.48	4.05	2.57	4.09	2.08	3.96

the Danish speakers in Germany and the German language group in Italy. Considerable economic restructuring and no associated language policy leads to low perceived support. In-migrants are regarded as offering little support for the languages.

The family, friends and the self constitute the language group and its relationship to collective consciousness. High and consistent scores indicate a commonality across the different subjects whereby they construct the language as an object in the same way, giving a collective structuring around the symbolic quality of the language object. Constructing the state as a negative object *vis à vis* the language group reinforces how language as an object becomes an ingredient of the construction of the 'us' within discourse that is opposed by the 'them' of the state and, in some case, other institutions. Some groups are perceived as having institutional support, either in the community or within the political and economic order; and aligned with this sense of group cohesiveness, this can be a very powerful force against how the state constructs itself.

There are groups where the respondents construct the social component in a positive way, side by side with a view of strong regional governance, religious institutions and a positive business world, even if the central state is not regarded as being very supportive. The greater the range of positive evaluation, the greater the sense of direction and unity. The language group is constructed as an outward looking social group rather than as a defence against the state. The most positive are the Slovene and German language groups in Italy, the Catalan speakers in Majorca, the Welsh and the Danish language group in Germany, followed by the Franco-Provencal speakers who lack institutional support; the Turkish language group which has the support of religious institutions, but little formal non-treaty political support; the Friulian speakers who lack purchase in the economic order; and the Corsican speakers who lack political and business support. At the other end of the spectrum are the Occitan and Sardinian language groups, Irish speakers in Northern Ireland and the Catalan speakers in Aragon. They perceive the strength of community support as low, and also lack institutional and political support.

The respondent takes in charge or does not take in charge the subject position which relates to objects and other subject places in specific ways within the statements. These subject places are what the orthodox perspective refers to as 'identity'. The statement 'Welsh is a dying language' contains an object 'Welsh' which is related to another object 'language'. In taking in charge the statement, the individual acknowledges the existence of this type of object relationship. The degree of strength of agreement obliges the individual who takes in charge the statement to occupy one or another subject position which bears a particular relationship to the objects under consideration. This approach is compatible with recent developments in psychology:

In recent years the study of human psychology has been undergoing profound changes . . . [involving] research programmes which pay attention to the languages of mankind, their diversity, and the very distinctive practices within which they play a major role. . . . accompanied by a sudden realisation that much of what passed as social psychology in the era of simplistic empiricism may be no more than a projection of local custom and practices, even local political philosophies.

(Harre, 1986:vii)

The following dimensions were used: instrumentality, status, and relationship to other objects. This symbolic representation links or relates objects, opening up the space for emotional commitment.

Most of the groups link territory and language, arguing for a close relationship between the linguistic distinctiveness and the 'character' of the region. Three groups disassociate themselves from such a direct relationship – the Occitan and Breton speakers, and the Irish speakers in Northern Ireland. There is a conception of regional identity which does not make the kind of link between subjects and objects which other groups are making. Non-speakers can assert a different link between identity and territory. Located on the edges of Greater Catalonia the two Catalan language groups pertain to long-standing political territories – Aragon and Majorca where there is a different link between territory and identity to that of Greater Catalonia and, in the case of the Majorcans, a claim that the language is not Catalan but Majorcan.

Results in Table 6.19 represent responses to the following statements, based on a five-point scale ranging from 1: strongly disagree to 5: strongly agree.

1   Other languages have more value than X.
2   X is a dying language.
3   Y would not be Y without X.
4   Lower class if X speaker.
5   Need X in public sector.
6   X is not modern.
7   Children should learn X in school.
8   X is not suitable for science and business.
9   X has value for social mobility.
10   X is old fashioned.
11   X is in admin.

The other statements can be drawn together into two components – instrumental and status (Figure 6.1).[5]

The Slovene and German in Italy, Catalan in Majorca, Welsh, Gaelic, Danish in Germany and Galician score highly on both dimensions, while

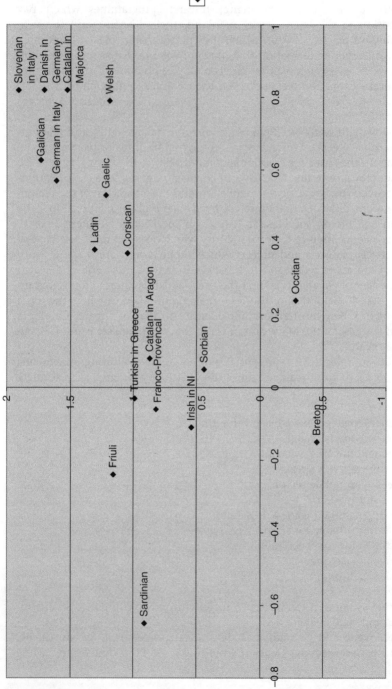

Figure 6.1 Instrumentality versus status scores by language group

Irish in Northern Ireland, Breton, Occitan, Franco-Provencal and Sorbian' score low on both. The Catalan in Aragon and Friulian have a high score on status and a low score on instrumentality, while the Ladin, Turkish and Corsicans have high instrumentality scores and low status scores.

Different scores on the two dimensions clarify the difference between status and prestige. The use of Turkish in work contributes to the high score on instrumentality. Despite it being a state language, the status dimension is low since, within the region, the group is allocated low status by outsiders. Religion and culture contribute to the closed nature of the group *vis à vis* the wider population. Language becomes a marker of a distinctiveness that spills over into general behaviour.

Control of the private sector in the regional economy provides high instrumentality for the Ladin. However, the language is viewed as a regional attribution, subservient to state languages, more of a dialect than a language. The language has been incorporated into education more as a measure to sustain the production and reproduction function than to facilitate entry into the labour market, accounting for the low status by reference to its broader potential.

The instrumentality score for Corsican is not extremely high, primarily because of its low prestige. The militancy by reference to extending the language into education and service provision in the public sector contributes to the relatively high score on instrumentality. There is also an awareness that this lack of purchase means that any comparison with other languages, most notably the state languages, reflect poorly on Corsican and its speakers.

The Catalan in Aragon draw upon the status of Catalan, a language with a large number of speakers and high prestige in greater Catalonia. The low instrumentality score reflects how the language is ignored by the Aragon government. The Friulian language has no place in education, and its entry into the labour market and work is more a consequence of public relations than of its value for work. Limited value in the world of work and not being absorbed into business and science is felt to have negative consequences for the ability of the group to reproduce the language in the future. The same awareness contributes to the relatively low score on the instrumentality scale. Yet there is an absence of stigmatisation within the contexts where it is widely used.

7 Other language groups[6]

Language-use surveys were undertaken in the Basque Autonomous Community in 1991 and 1996, extending to include Navarre and Iparalde in France (Basque Regional Government, 1989, 1996; Aixpurua, 1995). A total of 1800 Basque speakers and 1000 non-Basque speakers was found in the Autonomous Community; 800 Basque speakers and 500 non-Basque speakers in Navarre; and 917 Basque speakers in Iparalde. A proportional representative sample based on sampling points was used in the Autonomous Community and Navarre. In Iparalde random telephone interviews were used as the basis for discovering a universe stratified by age, gender and social class.

7.1 Basque in the autonomous community

Within the Autonomous Community, use in the home is more prominent than in the grandparental generation and there is consistency across the different roles (Table 6.20).

These figures are not dissimilar to the figures for the entire population across the three language groups, the exception involving the use made of Basque with the children which is considerably higher than the use of Basque with the partner or in the home, indicating an impetus to reproduce the language even within exogamous marriages.

Outside of the family the use of Basque declines (Table 6.21). The highest incidence of use of Basque is in the local markets which draw Basque speakers from rural areas. The regional government has reached agreement with the Church to extend the use of Basque and use with the priest is also high. Over a third of the friends of the respondents do not use any Basque with them. This is a smaller figure than the 70 per cent of the population which does not have any Basque language competence, suggesting that language does play a role in social networks.

Table 6.20 Intergenerational transmission – Basque Autonomous Community

	G. Parents	Mother	Father	Partner	Siblings	Children	At home
Basque	56%	59%	56%	53%	58%	66%	54%
Basque/ Spanish	9%	11%	6%	10%	11%	12%	15%
Spanish	35%	30%	38%	37%	31%	26%	31%

Source Basque Regional Government, 1996.

Table 6.21 Social context and language use – Basque Autonomous Community

	Friends	Shops	Market	Priest
Basque	45%	46%	82%	75%
Basque/Spanish	20%	17%	7%	8%
Spanish	35%	37%	11%	17%

Source Basque Regional Government, 1996.

Table 6.22 Language use at work – Basque Autonomous Community

	With colleagues	With superiors
Basque	38%	36%
Basque/Spanish	24%	20%
Spanish	38%	44%

Source Basque Regional Government, 1996.

Table 6.23 Language use with *locuteurs* in different institutions – Basque Autonomous Community

	Bank	Town Hall	Teachers	Health services
Basque	52%	54%	74%	24%
Basque/Spanish	12%	11%	6%	10%
Spanish	36%	35%	20%	66%

Source Basque Regional Government, 1996.

Basque is used considerably in work (Table 6.22).

Work interaction involves both bilingual and monolingual personnel, and status does not appear to play any role by reference to employment status and use within the enterprise. The use of Basque with key institutions within the community is similar (Table 6.23).

The incidence of use with the schoolteacher in Basque-medium schools is high, and the high figure for the use of the language in the Town Hall reflects official policy for the public services. The banks also have a language policy. The low incidence of use in the health sector is surprising. Language prestige within the Autonomous Community is high.

7.2 Basque in Navarre

The incidence of use by generation in Navarre is less than for the Autonomous Community, the incidence of use with the partner falling below 50 per cent. Use with children is higher than with the partner. The use of Basque in the home is higher than it is in the Autonomous Community (Table 6.24).

The incidence of use with friends is significantly higher than it is in the Autonomous Community. The use in the market is similar in both cases, but use with both the priest and in the shops is significantly less (Table 6.25).

The incidence of use of Basque only with both superiors and colleagues at work is higher for the Navarre language group than it is in the

Table 6.24 Intergenerational language use – Navarre

	G. Parents	Mother	Father	Partner	Siblings	Children	At home
Basque	65%	66%	66%	49%	59%	59%	57%
Basque+ Spanish	3%	2%	2%	7%	7%	7%	11%
Spanish	32%	32%	32%	44%	34%	34%	32%

Source Basque Regional Government, 1996.

Table 6.25 Language use with different *locuteurs* – Navarre

	Friends	Shops	Market	Priest
Basque	53%	43%	59%	62%
Basque/Spanish	22%	8%	7%	2%
Spanish	25%	49%	34%	36%

Source Basque Regional Government, 1996.

Table 6.26 Language use at work – Navarre

	With colleagues	With superiors
Basque	49%	40%
Basque/Spanish	10%	7%
Spanish	41%	53%

Source Basque Regional Government, 1996.

Autonomous Community. Those who use both languages at work are far fewer, suggesting there is a polarisation of language use at work (Table 6.26).

Finally, the incidence of use in the other institutions is presented in Table 6.27. The weaker official policy in Navarre means that use in the bank and the town hall is low. The use with teachers in the Basque language schools remains high. The figures for use in the health service are low. Language use is fairly extensive within the family, the community and at work. While it is not as widely used as it is in the Autonomous Community, it remains a self-conscious language group which uses the language in a variety of contexts.

Table 6.27   Language use with *locuteurs* in different institutions – Navarre

	Bank	Town Hall	Teachers	Health services
Basque	37%	37%	60%	26%
Basque/Spanish	5%	8%	12%	2%
Spanish	58%	55%	28%	72%

Source   Basque Regional Government, 1996.

Table 6.28   Intergenerational language use – Iparalde

	G. Parents	Mother	Father	Partner	Siblings	Children	At home
Basque	65%	54%	60%	37%	47%	33%	37%
Basque+ French	13%	18%	13%	16%	18%	15%	18%
French	22%	28%	27%	47%	35%	52%	45%

Source   Basque Regional Government, 1996.

Table 6.29   Language use with different *locuteurs* – Iparalde

	Friends	Shops	Market	Priest
Basque	31%	20%	52%	56%
Basque/Spanish	29%	18%	22%	17%
Spanish	40%	62%	26%	27%

Source   Basque Regional Government, 1996.

7.3 Basque in Iparalde

There are some significant differences when it comes to the Basque language group in France (Table 6.28).

In the absence of formal state support the incidence of use over two generations declines markedly, especially in the present generation, and the incidence of use with children is less than with the partner. Use among the grandparental generation was greater in France than in Spain, partly because of Franco's policy in Spain.

The use of Basque only with friends and in the shops is less than in the Spanish communities, but the overall use of Basque is not much less than the incidence in the other two language communities (Table 6.29). In the markets there is again a high incidence of use with the rural producers who are marketing their goods.

Table 6.30   Incidence of language use at work –
Iparalde

	With colleagues	With superiors
Basque	25%	13%
Basque/Spanish	15%	10%
Spanish	60%	77%

Source   Basque Regional Government, 1996.

Table 6.31   Incidence of language use with *locuteurs* in different institutions –
Iparalde

	Bank	Town Hall	Teachers	Health services
Basque	9%	21%	12%	6%
Basque/Spanish	16%	10%	7%	6%
Spanish	75%	69%	81%	88%

Source   Basque Regional Government, 1996.

Use with the priest is again fairly high, indicating support for Basque language politics in France.

Incidence of Basque use with work colleagues is considerably higher than it is with superiors, suggesting a cultural division of labour (Table 6.30). Use among colleagues is less than in Spain, because of a lower Basque language density in the region, and the lower prestige of the language and its relevance for employment. Many work in environments where the use of Basque is not tolerated.

The use of Basque in the public sector is not sanctioned by any level of government, but Basque speakers may be employed by local authorities, and the use of Basque is informal. Use with school teachers is not always evident, even with providers of the limited Basque language education (Table 6.31).

7.4 Irish in Ireland

Irish language-use surveys using the same format were undertaken in 1973, 1983 and 1993. The sampling frame in 1993 involved a random, two-stage, stratified sample of 976 respondents over the age of 18, based on a probability sample drawn from electoral registers.

Only a quarter of those raised in homes using Irish now use the same amount in their own homes. Irish language competence is the consequence of education rather than the family (O'Riagain, 1997). Only 40 per cent of the respondents used any Irish in the home, and only 12 per cent used it either 'often' or 'occasionally'. The incidence of use does not vary by social class.

Almost 90 per cent claimed never to use Irish at work, only 4 per cent used it at work on even a weekly basis, and the remaining 7 per cent less often than weekly. In all, 13 per cent of those in Social Class 2 used it on a weekly basis or more frequently, and 10 per cent of those in Social Class 1 used it less often than weekly. Also, 13 per cent of those working in the public sector used Irish at work each week, and 19 per cent less often, compared with figures of 2 per cent and 4 per cent for those working in the private sector. The use of Irish at work is concentrated among school teachers, police officers and civil servants. Fewer than 25 per cent attach any economic value to a knowledge of Irish and only 6 per cent felt it was of value in obtaining employment.

The survey was undertaken before the establishment of the Irish language television channel, but 40 per cent of the respondents claimed to watch Irish language television programmes, with 12 per cent doing so an a weekly basis. The higher the social class the greater the propensity to watch such programmes.

Two-thirds identified a relationship between being Irish and supporting the revival of the language, 60 per cent felt that Irish speakers were an essential ingredient of Ireland as a country, but only 46 per cent agreed that a knowledge of the language was essential to understand Irish culture, and 37 per cent regarded the existence of Irish as important in differentiating Ireland from England. This level of division prevailed by reference to the perceived future of Irish. As many as 38 per cent claimed they were indifferent to any attempts by the state to develop the reproduction of Irish. Yet 72 per cent felt that Irish speakers should have the right to use Irish with civil servants. Outside of the *Gaeltacht* those with the highest level of competence in Irish tend to be in the higher social classes, but reproduction is weakening as a consequence of the decline in the prestige of the language.

7.5 Frisian in the Netherlands

The earliest language-use survey of minority language groups in Europe was undertaken on Frisian during the 1960s (Pietersen, 1969). This was followed by other surveys early in the 1980s (Gorter et al., 1984), and in 1994 when 1368 interviews were undertaken, among which 601 were re-interviewees from the 1980 study (Gorter and Jonkma, 1995).

Within the family, 70 per cent used only Frisian at home and 7 per cent used both languages, compared with 73 per cent and 74 per cent who claimed to use Frisian exclusively with their father and mother respectively, while 1 per cent and 2 per cent claimed to use both languages with them. Regardless of age, 65 per cent claimed to use Frisian with their children, and a further 4 per cent used both languages with them. Only 28 per cent claimed to read Frisian language books, whereas 76 per cent claimed to listen to Frisian language radio programmes and 48 per cent claimed to watch Frisian language television programmes.

Over 40 per cent claimed that all of their friends speak Frisian, and 22 per cent claimed that more than half of their friends speak the language. Two-thirds claimed that they used Frisian with their child's schoolteacher, and more than half of the respondents (59 per cent) used it at the local police station. Also, 54 per cent claimed that they used Frisian only at work, and a further 20 per cent claimed that both Frisian and Dutch were used.

8 Conclusion

The stabilisation of discourse involves social practice as discourse, a patterned behaviour which is not necessarily conditioned by human rationality, but derives from how subjects and objects, including language and the speaker, are constituted in discourse, hence the predictable nature of human behaviour. The stability of the normative structures which condition social behaviour may or may not involve the use of minority languages.

The discussion of the institutional conditions for language use in earlier chapters is confirmed by the surveys of the use of language in these structures. We have identified the changing use of language in the family, the extent to which the minority language enters the educational sector, and the extent to which minority languages are used at work. It is now possible to summarise the preceding data and to develop a comparative analysis across the various minority language groups.

7
Data Evaluation

1 Introduction

The linear comparative scales constructed in the Euromosaic study provided clusters of cases which constitute different discursive formations with quite different meanings of 'language' and the related speakers as individual and collective subjects (see Appendix). How the state is constituted as the effects of discourse plays a dominant role in determining these meaning, relating to how universalism and particularism were different foundations of eighteenth-century state formation. The meaning of a particular language object is constructed differently by reference to 'education' for example, than it is by reference to 'family'. We again encounter the *demos/ethnos* dimension. Each context constructs the 'language' object by reference to the associated activity, and also constructs the subject position of 'speaker'. Institutionalisation is conditioned by this process of subject/object construction for each context.

Within these discursive formations the 'other' of language is not another language, but always the state. Where the language object is legitimised it becomes an integral part of the state, with the discursive positioning of the language and the state overlapping with the rational existence of the state. Even the denial of a language's existence must discursively construct the language, thereby confirming its existence. More common is to relegate the language to the realm of the emotional, the contrary of the rational state, a potential danger to the state that might require elimination. The discourse emanates from the place of the state – the minority language within education, for example, only becomes possible from this enunciative position. An independent subject only appears in the private sphere of the family and the community, and even this is denied by the discourse of democracy. Such issues clearly touch upon the issue of *ethnos*. The speaking subjects become the 'them' within the 'us' of the state, or a different form of 'us' can be involved. These issues have relevance for the relationship between diversity and democracy within the modern state, involving how the language is constructed as an object which can be accommodated within *'demos'*, or how it must be relegated from *'demos'* in order to insure the homogeneity of the inclusive 'us'. The social construction of some language groups as pariahs remains unchanged since the eighteenth century.

It is not necessary that the meaning of the language object is the same for all of the contexts designated re the potential for language use – education, family, community and the labour market – that is, it does not have the same meaning in all contexts. State discourses which only acknowledge a language in the private sphere construct the language as *'patois'*, as emotional, outside of the public space of reason. The minority language is constructed in opposition to the state and its official language. Language as an object always has a sense of ambiguity. Within the interdiscursive it is possible that two discursive formations will construct their categories and will choose the relevant lexeme from within a space of limited delimitation. It is here that the struggle over the meaning of 'language' as an object, and over the meaning of the associated subjects and the related notions such as 'nation' to which they may pertain is found. It involves a struggle over normativity.

The insitutionalisation of language as social practice is also the materiality of discourse, the pragmatic function wherein the individual takes in charge the subject position. Discursive materiality involves articulating the different contestations of discourse and meaning associated with each of the parameters of language use which exist within the analytic model. 'Explanation', based on the analytic model, involves a particular understanding of social and economic policy and how it relates to an official discourse that has implications across society. It is only one model, based upon the liberal, interventionist state. Neo-liberalism, with its emphasis upon free-market principles, would generate a different analytic model.

2 Analysis of scales

2.1 Introduction

Scores were allocated to each of the language groups on the seven main variables of the conceptual model that determine language group production and reproduction – family, community, education, prestige, culture, legitimation and institutionalisation. The identification of each individual case redresses the possibility of any miscategorisation of the variables. The analysis allows the cases to be ranked by reference to each variable and the total scores, and to isolate groups with similar scores (Table 7.1). A correlational analysis determines which variables relate to each other, in which way, while also establishing the strength of the relationship.

The range of scores for each variable extends from 0 to 4. However, a score of '4' is not indicative of a perfect situation and a score of '0' does not imply the complete absence of the relevant dimension.

2.2 Rank order and clusters[1]

Nine language groups have high scores across all of the variables – none scoring less than 3 on any of the individual scores. The top four scores can be distinguished from the other five, three of them are extraterritorial state languages in adjoining territories – German in New Belgium and Italy, and Swedish in Finland. The fourth case is that of Catalan in Cataluña, a proto-state which has increasing political relevance as the process of European incorporation on a regional basis proceeds. The size of this group is important in that it makes a number of relevant policies practical.

Three of the other five groups are located in Spanish autonomous communities. Luxembourgish is an official intra-territorial state language, but the case of Irish indicates that this in itself is insufficient guarantee of a high score. The final case is Welsh, a region which has recently achieved a degree of devolved governance. It is not simply the process of decentralisation that is of relevance, but how it encompasses the kind of language-related processes that pertain to the theoretically determined variables. All the language groups have either a state or a proto-state as their language point of reference. Legitimacy involves integrating the minority language into public-sector activities and into the education system at all levels.

Four further language groups from Spain – Catalan in Valencia, Basque in Navarre, Asturian and Occitan; five involving trans-frontier languages – Slovene in Italy and Austria, Turkish in Greece, Danish in Germany, and German in Denmark; two stateless languages – Ladin and Gaelic; and one state language – Irish constitute the second cluster. Most of them have a high level of state support, five of them on account of international treaties, four as a consequence of the action of the autonomous governments in Spain, and one through being a state language with status within the EU. The two non-Spanish stateless languages have different levels of voluntary support from central government. The groups have high legitimacy scores and often benefit from resources in the core area of the language.

Support, within the next cluster derives from civil society rather than the state, and instiutionalisation is fairly high. The low prestige scores indicate that the groups operate as community languages remote from the economic order. The two language groups in France and Catalan in Aragon lack any semblance of legitimacy. Three groups – Sorbian, Sami in Finland and Torne-dalen – have declining family support.

Groups in the fourth cluster have the same configuration as the preceding group. Language use focuses upon civil society and there is little evidence of either prestige or legitimacy. Among them are the numerically large Breton and Occitan language groups in France and Italy. This highlights the value of not treating minority by reference to numerism.

Finally, 12 language groups score less than a quarter of the total possible score. Four are located in Greece, a further four in Italy, and the remaining

Table 7.1 Cluster scores by variable

	Family	Culture	Community	Prestige	Institutionalisation	Legitimation	Education	Total
Cluster 1								
Swedish in Finland	4	4	4	4	4	4	4	28
Catalan	4	4	4	4	4	4	4	28
German in Belgium	4	4	4	4	4	4	3	27
German in Italy	4	4	4	4	4	4	3	27
Luxembourgish	4	3	4	3	4	4	3	25
Welsh	3	3	3	4	3	4	4	24
Basque AC	3	4	3	3	3	4	4	24
Catalan in Majorca	3	3	3	3	4	3	4	23
Galician	3	3	3	3	3	4	3	22
Average	3.6	3.6	3.6	3.6	3.7	3.9	3.6	25.3
Cluster 2								
Ladin	3	2	3	3	3	4	2	20
Slovene in Italy	3	2	3	3	3	3	3	20
Slovene in Austria	3	2	3	3	3	3	2	19
Turkish	4	2	3	2	3	2	3	19
Basque in Navarre	3	3	2	2	2	3	3	18
Danish in Germany	3	3	2	2	3	2	3	18
German in Denmark	2	3	2	3	2	3	3	18
Catalan in Valencia	2	3	2	2	3	3	2	17
Irish	2	3	2	2	2	3	3	17
Occitan in Spain	3	1	3	2	2	3	2	16
Asturian	2	2	2	2	3	3	2	16
Gaelic	2	3	2	2	2	3	2	16
Average	2.5	2.4	2.4	2.3	2.6	3.0	2.5	18.0
Cluster 3								
German in France	2	3	2	2	2	2	2	15
Friulian	3	2	2	3	3	1	1	15
Frisian	2	2	2	2	3	2	2	15
Croatian in Austria	2	1	2	1	3	3	2	14

Sorbian	1	2	1	2	2	3	3	14
Basque in France	2	2	2	2	2	1	2	13
Sami in Finland	1	2	2	2	2	2	2	13
Tornedalen	1	2	2	2	2	2	1	12
Catalan in France	2	2	2	1	2	1	1	12
Catalan in Aragon	3	2	2	1	2	1	1	12
Corsican	2	2	1	1	2	2	2	12
Average	1.9	2.0	1.8	1.7	2.3	1.7	1.8	13.3
Cluster 4								
Hungarian in Austria	1	1	1	2	2	2	2	11
Franco-Provencal	2	1	2	2	2	1	1	11
Irish in N. Ireland	1	1	1	2	1	2	2	11
Albanian in Italy	3	1	2	0	2	1	1	10
Sami in Sweden	1	1	1	1	1	2	2	10
Slovak in Austria	2	1	1	1	1	2	1	9
Catalan in Italy	2	2	1	0	1	0	1	8
Occitan in Italy	3	1	2	0	1	1	1	8
Mirandese	3	0	2	0	1	0	1	8
Breton	1	3	1	0	1	1	2	8
Average	1.9	1.3	1.4	0.8	1.4	1.2	1.4	9.4
Cluster 5								
North Frisian	1	0	1	0	1	0	2	5
Dutch in France	1	1	1	0	1	0	1	5
Slavo-Macedonian	2	1	2	0	0	0	0	5
Occitan in France	1	1	1	0	1	0	1	5
Sardinian	1	1	1	0	1	0	0	4
Bulgarian	2	0	1	0	0	0	0	3
East Frisian	1	0	0	0	0	1	1	3
Portuguese in Spain	1	1	0	0	0	0	1	3
Aroumanian	2	0	0	0	0	0	0	2
Grico	0	1	0	0	0	0	1	2
Albanian in Greece	2	0	0	0	0	0	0	2
Cornish	0	0	0	0	0	0	0	0
Average	1.2	0.5	0.6	0.0	0.3	0.1	0.4	3.3

five are divided across various states. Most of them, including Bulgarian or Albanian in Greece, French, Greek or Croatian in Italy, Portuguese in Spain and Dutch in France speak extraterritorial state languages. The two Frisian cases are detached from the core of Frisian speakers. Cornish is a language which was not spoken for centuries prior to its recent revival. Eight of the 13 cases are found in adjoining areas of the European periphery – in southern Italy and in Greece. The rapid decline in the use of Sardinian and the lack of a formal institutional context is indicative of a language group in crisis.

2.3 State and civil society

The relationships between the seven variables and a demography variable allows a consideration of the relationship between the institutional and social variables as they relate to the issue of power, and of the relevance of demographic factors. This redresses the limitations of geolinguistic work which prioritises its spatial preoccupation while demoting the social and political components of power.

The product-moment coefficients between each of the seven variables, and between these and the demographic variables (Table 7.2), establishes the extent to which there is, or there is not, a relationship between the scores on the various variables. There is a high correlation (0.801 to 0.888) between four variables – 'language prestige', 'institutionalisation', 'legitimation' and 'education' – which derive largely from the activities of the state. If the state involves a minority language in its activities, it will tend to do so on a broad basis.

The other three variables – 'family', 'community' and 'cultural reproduction' – are 'social' or 'civil society' variables, which allow a consideration of the social and cultural aspects of language group activity by reference to the relationship of a group to the state. The correlations between these three variables and the 'state' variables is lower, but still within the range 0.537 to 0.875. The correlation between culture and the state variables is high (0.756 to 0.810), indicating the influence of state policies on minority language culture, especially the media. The correlation is also high between community and the four 'state' variables (0.709 to 0.822), suggesting a relationship between the activities associated with state intervention and those operating within the community. It involves how state activities influence the status of the language group. Finally, the relationship between the family and the 'state' variables is much more variable (0.537 to 0.777). The highest correlation is between family language use and legitimacy (0.777), and the lowest between the family language use and education (0.537). The highest average score for all the cases from among the seven variables is for family language use (2.2), indicating that there is a greater range of scores across the other variables and that if the lower ranked cases were taken together, the negative relationship between the variables would be far clearer.

Table 7.2 Product-moment correlations for the seven variables

	Family	Culture	Community	Prestige	Institutionalisation	Legitimacy	Education
Family		0.553	0.845	0.631	0.711	0.603	0.537
Culture	0.553		0.727	0.799	0.774	0.756	0.810
Community	0.845	0.727		0.822	0.875	0.777	0.709
Prestige	0.631	0.799	0.822		0.874	0.888	0.807
Institutionalisation	0.711	0.774	0.875	0.874		0.841	0.801
Legitimacy	0.603	0.756	0.777	0.888	0.841		0.829
Education	0.537	0.810	0.709	0.807	0.801	0.829	
Correlation	0.769	0.869	0.916	0.938	0.942	0.921	0.883

It is possible to graph the relationship between the three 'civil society' variables taken together, and the four 'state' variables taken together (Figure 7.1). Cases above the diagonal display a degree of state support that is disproportionate to the ability of the civil society to produce and reproduce the language. Conversely, those language groups to the right of the line are obliged to rely on the efforts of civil society to a far greater extent.

Nine language groups score high (3.0–4.0) on both sets of variables: Swedish in Finland, German in New Belgium, German in Italy, Catalan in Catalonia and Majorca, Luxembourgish, Welsh, Galician and Basque in the Autonomous Community. Another large group of cases which score low (0.0–1.75) on both dimensions: Cornish; East and North Frisian; Greek in Italy; Aroumanian; Albanian in both Greece and Italy; Portuguese in Spain; Sardinian; Slavo-Macedonian and Bulgarian in Greece; Dutch, Occitan, Breton and Corsican in France; Irish in N.I.; Tornedalen; Franco-Provencal; Sami in Sweden, Slovak in Austria; Catalan and Occitan in Italy; and Mirandese in Portugal. Another group of six cases has intermediate scores (1.75–3.0) on both dimensions: Gaelic; Frisian in the Netherlands; Slovenian and Friulian in Italy; Sorbian in Germany; and German in Denmark. It is this group which could benefit from a greater degree of state intervention.

Only 11 groups have similar scores on both dimension, and there are only three cases where the degree of state support plays a significantly larger role in sustaining the language group than does the activities of civil society – Sorbian (1.33/2.50), Sami in Sweden (1.0/1.75) and Hungarian in Austria (1.0/2.0). State support lags behind the activities of civil society by reference to language production and reproduction for Albanian in Italy (2.33/1.0), Catalan in Italy (1.67/0.75), Occitan in Italy (2.0/0.5), Mirandese (1.67/0.75), Breton (1.68/0.75), Slavo-Macedonian (1.68/0.0), Sardinian (1.0/0.25), Bulgarian (1.0/0.0), Aroumanian (0.67/0.0) and Albanian in Greece (0.67/0.0). Four of these groups are located in Italy, and four in Greece.

Greece offers virtually no support, even for extraterritorial Balkan state languages. There are a few small language groups which appear to have little activity in civil society, but which do receive some degree of state support. States treat each case differently, not having a blanket policy for all minority language groups within their territory. This is the case in Britain, Italy and France. The size of the language group, its degree of militancy, the role of the language in the labour market, and the degree of devolution of administrative function are all contributing factors.

2.4 Individual variables

There is a relationship between the role of a minority language in education and the prestige of that language. Half of the cases show equal scores on both dimensions, but Turkish in Greece, Basque in Navarre, Danish in

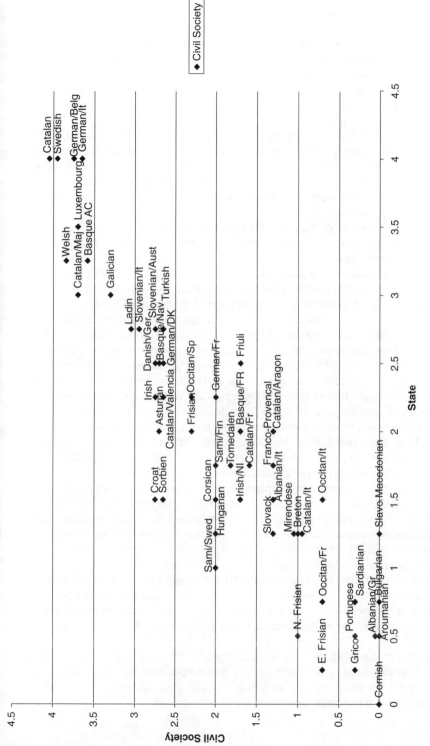

Figure 7.1 Influence of state and civil society variables

Germany, Irish in Ireland, Sorbian, Croat in Austria, Catalan in France, Corsican and Sami in Sweden are cases for which there is a greater support for educational practice than for the entry of the language into labour-market activities. For the Basques in the Autonomous Community and Catalans in Majorca, the extent of language use in higher education is not reflected in its use in the labour market. Northern and Eastern Frisian, Albanian, Catalan, Occitan and Grico in Italy, Breton, Dutch and Occitan in France, Mirandese and Portuguese in Spain have some educational support but no prestige. In contrast Ladin, Slovene in Austria, Friulian, Tornedalen and Franco-Provencal have a higher score for prestige than for education. These language groups control a portion of the labour market through private sector SMEs.

Over 60 per cent of the cases display a high correlation between legitimacy and prestige, and 56 per cent of the cases have a high correlation between institutionalisation and prestige. A quarter of the cases had no score for either legitimacy or prestige, and 15 per cent had no score for either institutionalisation or prestige. Most of the cases on the legitimacy/prestige pair where the scores differed had higher scores for legitimacy than for prestige. Only three cases – Friulian, Basque in France and Franco-Provencal – had higher scores for prestige than for legitimation. Legitimation does not necessarily involve labour-market activity, but economic relevance can be a consequence of legitimation. Where scores for institutionalisation and prestige differ, most have a higher score for institutionalisation than for prestige. The cases with higher scores for prestige are Welsh, German in Denmark, and Irish in Northern Ireland. The relevance of stabilised, non-economic language use for institutionalisation can be an important factor.

Apart from the Turkish language group, there is no formal educational support and no prestige value for any minority language groups in Greece. They rely upon civil society activity to sustain themselves. Trans-frontier activity is important in a comparison of language prestige and media exposure. The Danes in Germany, the Germans in Denmark, the Catalans and the Basques in France among other places benefit from trans-frontier media and other cultural activities, allowing cultural reproduction to be more relevant than prestige. Other cases allow media activity to increase the prestige of the minority language.

In a third of the cases family support is stronger than community support – as among the Portuguese language group in Spain, Croatian in Italy, Turkish in Greece and Mirandese in Portugal. The language does not appear to function either at the community or family level for the Cornish, or for Greek speakers in Italy. Over a third of the cases lack the community support that constitutes them as a language group. The Sami in Finland have a greater degree of community activity around the language than one would expect from the incidence of family use, but these language communities display little territorial continuity.

There is no clear linear relationship between the size of the language group and overall scores, but there is a degree of relationship between demographic size and the variable score. Of the 14 language groups which exceed 300 000 in size, 11 of them score 15 or more. The exceptions are Sardinian, Breton and Occitan in France. Three-quarters of the language groups have a demographic size smaller than 300 000, but some smaller groups such as Ladin, Occitan in Spain and German in New Belgium have high scores, and a number of language groups with membership of between 100 000 and 300 000 have low scores – Irish in Northern Ireland, Corsican, Catalan in France, Albanian, Aroumanian and Slavo-Macedonian in Greece.

2.5 Conclusion

The respective states do not treat all language groups in their territory in the same way. Also, some extraterritorial state language groups such as French and German are well placed, others are not. This lack of a universal pattern across what many feel are the main dimensions of language behaviour indicates a complexity that should be instructive.

Attention is now given to these factors by turning to a broader consideration of what has been discussed above. This involves stepping back from the detail of the data to consider the implications of the patterns discerned in the preceding analysis for the more general processes of social and economic change. This in turn obliges us to consider the relevance of the variables for that process and how that process serves to structure the patterns identified. In this respect the emphasis is very much upon causal analysis.

3 The restructuring of political and economic space

3.1 Introduction

The Euromosaic model suggests that economic restructuring influences regional migration patterns and the ability of families and communities to reproduce the respective languages. It is the extent to which the economic space – within which the language operates – is incorporated in the restructuring process that determines both the nature and the extent of social change by reference to the potential for production and reproduction of such groups.

Language groups must be capable of both production and reproduction within an environment which generates a desire to learn the language among non-speakers, and the need to ensure that speakers do not abandon the language. This demands a degree of co-operation in civil society and the state. The state must display an enlightened orientation and a tolerance towards diversity among its citizens, and the language group a drive for dignity through the use of the autochthonous language.

Language prestige can motivate both the indigenous population and in-migrants to produce and reproduce the language, reinforcing the other agencies of production and reproduction. Motivation involves the positive construction of subject places *vis à vis* specific objects so that the individual takes in charge the subject places associated with the relevant discourse. Constructing a language as an object which pertains to economic activity gives it a significance that relates to speakers as subjects. This significance transcends age groups and links with material advantage within the discourse on society, advantage and well-being.

3.2 Economic restructuring

The economic order is characterised by a constant thrust to sustain economic growth. Economic growth is not the smooth, constant process suggested by the linear, equilibrium models of neoclassical Economics, but involves cycles of growth and stagnation. The state stimulates growth while seeking to counter the effects of stagnation. Economic restructuring is a dynamic process that constantly changes the spatial division of labour. Industrial regions such as south Wales or Luxembourg are being transformed into economies that rely upon financial and other service activities. Other regions find it difficult to gain a toehold in the more dynamic activities. Prior to deregulation, the creation of the European Single Market, and the advent of innovation-based regional development strategies deriving from neo-liberal principles, these peripheral regions have been conceived as peripheries of state economies, each state having particular orientations towards its own economic space. Regional development tended to construct the state as the source of compensation for spatial inequality within its economic space. States directed specific economic activities to peripheral locations. Some such locations have become the source of retirement migration involving wealthier third-age migrants. Welfare measures often compensated for high relative and seasonal unemployment. Restructuring involves considerable circulation of financial capital, accompanied by the movement of people.

Peripheral economic structures are constructed out of the specific, often precarious, economic functions of locations – capital intensive, relatively short-term activities associated with primary-sector activities, with tourism or with locationaly strategic developments such as nuclear power plants are characteristic. A single sector, usually the service sector, dominates; activities such as tourism exaggerate the seasonality of activity; and developments are often short term. Unemployment and female activity, and part-time and self-employment rates are higher than in the core. New phases in the circulation of capital looking for the conditions to expand profit promote restructuring, and regions tend to be in competition for new capital and development.

4 The clusters

4.1 Cluster A

The extraterritorial state languages – German in New Belgium and German in Italy and Swedish in Finland – are increasingly becoming integrated into cross-boundary labour markets. Two of these groups are within the 'Golden Triangle' of the European core, as is Luxembourg. The economy of the Catalan in Catalonia is among the strongest and most integrated in Europe, at the heart of the Mediterranean Archipelago.

The other four cases are stateless languages outside of the European core. Basque and Welsh have a similar economic structure, being regions transforming from industrial production and an agricultural economy, contributing to the in-migration of a sizeable population from outside of the region. Galicia's economy has a heavy dependency on agriculture and fishing, and does not show the same degree of restructuring as the other regions, nor much recent in-migration. The economy of the Balearic Islands is dominated by tourism and has contributed to a pronounced immigration. These incomers show as little interest in learning Spanish, the state language, as they do in learning Catalan!

4.2 Cluster B

With only 3700 members the Aranese group confronting the recent influx associated with construction and tourism, similar remarks could be made concerning Ladin, which has only 56000 members. Asturian and Gaelic are located in sparsely populated areas with an economy devoted to fishing and agriculture, both subject to recent crisis management. Basque in Navarre and Catalan in Valencia are stateless languages, located in the shadow of the economy of the linguistic homelands. Resistance to promoting the language appears to be more political than it is economic.

The Slovene language groups in both Italy and Austria occupy regions with precarious economies, heavily dependent on tourism and agriculture. In-migration has not been pronounced and restructuring is a slow process. The same applies to the Danish and German language groups in north Germany and Denmark. The Single Market has realigned local and regional labour markets in such trans-frontier locations. Thus Germans and Danish in the border areas between Denmark and Germany, and the Catalans in France are likely to be affected. The Turkish language groups in Greece occupies the most economically peripheral of European regions. The Irish *Gaeltacht* is a region where agriculture and tourism dominate the economy. In-migration is not pronounced except for return-migration. The new Irish language media-based activities, and links with language-based activities in Scotland and Northern Ireland, may change things here.

4.3 Cluster C

Most of the language groups in this cluster have access to the main agencies of cultural reproduction and also have some form of educational support. The Sorbians with 15 000 members; the 31 000 Croat speakers in Austria; the 50 000 Catalan speakers in Aragon; the Tornedalen, which have a similar number of members; and the 4000 Sami speakers in Finland are small. In contrast the Friulian and the German speakers in France number over half a million; and the Corsican, Catalan in France, and the West Frisians all have over 100 000 members.

The Frisian group and the German speakers in France border the European core, attracting specific economic activities such as decentralised office functions which influence the flow of population in and out of the regions. The other groups are all located in the periphery. The predominance of tourism and retirement migration in some of these regions makes it difficult to reproduce the respective languages without the necessary status and institutional facilities. This is true of Corsican, the Basques in south-west France and, to a lesser extent, the Catalans in France. The Friulian and the Croats in Italy occupy rural areas which attract a certain amount of tourist economy, but which do not have a large influx of permanent new residents. The Catalan in Aragon are located in a region that is suffering from the current depression in the agricultural economy. This is even more so of the Tornedalen and the Sami in Finland. The later have male exclusion rates that are amongst the highest in Europe. Occupying a large sparsely populated area, the size of the group is such that it only requires a small influx of people to make a difficult task even more difficult. Already the language density is reduced to little more than 30 per cent. Finally, the Sorbians are located close to a region which is involved in profound structural changes.

The 25 000 first-language Corsican speakers, and the 100 000 who do use the language, indicate a decline of about 25 per cent during the past 15 years. The massive in-migration, and the parallel out-migration, means that half of the Corsican population was born elsewhere. This disruption of the demographic base of the local community that relates to tertiary-sector changes, especially tourism, limits the ability of the language group to produce and reproduce itself.

The 85 000 Basque speakers in Iparalde constitute a third of the local population. In-migration contributed to a population growth of 25 per cent between 1961 and 1991, and 43 per cent of the population in the district of Lapurdi are in-migrants. Tourism and retirement migration are strong. This language group receives even less recognition and support from the French state than does the Corsican group. Proximity to the Autonomous Community provides media and other resources.

The Friulian language group in north Italy has not been subject either to the same degree of population movement nor economic diversification, and the local economy retains a particular focus upon the service sector, agriculture and agriculturally related activity. Unemployment is low, while per capita income figures are relatively high. This has a positive effect upon language status. The local industrial parks in the area are of limited scale and focus upon local development through local actors. Developments that have focused upon tourism, electro-mechanical engineering, chemicals and micro-electronics have prompted some degree of in-migration.

The movement of financial and other enterprises out of the core into the semi-periphery of Friesland derives from the high cost of real estate and labour, and contributes to an economic restructuring focusing upon the service and retail sectors which employ most of the regional population. It shares with other peripheral locations the tendency to be treated as a retreat for the core population. The language group is quite large, and the institutional structure is such that there is potential for accommodating structural changes.

4.4 Cluster D

Most of these groups lack the necessary degree of state support to promote reproduction, and the irrelevance of the language for labour market activity makes production unlikely. The extremism of the French state's cultural and linguistic homogenisation project, and the associated denigration and neglect of minority language groups, has generated a profound negative identity among members of the Breton and Occitan language groups. The current benign neglect betrays a lack of any policy to redress the situation. Both regions have experienced considerable economic diversification involving some industrialisation, a commercialisation of agricultural activity and a pronounced increase in tourist-related activity. In-migration has not been as pronounced as in other locations. The absence of state support for the agencies of production and reproduction, the exaggerated negative identity, and the way intergenerational occupational and locational continuity has been ruptured by the process of economic restructuring have, between them, contributed to the changes since the Second World War.

Two of the language groups in Italy – Occitan and Albanian – have about 80000 members and about 100000 members respectively. Albanian extends from Abruzzi to Sicily in one of the more depressed areas of the European periphery. Out-migration to the industrial locations of Italy and the rest of Europe is high, and the standard of living is low. The agricultural and craft sectors have suffered, and much of the rest of the employment is in the service sector. The low socioeconomic status of the language group, and the absence of official support, contributes to the negative identity and rapid decline of the language group. The Occitan occupy a rural environment of impoverished small towns and villages of the Piedmont. The depressed nature of the economy has contributed to massive rates of out-migration.

There are about 15 000 Catalan speakers living in Alghero, in north-western Sardinia. The small population and its restricted territory makes it difficult to view this as a social group. After 1950 many left the area for other parts of Italy, while rural industrialisation and tourism promoted a parallel in-migration. Tourism and services account for almost two-thirds of the labour force, a small agricultural sector and small industrial sector, together with construction, employ a further 32 per cent. The absence of prestige, the lack of an official institutional context, and the negative identity means that the recent change in the size of the group is significant.

The Franco-Provencal language group is located in two different regions – Val d'Aosta and the Piedmont – and there is doubt that they exist as a single, coherent language community. A third of the population of Val d'Aosta region consists of in-migrants working in tourism, commerce and industry. A special statute promotes Standard French which is spoken by about 5 per cent of the population. Franco-Provencal suffers by comparison, being seen by many as an inferior form of French. About two-thirds of the 68 000 speakers of Franco-Provencal live in this region. In contrast, the Piedmont is a relatively impoverished location with limited economic diversity occupied by the remaining third of the language group.

4.5 Cluster E

These language groups lack any legal status, have no official support infrastructure, and rarely use the respective languages in either the family or the community. Many of them are small in size. Greek in Italy, Cornish, Portuguese in Spain, East and North Frisian, Dutch in France, and Bulgarian have a membership of less than 30 000. Of the remainder, the largest is Occitan with an estimated 2 000 000 speakers, followed by Sardinian with over a million and a quarter members, and Aroumanian with 200 000 members; then Albanian and Slavo-Macedonian in Greece each of which has an estimated membership of between 100 000 and 150 000.

Several occupy peripheral locations where diversification and restructuring have been minimal. The three language groups in Greece, Portuguese in Spain, and Greek in Italy occupy very poor areas with per capita incomes that are the lowest within the EU, leading to out-migration and low self-esteem. Attempts to improve the economy by external forces and encouraging in-migration will result in the demise of the majority of these groups.

Sardinian and Dutch in France can claim to be neither small, nor located in the extreme, undiversified periphery. The demise of the European coal industry has contributed to the economic decline of the Pas de Calais, while the economy of Sardinia has not been amongst the most dynamic. With between 20 000 and 40 000 speakers, and a geographical proximity to the same state language, the Dutch speakers should be in a much stronger position than they are. The low language density, the absence of state support in education, cultural reproduction and so on means that language reproduction is difficult, and language production impossible. Non-reproduction is prominent, leading to a pronounced intergenerational decline in ability. Sardinian suffers similarly and is in a process of rapid retreat. Language use is institutionalised to the extent that its contextual flexibility is impaired. The restructuring that accompanied a degree of political devolution has not been beneficial, since it includes movement to locations where associations are not based on the customary knowledge of personal relationships which language use relies upon. The focus of the economic activities associated with the higher social classes in the urban centres means not only that the language is either privatised or class specific, but that it is increasingly confined to rural locations. The relationship between language and life-style is crucial and has an important bearing upon the strengthening of a language-related negative identity. A Bill passed by the regional government to introduce Sardinian into education and public administration may be a step in the right direction.

4.6 Conclusion

The preceding discussion suggests that language policy and economic policy rarely overlap. Language is not relevant to economic development, even if it affects the salience of minority language groups. The relationship between different levels of the labour market is influenced by the relationship between capital and labour within the dynamics of economic restructuring. However, the discourse of development is changing as neo-liberalism replaces compensatory mechanisms, and the New Economy emerges (Williams, 2000a).

Most of the groups in Clusters A and B are located in the core or semi-periphery and have been able to withstand the process of restructuring, or have occupied specific economic niches. The high degree of in-migration is negated through labour-market segmentation and how it promotes the prestige of the language. However, each cycle of economic restructuring circulates capital and labour, and takes its toll on the size of the language group. The groups are constantly obliged to innovate in developing a response that insures any degree of success. Where the state is not supportive and proactive in this respect, the struggle to adapt is intensified.

'Language' and 'speakers' are constructed similarly for the language groups in Cluster A, and to a lesser extent for those in Cluster B. Language is a dynamic object which has value beyond the private domain, it operates within education so that it has relevance for the regional labour market. This is legitimated by how the discourse on the state allows these objects to be accommodated within the conception of public policy. This legitimacy links the objects to space in that it defines the territory to which the language pertains. This territory is also a social construct that is given meaning partly by reference to language. It is legitimated also by linking space to time through a sense of history within which the territory has somehow or other achieved a meaning. The subject as speaker of the language achieves meaning by reference to these dimensions.

Few of the language groups in Cluster C have been similarly exposed to the consequences of economic restructuring. Where this has occurred, and where in-migration is pronounced, the language group is threatened. Language groups in Cluster D are more likely to be in peripheral locations subject to restructuring and high in-migration. Finally, the language groups in Cluster E are small groups in the periphery, which have not been subject to a high rate of in-migration and have been little affected by the restructuring process. Their condition is a measure of their exclusion from positive state influences.

The state refuses to acknowledge the existence of groups in Cluster E. In so doing, it confirms their existence. The individual subject is not constructed as anything other than a citizen of the state. The language is often denied existence in the private domain, but in most cases it is acknowledged as having private relevance, though always within the context of a 'tradition' that is in the process of disappearance through 'modernisation'. This is the orthodox discourse of the modern state discussed in the introduction.

5 Conclusion

There are four different contexts for the relationship between economic restructuring and language groups:

- Locations with little evidence of the effects of economic restructuring have high status, with state-supported language groups capable of sustaining themselves from existing resources.
- Locations aloof from the impact of economic restructuring, but which experience considerable out-migration and low socioeconomic status is matched by a low group status. Language groups receive little or no support from the state and are faced with elimination.
- Locations which experience the full brunt of economic restructuring, where the language groups receive little state support, and lack the institutional resources to sustain themselves.
- Locations subject to a high degree of economic restructuring, where language groups have considerable state support, can accommodate the change and even benefit from it.

The issues of scale and economic process facilitates an understanding of the relevance of the state in the general process of sustaining language groups.

The absence of any relationship between cultural diversity and economic development is consistent with the modernist claim that economic growth is best promoted through a process of a cultural homogenisation that leads to universal rationalism, a view that characterises how neo-classical Economics has considered the relationship between the core and the periphery of the state's territory. The economic transformation of the periphery depends upon two factors, breaking down isolation through facilitating communication, and eliminating cultural difference in order to promote 'rationalist' economic orientations.

Placing the onus for adjustment upon the minority language group and its speakers involves attempts to institutionalise the use of the minority language in contexts hitherto reserved for the state language. It engenders resistance and open opposition. Given the forcefulness of the concept of freedom and liberty in the discourse on democracy, such a reaction carries substantial weight. The co-operation and commitment of the state is essential for sustaining diversity.

The vitality of minority language groups depends upon the extent to which language can enter the economy. Individual mobility within labour markets is central to the discourse on economic well-being. Success involves the individual's ability to obtain the prerequisites necessary to master the challenges of the economic order. How the individual deploys language is a feature of this mastery, providing the language used has relevance for such behaviour. The 'good life' within the discourse on democracy constitutes the link between economy and democracy. This emphasis upon neoclassicism is changing in the face of the emergence of the Knowledge Economy and the neo-liberal principles which are driving it.

The combined effect of ICT and the globalisation process is leading to a reassessment of the economy. Neo-liberalism involves an economy operating in accordance with social needs and desires and unhindered by state intervention. Society is seen as the product of human agents obeying rules that operate as tacit knowledge. It is these rules that inform the free market and insure that economic planning is futile (Giddens, 1994).

Economic development involves the capability of regions to compete on their own assets and competencies; a concern with human rather than financial capital; and a concern with the ability to stimulate constant innovation. This opens the space for diversity within the relevant discourse. The relationship between innovation, language and the social construction of meaning assumes a new relevance for economic development. Languages construct meaning in different ways, and the mix of such structures can be the basis for new knowledge formation. Knowledge creation and knowledge management involves language playing a central role in the relevance of reflexive learning and the development of networks for innovation. Innovation is best facilitated at the regional level because of the significance of regional identity for this process. The community attains a new significance, becoming the source of responsibility, accountability and transformation.

The reconstitution of the language object involves its construction as the basis for knowledge development, and its value for networking within an innovation process that relies upon knowledge exchange through interaction. What is not happening at the same pace is the extension of this re-evaluation to accommodate all languages and associated subjects. The arguments are made by reference to state languages, and not to language *per se*. The reluctance to move away from the modernist constitution of *ethnos* and *demos* is clear. The shifting of responsibility from the state to the individual and the community may well result in a failure to undo the stabilisation of discourse that has resulted in the precarious position of most European minority language groups. The absolution of the state from responsibility will lead to the blaming of the victim, and a confirmation that the language community has no interest in sustaining itself. Most of the language groups we have discussed will disappear during the present century and Europe's diversity will be that much poorer.

8
Diversity and Democracy

1 Introduction

The remarks in the Introduction indicate that the modern European state has been constructed on two pillars – the autonomy of the individual state and a particular sense of democracy, the two main components of industrial capitalism. Minority language groups have either been excluded or marginalised from these developments. However, we are on the cusp of a profound change. European integration involves a weakening of the state in public and private life. Liberalisation and globalisation are sustained by a global neo-liberalism. Simultaneously, industrial-age economy is giving way to the New Economy constructed out of a new technology and an associated re-evaluation of the principles of economic growth. *Ethnos* and *demos* are being destabilised.

The concept of democracy seems akin to the role played by Christianity and Civilisation in nineteenth-century Western discourse. So pervasive is it that to challenge it is akin to heresy, and it seems inconceivable that future development can be detached from it. It is constructed as the antidote of alternative principles of governance that are constructed as 'evil'. Yet it is by no means a uniform and stable notion.

The question we are obliged to ask in this final chapter addresses the extent to which these new conditions are, or can be, favourable in reversing the apparent fate of Europe's linguistic diversity. The rejection of the arguments about the specific direction of 'progress' and 'development' within the social sciences gives such a question new relevance.

The notion of democracy was premised upon the idea of a united Europe and the need to develop democratic political cultures. European integration is well under way, while the issues associated with democracy remain relatively undebated (Seidentop, 2000). This debate will be about linguistic diversity and pluralism if a new form of united polity is to be forged. A lingua franca as the means whereby democracy across diversity will be conducted may prevail. Already the European Commission primarily operates two such languages – English and French – while paying lip service to the use of the other state languages. The 'language which is the vehicle of money' within the international labour market is English, the second language of all of the European states (Balibar, 1985:190). Those who subscribe to neo-liberalism, and the associated commodification of everything, argue that market forces will determine the outcome of the role of the respective languages in the United Europe. The question remains, is 'the democratisation of language' (Balibar, 1985:194) the product of such a discourse? If it is, what are the consequences for a democracy premised upon diversity and pluralism? These are questions which pertain to all European languages.

The emergence of a proto-federalism and the associated removal of regulatory and other powers from the various nation states obliges rethinking the spatial configuration of society. The unitary nature of one society for each state, deriving largely from the legislative and economic regulating powers of the state, would appear to be redundant. The state was legitimised by a normative order which defined the deviant or non-normative. Moving towards a united Europe raises the question of the new normative order and the redefinition of deviance. Language plays a role in defining language groups as social groups. The link between the new normativity, the emerging concept of a European society and deviance demand a debate about the relationship between European democracy and diversity. It has particular significance as we move from an industrial society to an information society.

An 'event' (Foucault, 1969:231), or how a situation is placed within a field of social forces, is not the cause of change, but a locus of chance reversal, the discontinuous moment when a transformation is evident. It involves a critique of an existing order of discourse and the transformation of social practices. Any one conception of the norm and its action leads to a different norm and the different social relations associated with it. Normativity, social relationships and the insertion of individuals as subjects in the networks which these relationships constitute are questioned, leading to different definitions of subjects and objects, and their relationships to the constitution of meaning. One outcome of the event is the ability to question the assumptions or the taken for granted of previously stabilised discourses which are now destabilised.

2 Diversity and democracy

The history of nation building in Europe and the denial of minority language groups implies a contradiction between democracy on the one hand and diversity and pluralism on the other. Democratic liberalism, Republicanism and the idea that a democratic culture protects diversity are the basis for the relationship between pluralism and democracy. This derives from the Christian moral tradition and the Christian Natural Law tradition. The pre-individualistic social and intellectual context gave rise to the discourse of classical Republicanism or citizenship, and the French and American Revolutions transformed this tradition into a political venture based on the civic virtue of patriotism, with the collective as the basis for principles of justice or equity. Medieval Law theory gave way to the social contract of the seventeenth and eighteenth centuries, the basis for both Political Science and Sociology. It rested on the moral equality of humans, and leads to a legal order based on the rights and duties of individuals rather than collectivities, on the separation of the private from the public sphere, of civil society from the state, and the struggle between particularism and universalism.

However, European states have evolved differently during the past two centuries. Each European nation state has its own political culture and quite different relationships between '*demos*' and '*ethnos*'. Civil society is where individuals can exercise choice according to conscience and are protected by rights. The discourse of democracy, especially the version of American Republicanism, constructs both the family and the community in a particular way in accommodating them within 'democracy'. This explains some of the preceding findings. In many European states, democracy has been unable to reconcile the universalism of citizenship with the particularism of identity. In contrast to the American Revolution, the French Revolution abandoned the question of the relationship between liberty and the form of government which could guarantee liberty in favour of a politics of pity (Arendt 1967:82–165). This involved the spectacle of suffering or the privileging of observation over action. It leads to a politics of justice involving meritocracy and the normative evaluation of the respective merits of different citizens (Boltanski, 1993:16). This politics of pity does not involve a relationship between the fortunate and the unfortunate, but rather that between 'the great' and 'the small', that is, in accordance with the value of people (ibid:16). This judgement was not made by reference to individuals, but to collectivities. Universalism located minority language groups in the same camp as the aristocracy, outside of reason, at best on the margins of pity and justice. They became the '*baragouiner*', incapable of even appealing for pity because of the yoke of language.[1] The discourse on particularism was much better placed to develop a discourse of justice constructed out of diversity and pluralism.

We still encounter the evolutionary thrust of the particularism/universalism debate in the current discussion of democracy in Europe, partly since liberalism derives from the work of Kant, who was among the most vocal champions of a political reform which encompassed the principles of universalism. It is akin to Schumpeter's (1947) economic model of democracy. Thus Siedentop (2000), argues that a pluralism premised upon group rights will not work in Europe because the regional identities which are conveyed are representative of a culture which somehow lies outside of the principles of individual liberalism. Earlier, the eighteenth-century *philosophes* argued that universalism merely played into the hands of feudal power holders, thwarting the drive for modernism. Such an evolutionary view is not only disingenuous, but offensive to those who have spent 200 years within liberal democratic systems which have steadfastly refused to acknowledge their interests. Language groups within such systems have operated within fully developed voluntary associations, nurturing democratic principles and debate, and contributing actively to local and regional civil culture. A democracy which encompasses a link between a civil society which debates and discusses its needs in relation to the state must address the needs and expectations of that community, rather than try and shape it to the form which makes it commensurate with a centralised culture and system. Others (Touraine, 1994; and Pusey, 1998 *inter alia*) have rejected this corner-stone of the discourse of democracy.

Democracy requires a citizenship that is actively engaged in shaping policy if it is to become part of a public process with specific goals. The pursuit of private ends is legitimated and protected in so far as they are consistent with justice. The creation and protection of individual rights, the instrument of civil equality, is the state's responsibility. Nonetheless, the citizen is meant to be able to attend the assembly and share in public power. Any government or political culture promoting an assimilationist policy, seeking to denigrate a language group and an associated culture within its territory in the name of unity, uniformity and the state, will find this difficult to achieve. Regional identities and loyalties in Europe are claimed not to be so closely tied to the rule of law or democratic principles as they ought to be. Regions may have created a political culture, but these political cultures have not been allowed to express a specific form of regionalism, expressed in particular languages. The claim that the populations of the regions are in danger of abandoning civic cultures and democratic norms in rejecting the central state (Siedentop, 2000), merely pampers to a displaced belief in paternalism and a lack of faith in the nature of non-normative civic culture.

Charles Taylor (1992) emphasises that there are two ideal-type models of modern liberal democracy, one favouring the 'politics of equal respect, as enshrined in a liberalism of rights', but is 'inhospitable to difference because: (a) it insists on uniform application of rules defining these rights, without exception, (b) it is suspicious of collective goals'; and the other is a model that finds different answers to the problems of (a) and (b) This form would not:

> call for the invariant defence of certain rights . . . There would be no question of cultural differences determining the application of *habeas corpus* for example. But they distinguish these fundamental rights from the broad range of immunities and presumptions of uniform treatment that have sprung up in modern cultures . . . they are willing to weigh the importance of cultural survival, and opt sometimes in favour of the latter.
>
> (ibid:61)

Such a model would, in the last instance, not be grounded in procedures, but in judgements about the good life. Individualism undermines accommodating how sharing is the essence of the true community.

In the United States people remain in their specific, often ethnic, communities, whereas in politics they are highly individualistic (Walzer, 1992). The size of the ethnic groups means that no single ethnic group can control political institutions. This reference to ethnicity involves self-identity rather than developing the basis for institutional control that would guarantee the linguistic and cultural distinctiveness of the language group, so that the US system is both assimilationist and allows everyone to assert their difference. This is also true in Europe, with voting patterns in regional and local elections being quite different from those in state elections. However, the American version of democracy fails to encompass sustaining cultural diversity as opposed to guaranteeing individual liberty.

Siedentop's rejection of diversity is redressed by Dworkin (1977) who discussed the relationship between equality and liberty. He argues that constitutional politics must balance equality and freedom. He distinguishes between the right to equal treatment and the right to be treated equally. One alternative involves everyone receiving the same goods or chances, while the other refers to equal treatment in the decision-making processes which decide how goods and choices are distributed. If the first is over-emphasised, the equilibrium between social rights and individual freedom is affected so that social rights might replace individual liberty. There is an intrinsic connection between political and social rights.

Obtaining adequate protection from the authorities rests on the importance given to established principles and to ethical values – principles of equality, solidarity, tolerance, pluralism and freedom of opinion. A principle leading to a policy of minority protection becomes one of affirmative action in favour of social groups and individuals. It rests on redistributive capacity and the inclusive capacity of disadvantaged groups. The protection of minorities ceases to be a mater of rights and becomes a question of politics (Carrozza, 1992:217). Liberals insist that the normative reason for collective rights involves a value of individuals rather than the collectivity. Thus members of minority groups should be protected against devaluation of their cultural membership as well as against group oppression (Kymlicka, 1996). The American model of liberal democracy as modernism has become a meta-discourse that constructs the subjects and objects that relate to specific problems in specific ways, obliging an evaluation of social problems by reference to this discourse, and limiting the basis for their solution. It is exacerbated by how the neo-liberal discourse, the associated demise of welfarism, and the declining role of the state in economic decision making, lead to a politics of fear and risk (Beck, 1986). Democracy is heavily reliant upon trust, especially within civil society and between civil society and the state. Its absence creates the danger of a fear of superior force, precisely the condition characterising much of the relationship between minority language groups and the state since the emergence of the modern state.

Diversity is important for democracy in how it disperses power, and builds human character. Any political system that serves an extended territory must foster diversity if it is to remain sensitive to the wide range of spatial, social and cultural differences within its territory, while also encouraging innovation and experimentation within the broad limits established by justice. This means creating different spheres of public authority and withdrawing the power to alter those spheres unilaterally from central government, that is, creating federalism. The dispersal of power and character building and self-reliance leads to active citizenship by guaranteeing local and regional autonomy. It conforms with the chief conviction of modern Western societies – that freedom is a prerequisite of a moral conduct which derives from a consensus within society. It is not akin to a normativity since it springs from consciousness, and that consciousness should pertain to local and regional sensitivities.

3　Devolution in Europe

Siedentop's evolutionary and paternalistic argument is that it is only when the connection between moral equality and the claim of equal liberty is fully understood that a secure base for self-government within any society is possible. Only then can representative or free institutions develop. He claims that the Northern Protestant nations have developed more durable traditions of self-government than those of the Catholic South. Germany and the Netherlands have developed a rhetoric of federalism in contrast to the bureaucratic and, at times, populist thrust of French democracy, or the communal and even anarchic nature of democracy which he claims prevails in Italy. The foundations of liberalism in Southern Europe are influenced by how the rule of law is associated more with the central imposition of rules than with the forming of popular attitudes and habits. He contrasts Roman Law with the importance of Common Law in the United Kingdom. He could have referred to the commonality between the UK and Germany, based upon the historic influence of Burke's thinking on Germanicism (Losurdo, 1992). Chauvel (1995), also claims that the states of Northern Europe are far more homogenous by reference to regional differences and values than the fragmented South.

It is the center-right and center-left in Europe that have been most in favour of a devolved democracy. Across Europe the left and the right average about 40 per cent of the vote in elections, with the middle vote shifting direction in determining superiority. The relevance of this for the future of devolution is unclear, especially when some former left parties espouse centre-right neo-liberalism. A structural analysis of regionalism and devolution is plagued by the persistent evolutionary tendency to treat local and regional organisation as 'traditional', rather than treating them as stabilised discourses capable, under specific circumstances, of linking subjects and objects in ways which are conducive to highlighting the region and its claim to authority. It is an inherent feature of the American brand of democracy.

Comparing federal and centralised states requires caution if we are focusing on a regard for linguistic diversity. The influence of American Republicanism is in the treaties, discussed in Chapter 2, which were established on the principle of cultural nations, and Woodrow Wilson's insistence on 'making the world safe for democracy'. However, it is dangerous to take these treaties as representative of current democracy and pluralism in these states.

There are six federal states, not all of them with a concern for regional interests. Spain, Belgium and, to an extent, the UK have a form of governance that accommodates the historic regions, and the acknowledging of their right to encompass regional languages and culture in this devolution. Power has been dispersed in changing the relationship between the state and civil society. In the UK, neo-liberal principles shift responsibility and accountability from the state to the individual and the community. This may bring government closer to the people, but conforming with the principles of democracy by giving the individual and the community a direct role in policy formation and decision making has yet to be seen. Also, party control from the centre still prevails. In Spain, power and legislative and revenue-raising potential has been devolved to the Autonomous Regions which, within the constitutional constraints, become entirely responsible for their policy for sustaining linguistic diversity. Yet attention to diversity often depends upon which political party claims power. Devolution is no guarantee of diversity and pluralism.

In Belgium, devolution has progressed to the point where some claim that 'the state itself would implode' (Sassoon, 1999). 'Linguistic autochthony' is at the heart of its devolution. The distinction between the Flemish and the French language groups encompasses religion and politics, with the Flemish being primarily Catholic and centrist, while the Walloons are socialist and more secular. Cultural autonomy was institutionalised within each of the three 'communities' – French, Dutch and German. De Rynk (1998) identifies a higher level of civic involvement among the Flemish language group than among the French speakers, whereas the incidence of clientism is higher among the Walloons, but claims that these internal variations hide a general uniformity within Belgium. We should not give too much value to this kind of work, given the criticism that Putnam's (1993) similar work has rightly received, and the doubts which must remain about the claim for a direct relationship between social structure and democratic principles. The relationship between devolved governance and level of 'civicness', and interaction between civil society and regional government, involve an overlap between the two subject positions that pertain to the local community, or civil society, and regionalism. The Flemish communities did gain their regional status through reaction at the level of civil society against the *status quo*.

The competences of these subnational governments overlap with the supranational government in Brussels, having devolved responsibility for European affairs and the associated need for relevant information. Many of these subnational governments represent historic regions, having a basis of collective action largely constructed out of the link to language and culture. They contrast with the regions which are defined by reference to their political responsibility *vis à vis* the state. A strong associational culture is claimed to be that which represents social trust, education and other social forces which lead individuals into closer relationships with their neighbours (ibid.).

French regionalism involves a discursive relationship between the region and the state that is functional, the region serving as the basis for state action. The political culture of such states involve law and public policy as the domain of the expert or of strangers who have an advantage over submissive and passive locals. The locals are mere spectators of the political process, and the state is centralised and remote from the regions. Decisions tend to be arbitrary and well-placed groups and interests shape decisions. Central agencies can be used to quell local interests, generating the view that power is always in the hands of others. Since 1981 decentralisation has involved a quest for a balance in the departments between the prefects, who are agents of the state, and the popularly elected councillors. Regional and local authorities have gained the power to raise taxes and to borrow, and have more jurisdiction in linguistic and cultural affairs, but this is always subservient to principles laid down at the centre. The decentralised activity has involved economic and social planning and the co-ordination of resources. This changes civic life at the local level, making it a more democratic system. If these developments are to extend the ability of language groups and cultures to sustain their identity while protecting local autonomy, considerably more is required. Some regional Presidents claim regional autonomy to implement regional development principles deriving from Brussels (*Le Monde*, 16/12/1997). Yet, central government ministers resign for fear that ceding regional autonomy will threaten the Republic (*Le Monde*, 29/8/2000).

The ambivalence in French civic society about participation in group life is held to derive from a lack of belief in co-operation and the existence of legal restraints on associational life. This and Republicanism make groups hostile to serving as intermediaries between the people and the state. State subsidy is primarily to political associations which reinforce existing social divisions rather than to promoting the emergence of social and fraternal groups. The electorate is suspicious of authority and looks to representation as its protection against arbitrary government, leading to a suspicion of parties who seek to promote political reform.

The French model applies to both Sweden and Finland, which have centrally appointed regional governors who oversee the administration of government interests in the periphery. The absence of power in local government means that action is constantly by reference to central affirmation. In the absence of a powerful elected regional body, the Sami are obliged to take their problems to the capital. A strong municipal government and a unitary state in Sweden, as indeed in the Netherlands, militates against developing regional government. Resistance to devolution is also strong in Portugal where a 1998 referendum rejected regional elected assemblies.

The German constitution creates different spheres of authority and a powerful constitutional court minimises the risk of encroachment from federal government. Postwar Germany created a rule of law, a strong civil society and an American-inspired federalism which could limit the power of central government. The constitutional court serves as the check and balance *vis à vis* decision making, this limiting the development of an all powerful elite. The constant bargaining between the *Lander* and central government is assisted by the quasi-corporatist German society, with a network of national associations lying behind the German political class, creating a political culture that places a premium on consensus. Deference to authority means that the public plays only a minor role in shaping the political class.

Britain relies upon precedent and custom, and has a consensual model of government where custom is to the fore. It derives from a tradition of an informal decentralisation, linked with Parliamentary sovereignty. This gave extensive local autonomy and an important role for internal bodies and voluntary associations, including the Church, the legal profession and universities. Political culture was consensual which maximised the role of public opinion. There is no British constitution, and the current thrust of decentralisation and devolution must go further if it is to lead to increasing political participation. Recent devolution is premised on neo-liberal principles giving the historic regions of Wales, Scotland and Northern Ireland a semblance of autonomy that does appear to be benefiting the shift towards accommodating diversity.

The strength of the Northern League has forced the left to expand its commitment to devolution in Italy. The absence of a devolved system which accommodates regional identity, is partly because the state is so weak, lacking the means to establish a formalised system that will balance north and south, and a constitutional system that informs a distribution of power between core and periphery. The Italian constitution is one of the few in Europe to make specific reference to the protection of minorities. It states that the Rights of Man should apply not merely to every individual, but also to social groups. Outside of the wealthier northern regions, and the extraterritorial language groups that occupy them, progress has been slow. Attempts to establish a legal framework allowing regional authorities to protect linguistic and cultural minorities were blocked by a Parliament which affirmed that any such law could only pertain to the state. As in France, universalist principles are used to reject minority groups and cultural differences. The priority allocated to the state and the weakness of the regional authorities leads to the legal system being viewed as a means of controlling minority groups. A general law of the minorities has been proposed, but never voted upon by the Italian Parliament.

Supposedly politics in Italy penetrates the community through a patron-client relationship that colours the bureaucracy. Power brokers are claimed to have such a hold on local society that the state finds it difficult to govern. The public sector is divided among the parties, developing networks of influence and reciprocal loyalties, generating a kind of ruling class. Activity at the community level involves these political parties, which have their own media and a well developed party machine. Penetration of social life is clearly highly pronounced. Similarly, the Catholic Church, whose authority resides in the Vatican, is often in close alliance with the Christian Democratic Party, the largest and most stable political party in Italy, against the Communist Party (PCI). The north-east is under the hegemony of the former, whereas the central belt is controlled by the PCI where forms of identification which mobilised territory and local communities were replaced by class integration in the political discourse (Bagnasco and Oberti, 1998).

Subjects were constructed as members of a social class operating within universalist principles and Fordism was meant to penetrate the entire population of the state. Internal community divisions often invoke the anti-clericalism which opposes the traditional power of the Church. Indeed, the hierarchical organisation of the Catholic Church and the Italian Communist Party are remarkably similar. Between them they are responsible for organising much of the social activity at the local level around the family, local identity, and artisan and entrepreneurial traditions. The regional authorities created in the 1970s were based on historic territorial space, but the centralised universalism of the *demos* of both the Church and the main political parties makes any integration between the community and new regional bodies difficult. This clientism is not universal in Italy, and Putnam's analysis claims that northern regions display a much higher degree of civic culture or political and social participation. He has been rightly criticised for the excessive emphasis on the legal-rational model characteristic of American democracy (Ritaine, 1998) and how this fuelled the emergence of the Northern League.

Greece purports to operate European democracy and the associated Christian moral beliefs. The creation of the Greek state and the separation of the Church from the Constantinople Patriarchy, which represented the orthodox ecumenical, led to a nationalist Orthodox Church. State centralism involves an inability to accommodate opposition. The state is there to protect the entire territory. The messianic attitude of the Orthodox Church involves defending its orthodoxy against any heresies or any other religious doctrines. It is difficult to view the Greek state as a lay state. The 1975

Constitution is promulgated 'in the name of the sacred, consubstantial, indivisible Trinity', and defines the development of 'the national and religious consciousness of Greeks' as among its missions. Its assimilationism extends to not recognising linguistic groups other than those to whom its international treaties refer. National integration leads to this lack of pluralism which covers both language and religion, and local powers are far too weak to contest central government.

As a state which displays a strong tradition of local politics based upon the municipalities, the Netherlands involves oligarchic provincial cultures adapted to a democratic national culture. Provincial government plays an intermediate role between the central state and the municipalities, but has a limited role in democratic governance, partly on account of the centralised budgetary control. Decisions taken at either municipal or regional level can be annulled by the state.

Different state forms relate to different forms of political culture and political elites. The preceding allow the separation of those states which have taken the most positive steps by reference to sustaining minority language groups, from those whose efforts in this respect have been limited by reference to political culture and the associated political structure. It is also necessary to consider variation in civil society across the different European societies.

The Roman Law tradition regards regional and local units of government as mere appendages of central government. Its doctrinal position makes it difficult to accommodate different opinions and factions, but takes a prime place in the socialising process. In contrast, Christian Natural Law fostered an individualism within civil society. The struggle between social privilege and protest engulfed the Catholic Church, which was seen as the instrument of social control at the community level on behalf of the ruling class. The associated anticlericalism is sometimes evident. The Second Vatican Council was an attempt to shed the divisive role in Europe, and to develop a discourse with Christianity as the precursor of representative government and the defence of human rights, the essential principles of liberalism. Some regional clergy have used these directives in affirming their, and the Church's, allegiance to that region. In other cases this has not happened. Community organisation within those states where Catholicism is hegemonic is distinctive and the Church continues to play a central role in this organisation. The extent to which the regional clergy has played its hand can have enormous significance for the ability of language groups to reproduce themselves.

In contrast, Protestantism places emphasis on conscience and voluntary assent rather than on authority and obedience. It encourages self-administration and political apprenticeship, and separates community-based voluntary associations from religious activities to a greater extent than in Catholic communities. Indeed, Bonald feared that Protestantism represented the kind of privilege which lacked reason, and which opened a particularism which diluted the social in the individual (Bonald, 1985).

Viewed from the periphery, all European states appear unnecessarily centralised. When each state had its own economy and labour market, as well as the regulatory powers to intervene in economic planning, 'development' was criticised for being premised upon core interests rather than on removing core–periphery disparities, for involving a paternalistic core offering the 'benefits' of welfarism during recession and core-focused development initiatives which offered employment, but little value-added benefit to the periphery during periods of growth. Such state initiatives were justified by an appeal to the principles of liberal democracy that were meant to insure if not equality, then an equality of opportunity. The trend towards devolution is open to the same suspicions.

Another side to this discussion about a democratic Europe and how it pertains to a liberalism formed out of Christian moral principles involves the need to accommodate group rights. Berlin (1999), for example, draws this from the particularist tradition. As moral minorities, many minority language groups view rights in terms of the collectivity, while acknowledging the need to accommodate individual rights. Multiculturalism and tolerance involve a critique of how the abstract concern with individual liberty and human rights ignores the essence out of which collectivities are constituted. How the state constructs the individual depends on the discourse of citizens as a collective with specific loyalties and prejudices not only denigrates the non-normative, it also leads to creating a range of political cultures that succeed in raising the issue of pluralism within a united Europe not by reference to minorities, but only by reference to the moral majority.

The insistence on individual rights, by polarising pluralism and liberalism, stems from the evolutionary thrust of universalism, resulting in a Eurocentrism premised upon the centrality of Christianity, and a claim that the infidel cannot accommodate democracy. The 'us' that establishes the boundary at the confines of Europe involves transcending state boundaries, much as the ethnicity which derives from particularism and Germanicism has done in the past. No one can lie outside of this commonality, and how the 'Other' is constructed obliges all Europeans to fear and offend the infidel. Christian ontology is held to serve as the premise for moral equality. The outcome is either European isolation or that the rest of the world must assume the same principles of moral equality as those found in Europe. The argument appears to be little more than an extension of the missionary zeal of Christian global dominance. Yet it is highly relevant as we enter a globalisation within which Europe and the United States present themselves as the moral and legal arbitrators of moral consensus.

Is a form of democracy that not only encompasses diversity but does so by blending both individual and collective rights possible? Subsidiarity must be given a constitutional standing by defining areas and spheres seen as capable of generating legitimate claims on the state. The legitimacy of regional interests and identities should be recognised and catered for by an adequate political system. A political culture must be rights-based and should accommodate language rights. While the right of appeal against injustice remains in the centre, and is arbitrated by reference to central interests rather than universal norms of justice and moral principles, it is unlikely that it will be conceived of as fair by those making the complaint. Rather, it will confirm the system as one imbued with injustices operating in the interests of the centre.

The language of economics has replaced the language of politics and constitutionalism, obliging us to subordinate values and principles to the logic of the market, at a time when the link between perceived rationalism and economic behaviour is being questioned (Williams and Morris, 2000). This utilitarian philosophy replaces the issue of who controls public power, ensures accountability and political participation. Neo-liberalism has replaced both socialism and liberalism; a greedy individualism, devoid of the liberal doctrine of citizenship and public duty or of compassion for the unfortunate of socialism transpires. Yet it also transfers responsibility to the individual and the community rather than the state. This devolution, if handled delicately, can resurrect the role of the community within civil society. Mutual involvement requires more than an appeal to a sense of community. A sense of civic virtue as a devotion to the collective cannot be achieved if, at the same time, the state refuses to acknowledge the particularity of the region and the community. Minority languages are left outside of the terms of a citizenship premised upon a knowledge of the state language and the capacity for reason which is held to accompany it. Within the discourse of citizenship, freedom remains construed as the ability of the minority language speaker to liberate herself from the minority language, and thereby discover citizenship and its privileges. Some states, most notably France, have temporarily resisted the rhetoric of neo-liberalism by insisting that the state retain a role in shaping the market place.

This is a much broader discussion than merely about the extent to which the future Europe can involve diversity, it is an inquiry that focuses upon the relevance of diversity and pluralism for democracy, it is about the relationship between the state and civil society. This incorporates the current debate about the nature of the state and what is meant by civil society. The relationship between the two realms is far more complex than the conceptions provided by the early social thinkers. It is particularly apt for a Europe that appears to be in the process of uniting states into a federation, despite some misgivings (Siedentop, 2000).

The pendulum has swung from a legitimisation of universalism, to a growing emphasis upon the particular, accompanied by a growing conservatism and an increasing tendency towards the exclusion of many within Europe. Must the advantages of a discourse that espouses diversity of necessity be accompanied by a tendency towards conservatism or, conversely, is equality inherently related to uniformity? Certainly this was the view of Kant and his followers in the eighteenth century. Discussion must involve how this re-evaluation of diversity pertains to the new discourse on the economic order.

The notion of historic regions contrasts with how the official discourse of the EC constructs 'region' as the next level of government down from the state. If social constructs partly derive from how subjects and objects are stabilised in prior discourse, the essence of a historic region is how this prior discourse and the stabilised subjects and objects feed into the present. The same is true of languages, and how they are constituted. An autochthonous language overlaps with a particular historical region. It is axiomatic that any region is part of a larger spatio-political arrangement. The state lays claim to being the point of reference for any region, and it is the state that has systematically sought to eliminate the languages which have served as one of the defining bases of the historic region. This is being challenged as the defining referent of 'region' by the mere existence of European 'regions', destabilising the 'region' as an object by obliging a clarification of the nature of the preconstructed referent.

Breaking with the modernist discourse which has stabilised the state as the preconstructed referent, and with paranoia about the minority languages and the historic regions, involves reconstituting the historic regions and the minority languages as political forces: the *ethnos–demos* relationship is thus reconstituted. This opposes those such as Putnam who see the process of region formation as rooted in the rationalism of modernism. Space is reconstituted, and both region and language become the objects around which community capacity building is mobilised. The civil society and the capacity for political mobilisation is already in place, albeit that it must be restabilised within a new discursive context. They must be transformed from linguistic and territorial cultures into political cultures. This is already in progress; however, it operates by reference not to the context of the industrial society that was heralded by the modern 'national' (*sic*) society, but by reference to the information society and its relationship to a global economic order. Normativity and social order yield to a relationship to do with the capacity of a region to accommodate a positive engagement with the new global economic order. Of necessity it involves a reassessment of the nature of 'ethnicity'.

In some respects Seriot's reference to *ethnos* and *demos* involves how the nation state creates its subjects at citizens around the centrality of the political, which has the capacity to construct the citizen as coterminus with its territorial space in relationship to historic time. The regulating activity of the state is in retreat, and this relationship between time, person and space is being reconfigured, involving new significations and representations. There is a redefinition of the right of the state to intervene in private space, and of the nature of the state that claims this right. It is a process that has yet to be worked out. The contest between the moral and the legal, explored above in terms of the quest of minority language groups to incorporate a colingualism that legitimises their existence, may well shift to a new form of contestation involving the place of the nation-state in the European space (Balibar, 1993). The nature of *'ethnos'* will shift, and with it the struggles over identity. How the local regulation of the relationship between *ethnos* and *demos* operates will determine the nature and extent of European diversity.

The political parties have been constructed out of universalist discourses. They are now beginning to separate the general principles of their ideologies from this universalism, developing organisational structures which accommodate different territorial aggregates. Simultaneously, neo-liberalism breaks down the right–left distinction, drawing the political discourses of the respective parties ideologically closer. The implicit relationship between neo-liberalism and the emergence of a fascism premised upon populism must be avoided. Retaining the ideal type of liberal democracy against the benefits of solidaristic relationships constructed out of a cultural civil society is counterproductive. Similarly, regional development strategies, tied to a discourse which emphasises the role of the state, Keynesianism and inward investment yield to the neo-liberal focus upon indigenous investment, sustainability and entrepreneurialism dependent upon self-responsibility. A positive evaluation of a regionalism constructed out of the indigenous diacritica of the region becomes possible. The region as an object links with subjects who are empowered to find their own destiny in a way that the state has failed to provide. Diversity assumes a new significance. Yet simultaneously there is a profound shift in the relationship between discourse on society and that on the economy, from the industrial society to the information society. Minority language groups are locked in a new struggle associated with the need to integrate with the information society and the New Economy.

4 Governance, digital democracy and the New Economy

The openness and interdependence of the international economy means that governmental bodies must play a central role in the New Economy. That is, policy promotes innovation and customer oriented government. The polity must become more flexible and responsive, partly on account of how electronic means generate productivity and income gains, while also increasing the quality and cutting the cost of government services. The operational systems of the New Economy involve new forms of govermentality resulting in specific policy orientations which are essential for promoting the information society. It is highly dependent upon neo-liberalism and upon how shifting responsibility and accountability from the state to the individual and the community obliges a re-evaluation of service provision.

Services no longer involve providing policy to passive recipients or consumers, but rely on a dialogue within which consumers actively formulate policy. Service provision involves meeting the needs and expectations of the citizen. Interactivity involves interoperable digital sites and the transformation of representative democracy into a democracy which accommodates participation (Williams, 2001).

Local action is premised on both the significance of the community as a form of social order and on the idea of partnership. Partnerships involve shared meaning and understanding, and a common orientation to problem resolution for institutional contexts that have ingrained interests and operational practices. Digital democracy as the basis for consultation between the various agencies and the communities they serve, as well as for the integration of the community into these partnerships, plays a central role in this development (Williams, 2000b).

A new organisational framework replaces how the modernism responsible for establishing the modern state has prevailed over social planning and political practice. The will of the people was to be expressed not only as citizens, but also as voters within a pluralism that granted them a right to select their local representative who represented the political-economic positions of parties. As the source of reason they could transcend the lack of reason associated with the masses who voted for them. The parties are the source of rational debate *par excellence*. The state is subordinate to government and, thereby, to the party in power, becoming the administrative and legislative manifestation of the will of the 'nation'. It gives the threefold distinction of state/society/nation that is quite distinct from that of state/nation/individual or state/civil society/political society. In some cases the party dominates the state. In most cases it has assumed the state's capacity to both regulate internal affairs and to relate to other states, doing so on the basis of political philosophies involving different conceptions of the relevance of equality and its significance for the greater good and the good life. The parties represented social movements, and in this respect laid claim to being a manifestation of the will of the people who were locked into these social movements. Over time these parties have become institutionalised to the extent that they have become transformed into electoral agencies, no longer being capable of representing social movements and no longer representing a defence of any social project.

The crisis of representative democracy involves the profound decrease in participation, the cases where the majority of the citizenry sanctions representation becoming increasingly rare. One argument claims that the social bases of political life are enfeebled, or dislocated through the shift in the industrial base of a society that was dominated by the opposition between the employer and the employee. Most European societies pertain neither to the working class nor to the bourgeoisie, and the main defining condition of such societies are consumption and mass communication, social mobility and migration, the variety of mores and the defense of the environment. The industrial production upon which representative democracy was founded is irrelevant to such circumstances. Neo-liberalism shifts the debate on inequality away from social inequality and class analysis to exclusion.

It becomes impossible to base political life on debates and actors that do not correspond to present reality. Political parties have become teams of government from among which the electorate must choose. The collapsing of the political space between the main party protagonists undermines the rhetoric of public choice. It is not the necessary dependence of political forces in relation to social demands that is transformed, but their nature. The action of classes linked to relations of production cannot be disassociated. The 'objective' definition of the social actors has changed, without there being an associated shift in the necessary link between political choice and the interests or values of social actors defined by their position in the relations of power. Rather, the 'objective' definition of social actors gives the political parties the monopoly of the meaning of collective action. Once social action is defined as the revindication of freedom, defence of the environment, struggle against the commodification of all aspects of life and so on, there is a sense in which it becomes possible to impose priorities on a party that is reinforced by such issues.

A politics based around the relations of production involves the danger of reducing social actors into a mass, the electorate being constructed as an object that is no more than a political resource, subordinating social action to the political intervention where power pertains to 'The Party'. This reified 'Party' is constructed as an object with an identity and a life force which insists on perpetuity and allegiance. Local or regional issues are subordinated to this conception, and to how state power overlaps with the power of 'The Party'. It confirms the authoritarianism that democracy is meant to hold in check. Equating the interests of the state with those of the nation, again conceived of as a mass, involves parties which subordinated their action to the interests of the nation. These interests were constructed out of simple bases of identity, devoid of any sense of multiple identities. Minority language groups that occupy part of the state's territory are locked into a system which is of relevance to the totality of that territory and the population that occupies it. Herein lies the appeal of regional autonomy for minority language groups.

Globalisation and the mobility of capital undermines the ability of labour to mobilise and to be mobilised. The state is deprived of its regulatory capacity and the ability to express itself via a monolithic political philosophy through different conceptions of welfarism and social policy. The efficacy of the 'Party' is undermined and with it there appears a distantiation of the social subject.

The classical opposition between direct democracy or political self-management and representative regimes is in danger of collapse because the direct popular government which Rousseau conceived of has been associated with the political rationality of Enlightenment philosophy, where the interests of each one, and those of the integration of the collectivity, are associated with the state and its link to a single society. Representation introduced the separation of represented and representee, the distinction between demand and offer of the political market – between social and cultural demands and the functions of government. Universal suffrage and the working-class movement led this along the path of industrial democracy and social democracy. The role of political parties involved the claim that social struggle was the basis for political life. The mass parties established a correspondence between social interests and programmes of government, and the parties were permitted a central control of the electors over the elected, limited perhaps by the party heads. The subordination of the political to the social limits political power. Linked with this, the globalisation of the economy, involving the international system of production ruled by international markets, is distinct from the state political systems that speak in the names of their different 'nations', and which link with programmes of government. The later seeks to address the problems of particular groups and the life chances of individuals, whereas such issues are increasingly determined by the former. Does this lead to a new system of representation, or a democracy involving a new conception of participation to a new conception of the relationship between the state, political society and civil society?

Some claim that the state increasingly invades civil society so that it is destroyed by the state, which pretends to be in a direct relation with the people, or which presents itself as the direct expression of social demands. Also, the practices of political parties can organise the control of social groups by a party-state rather than by the free expression of popular demand. The direct relationship between the state and the social actors is impossible, making some form of autonomous political system essential. Democracy is the most coherent form of that system. Social demands must have priority over internal exigencies of government, or the 'play' of the political, but these demands tend to be formed by particular interest groups, resulting in a multiplicity of such groups that represent the general problems of social organisation. The weakening of the state leads to the political system entering the domain of the state in the name of civil society. Collective action in the form of political organization becomes a political resource used by the parties and their leaders.

Some system whereby participation increases and there is some semblance of control from within civil society over the political parties is essential. Individuals cannot engage with politics once every few years by voting for an individual they might not know, who espouses party politics, and who, if elected, enters Parliament only to be sidelined by the party leadership and the party machine, becoming little more than a glorified social worker, often for those who never even voted for him/her. The rolling back of the state, and the establishment of regional bodies, coincides with the demise of the modern state and the integration of the regions with a European dimension. The central state will continue to contest with Europe the right to determine the destiny of the regions, but this will involve the right to distribute funds allocated at the European centre by the European Parliament. Meso-government derives from such developments. It is also in response to such issues that the call for a new form of participatory rather than representative democracy derives.

5 From representative to participatory democracy

The history of democracy is the history of the struggle between the idea of direct democracy and that of representative democracy. The first seems to be popular and the later political, but the opposite is true. The definition of democracy as the power of the people subordinates the diversity of society to the unity of political power, making 'the people' a clumsy transcription in social terms, such that the theme of representation implies the priority and autonomy of social actors in relationship to political agents who are more or less directly submitted to their decisions. The idea of popular power has nourished many of the authoritarian ideologies, while representative democracy has not given political parties an autonomy which is transformed into independence and domination. Political parties are subordinate to related social movements.

How do we confront the relationship between the individual and direct democracy as a manifestation of the general will or the collective conscious-ness of a particular community without reverting to the culturally homoge-nising goal of the central, modern state which denies the will of diversity? Direct democracy should not be reduced to the strategies of minorities seeking to redress this tendency. A representative democracy linked to public liberties, and the recognition of the pluralism of opinions and interests, invokes suspicion that soliciting public opinion merely leads to opinion satisfying and the need for political parties to influence opinion formation. The tyranny of the majority and the subordination of local interests to party interests has undermined the faith of many in representative democracy. Political pluralism is currently receding as neo-liberalism drives political philosophies towards a common centre. The withdrawal of the majority of the public from participation in the formation of laws and rules of collective life and the protection of private life leads to a crisis of democracy. The nineteenth century was dominated by a search for both a social democracy and political democracy, leading to the inclusion of the excluded and to direct confrontation between employer and employed. The focus on class struggle contributed to ignoring the culturally homogenising influence of this form of democracy. The idea of popular sovereignty associated with the rights of man sought to limit the power of the state in the name of a principle superior to all social reality, giving pluralism a central importance and according minority rights as much importance as the government of the majority. Three ideas have therefore been central to democracy:

1 citizenship,
2 the limitation of power by the respect for fundamental human rights,
3 pluralist representation of interests and opinions.

Liberty insists on the plurality of interests, with solidarity being the concrete expression of citizenship. Citizenship as the principle of unity; representation as the principle of diversity; the complementarity of the appeal to a universalist principle; and the taking in charge of situations and of real social relationships relies on the idea of reason and homogeneity – thereby including a limited conception of diversity. It is threatened by state nationalism, the dictatorship of the proletariat, the subordination of the economy to the financial world, the inability of the state to effectively intervene in economics and social policy, and the hegemony of the state.

The complementarity of the citizen as a principle of unity and of representation as the principle of diversity have been operationalised on the assumption that the citizen carries a homogenous culture, but is socially variable. Representation involves how political parties represent different social interests. This constrains interests within politics, and excludes a politics of diversity by relegating it to the world of the non-rational, of the emotional. Emphasising the inclusion of women or minorities among the representees does not extend representative democracy beyond the social basis out of which it is constructed.

Subordinating the state to the market is disturbing. Neo-liberalism derives from two distinctive lines of late eighteenth-century liberalism. One focused upon liberty, asking which is the most effective means of delivering it. It contrasts with a liberalism that focused upon pity and compassion. The first was associated with the American Declaration of Rights, and the second with European liberalism. It is the first that predominates in the current neo-liberal focus, asking how the individual or the community can be enabled to fend for itself rather than relying on welfare dependency. It lacks an ethical dimension and focuses upon a mechanical efficiency, having little to do with reducing inequality. Engaging with participatory democracy rather than focusing upon responsibility and accountability requires an ethical dimension. Democracy must have an ethical base. Currently, the ethical rests in the community, and the regional authority, where it exists, provides a technical response to these ethics, the central state setting out the general principles of governance and relating to international relations. Participatory democracy becomes little more than the means of facilitating the operation of the ethical community. If the community is the unit of accountability, it must have a role in governance and must be appropriately empowered. Community is currently seen as a regional rather than local entity, and even as an ill-defined amalgamation of shared interests or activities.

Within the neo-liberal discourse there is the danger that the citizen becomes nothing more than a person enabled by a state which fails to deliver guarantees that derive from responsibility. Democracy is premised on both the idea of liberty and the collective capacity for action. It is not possible to separate liberty from responsibility, so there must be some accountability to the people. This accountability resides not with the party or the state, but with the elected representative. S/he is accountable to all the residents of the constituency, whether they voted for her or not. This responsibility is controlled via hierarchical party management that is anathema to the concept of democracy. It begs the question of the relationship between an elected regional body that is dominated by a single party and a central government dominated by a different party. Sovereignty will prevail, but accountability will not! To what extent should responsibility for decision making involve the people? Do we resort to a context in which the state withdraws from resolving the crisis of society by reverting responsibility to the individual as a form of individualism that is indifferent to public affairs, but reinforces the intervention of social actors in public life? The self-responsibility of the individual, would constitute a new form of governmentality.

A conception that allows the individual to regard the political process and with it a politics of observation, is emerging. It contrasts with the current focus on liberty and the form of government that can guarantee this liberty. Politics moves away from action to observation, linked to a total accountability. Information and communication technology (ICT) allows the breakdown of space, allowing all of us 'to be there', collapsing the distinction between 'here' and 'there', obliging us to take in charge the distance between them. Politics ceases to be a spectacle and becomes an engagement. One of the specific tasks of modern politics was the unification of territory by putting 'durable institutions' in place that can create an equivalence between 'local' situations in time and space. The extreme of this was the welfare state.

To be structural, the local must be representative – what happens in one locality can happen in another. However, the level of action or the political focus shifts from the state to the region, leading to interregional rivalry and competition over resources. This operates within a context of fair play and effectiveness – the most efficient region wins the prize. The region must be treated as a collective person, which means that it must be disassociated from the other collective person – the state.

Democracy is the discursive and argumentative processes of forming a common will (Habermas, 1996). The impetus shifts to the surveillance of the institutions and rights by the citizens. Representativity, and the associated responsibility, must be linked with a new form of accountability. Yet it is equally likely that the time of representativity as constructed by modernity is ending, and that it will be replaced by a democracy constructed out of participation. ICT allows the electorate to be part of the debate rather than to dispatch a representative. The closed corridors of politics can be open fields. We can show how this is possible, but cannot dictate what the nature of this democracy should be. Yet neither do I believe that this should be the prerogative of those who currently hold power.

6 Conclusion

The shift in economic organisation since the 1980s has involved a series of changes in the mode of enterprise management, and a 'new spirit of capitalism' that conveys a new general presentation of the economic world is developing (Boltanski and Chiapello, 1999). The shift in the discourse on regional development is from a focus upon neoclassical, macroeconomic principles to a distinctive, multidisciplinary focus on human capital and ICT. The abstract market is replaced by social networks linked to shared meaning in social partnerships. The focus on tacit knowledge queries the relevance of the rational human subject. Institutional behaviour rather than the rationality of optimisation within reified markets conditions economic behaviour. The focus encompasses regional enterprise clustering as a community. New models of the enterprise and of wealth creation are emerging.

The state-driven, or command, economics yields to interactive relationships and an openness replaces the rule-driven thrust of modernist planning, encompassing the possibility that different regions will develop in different ways, with the focus on diversity, and a move away from linear trajectories and uniform progression of the modernist link between development and progress. The change in the social consciousness of a community is to be achieved through negotiation and institution construction. The focus is on supply-side measures such as the circulation of information, training and skill formation, knowledge-transfer network formation, the integration of supply chains between enterprises, and the use of effective support systems for innovative action.

The promotion of liberalisation; the rolling back of the state from a direct, interventionist role in favour of market mechanisms; privatisation and the parallel reduction in the centrality of the public sector – all draw on the need for community as the locus of responsibility and accountability. This is both an opportunity and a threat for minority language groups. Those groups which have established a presence and a legitimacy in the public sector may find this foothold undermined, while the solidaristic nature of communities structured out of language and culture could be activated. Language and speakers must be constructed by reference to an openness that involves autonomous channels of communication with the centre. If states recognise the value of such communities, and if they have the courage and confidence to use the technology to develop a truly participatory democracy, the probability of the basis for Europe's diversity surviving will be enhanced.

Some postmodernists persist with the evolutionary principles of modernism in opposing a politics of rational interest with 'tribal loyalties' (Bauman, 1992). It betrays an allegiance to the state which prevents the including of autochthony as a territorial entity – the state is the only, exclusive territorial entity, and the source of reason. The ethnic group, life-style or a way of life is cast in opposition to this as the realm of the emotional. How these concerns are capable of mingling with 'traditional modern politics' is questioned. Bauman (2000:176) express a disdain of *'ethnos'* by claiming that it involves an exclusivity within which the 'us'/'them' distinction exerts a form of closure that inhibits choice, the very limitation which the coercion of the state as the corner-stone of reason and order has placed upon minority language groups, precluding many from survival, let alone from determining the terms of closure. Linked with a denigration constructed out of difference, and the blaming of the victim for that difference, this coercion becomes the converse of a democracy premised upon freedom. In Luhmann's (1998) terms, the action of the victim must involve *autopoiesis* or self creation. An enlightened politics would couple the potential for sustained diversity with the possibility of inclusion of everyone within that diversity.

The dissolution of evolutionism, the faith in inevitable progress, and the demise of historical teleology question the discourse on democracy. The distinction between modern and tradition disappears. Durkheim's claim about freedom involving the individual submitting to society as the condition of her liberation, with society constituting the intelligent force which protects the individual, is questioned once the link between the state and society is put in jeopardy. The faith in reason flounders when considering language and reason, leading to questioning the entire edifice of modernism. Claims about progress involve a vision of the future. Discursively this involves constructing the future with the enunciative positions of the understanding of the present. It involves modalities in the sense that there is an attitude on the part of the universal *enonciateur* towards the future. Also challenged are the subjects and objects which are implicated in the certainty associated with 'progress'. The link between reason and progress was premised upon specific relations between particular subjects and objects, to the exclusion of other subjects and objects. A stake in 'progress', and the associated rewards, was available only to those subjects who coexisted with the relevant objects. Conformity with the normative was essential. Questioning this results in 'the end of definition of the human being as a social being, defined by his or her place in society which determines his or her behaviour and actions.' (Touraine, 1997:368). Denying the inevitability of progress does not mean that progress is not conceivable, but that a world which is 'centrally organised, rigidly bounded, and hysterically concerned with impenetrable boundaries' (Jowitt, 1992:306) has shifted. The link between subjects and objects proclaims the centrality of agency, which is now destabilised. Neither is normativity denied for existence cannot be devoid of a sense of discursive stability, giving the relationship between subjects and objects a sense of continuity. Rather, it is a matter of releasing the normative from narrow constraints, so that diversity and tolerance become a feature of normative order. It involves a retreat from what Bauman (2000:25) calls 'The totalitarian society of all-embracing, compulsory and enforced homogeneity . . . the sworn enemy of contingency, variety, ambiguity, waywardness and idiosyncrasy . . . .'

Democracy is constructed out of reason and progress. The weakening of the pillars raises questions about how the discourse of democracy has emasculated minority language groups to ensure that the constructed normative order proclaims its superiority. The state as guarantor of progress for the internal, homogeneous nation as collectivity is increasingly at the mercy of global capital. In its place the individual is increasingly responsible for her own destiny, for her own planning and progress. This opens the space for new alignments for subjects and objects within the modalities of certainty. Yet the certainty that links to order is no longer the domain of the state, but is a global order, defined, protected and preserved by what increasingly comes to resemble a global legal force, and a narrow and dogmatic conception of 'democracy'. The weakening of the state opens the space for different levels of 'us' and 'them' in the quest of a unity constructed out of difference and diversity.

The New Economy gives compelling reasons for merging language planning (LP) and regional development. LP can no longer be the residual activity of those interested in sustaining language for emotional reasons, but becomes part of the process of sustaining the very resources which any knowledge economy depends upon. The constitutive elements of minority language groups provide a value for everyone in Europe, not merely those who share the relevant language and culture. It is this transformation that will insure their reproduction.

To create is to challenge the normative, the orthodox. The presence of fixed meaning is broken, the challenge of ambivalence and ambiguity, the very essence of language is accepted. This is the challenge of diversity, to accept the conditions that allow new meanings to derive from linguistic diversity, not necessarily in the name of progress, but in the name of democracy and freedom. Only then can the individual take in charge the meanings that condition their lives.

Appendix: Scales

Cultural reproduction

4 Full range of TV and radio available, produced at home or cross-frontier; daily newspaper/s; large number of new books every year (>1 title per 5000 speakers).
3 Full range of radio available and some TV programmes, produced at home or cross-frontier; bilingual daily newspaper; considerable number of books (>1 title per 10000 speakers).
2 Some radio programmes, a little TV daily, a few magazines, fair number of books (>1 title per 15000 speakers).
1 Occasional books, virtually no TV, less than 10 hours per week radio coverage; small number of books (>1 title per 20000 speakers).
0 No magazines, no radio in L; language not written in accepted form.

Family

4 Virtually all young families speak their language (L) with offspring as do most L-speakers in mixed families.
3 Some young families speak their language with offspring, but mainly the older generation; a few L-speakers in mixed families also use L.
2 Only about a half of families speak L with offspring, mainly the older generation.
1 Only a minority of families speak L with offspring, mainly older people; people have heard grandparents speak the language.
0 Virtually no families, except for the very old, use L in the family.

Community

4 L is freely used by L-speakers in the community in most kinds of social activities, including formal and informal associations throughout the country. There is widespread use of L in the neighbourhood.
3 L is used by L-speakers in the community in some kinds of social activities, including formal and informal associations in most of the country. A large number of L2-speakers claim to have learned the L in the local community.
2 Some of the civil organisations use L in their activities, including in their own bulletin; L can be heard fairly frequently in the street.
1 Little use of L in the community, restricted to informal social networks.
0 The L is hardly ever used in public by anyone, no civil organisations use it. Older people remember its use in their youth.

Prestige

4 Knowledge of L is very often a job requirement in both the public and private sectors (media, education, public service, receptionists, salesmen, . . .); L is widely used by firms in their dealings with the public.

3 Some jobs require a knowledge of L, mainly in the public sector; L is quite widely used by firms in their dealings with the public; L-speakers tend to earn similar salaries to non-L speakers.

2 Very few jobs require a knowledge of L and only in the public sector; L-speakers tend to hold less well paid jobs than non-L speakers.

1 L is only used in a few marginal and traditional professions.

0 Knowledge of L is never a job requirement.

Institutionalisation

4 In most contexts the use of L is taken for granted by almost everyone as being normal and unmarked.

3 In some contexts its use is taken for granted by most people as being normal and unmarked.

2 In a few specific contexts its use is regarded by most people as being acceptable.

1 Its use is always regarded as marked and deliberate.

0 In virtually no contexts, except perhaps for the most informal ones, is its use regarded as being acceptable.

Education

4 All or nearly all schoolchildren in the L-speaking areas receive most of the main subjects in their pre-schooling and primary and secondary education through L, and future teachers are trained appropriately; in the demographically larger communities many university courses also use it.

3 There are some L-medium bilingual pre-schools and primary and secondary schools, though not throughout the territory , and L is a compulsory subject in all schools.

2 L-medium and/or bilingual instruction at the pre-school and primary level is available in some parts of the territory. It is taught in most schools as a compulsory subject.

1 L is a voluntary subject in many primary schools, but is not compulsory. There are some voluntary evening or Sunday classes.

0 L is not taught in schools.

Legitimation

4 L has a legal status which defines language rights. Central government bodies in the area use it. Regional and local authorities have it as their usual L. It can be used in the courts. There is an official language policy and a language planning (LP) organisation to promote its use..

3 L has an official status which enables language to be used. Regional and/or most local authorities in the area have a language policy and use it to some extent. It can be used in the courts under certain conditions. Quasi-official LP organisations promote its use.

2 L has an official status, but lacks the necessary implementation structures to translate status into use. There is some symbolic use of it by some authorities (bilingual speeches, place names, . . .).

1 L does not have an official status, nor is allowance made for it in social policy.

0 Social policy offers a disincentive to the language

Notes

1 Conceptualisation, data and method

1. By the same token, for most, a language is nothing other than the homogeneity of a system for all speakers.
2. This is only too evident in the Council of Europe's 'Project for a Regional and Minority Language Charter' which, after clarifying its goal, proceeds to claim that its intention is to '. . . organise the protection and the promotion of languages and not of linguistic minorities' (Quoted in Balibar, 1993:102).

2 Legitimation

1. This composition and the rules which regulate it obviously have implications for the two in opposing factions in the Slovene language group. The advisory board of the Federal Chancellery thus consists of the Catholic Church, the political parties at the state level which have seats in the regional parliament, and the two Slovene groups – ZSO and NSKS. Its function is merely consultative. However, it is the Federal Chancellery which funds Slovene activities to the tune of about €0.5m, which is only half of the level of support given by the Slovene government.
2. In this section I draw heavily upon O'Riagain and Tovey (1998).
3. Recently this structure has been revised to accommodate cross-border partnership.
4. An elaboration of this section can be found in Williams and Morris, 2000.

3 Education

1. An exception in this respect is O'Riagain, 1997.
2. It is only in Portugal, Ireland and Italy that more than 40 per cent of those who take initial degrees in the natural sciences and/or mathematics are women. In none of the member states are women more than 20 per cent of those who take degrees in engineering, architecture or transport.
3. This section draws on Eurydice, 1990 and 1994; and Vaniscotte, 1989.

4 Reproduction: family community and household media use

1. For a discussion of this issue, see Williams, 1999a.
2. An interesting account of how the sociological meta-discourse has discussed family and the community can be found in Elias and Scotson, 1994: 182–6.
3. This opposition is developed in Williams, 1992a.
4. How Breton regional identity is signified more by music and dance than by language is also true of Ireland. It involves the undoing of the nineteenth-century focus on the standardisation of music and dance as classical. As the belief in the superiority of High Culture declines, regions free themselves from this straight-jacket.

6 Institutionalisation of language use

1. A critique of Bourdieu's work from the position I adopt can be found in Williams and Morris, 2000.
2. These language use surveys can be found at: www.uoc.edu/euromosaic.
3. At the time of writing a Breton language television channel had started operation, broadcasting 17 hours of Breton daily.
4. A criticism of the domain concept argues that it is not so much the partition of language use by domains that is at stake, but the opportunity to use that language (Williams, 1992b).
5. In developing Figure 6.1 the scores have been rearranged by classifying 'neither agree nor disagree' as 0, with the disagreement scores being ranked as negative scores and the agreement scores as positive scores. Second, the statements have been arranged so that the direction of the evaluation is similar for all statements. Third, the instrumental scores consist of the sum of the scores for items 1, 5, 8, 9, and 11, while the status scores consist of the sum of the scores for items 2, 4, 6, 7 and 10.
6. Wherever possible an attempt is made to focus on similar issues to those discussed above. The two sets of data are related in the evaluation exercise of the next chapter.

7 Data evaluation

1. The clusters are based on arbitrary boundaries rather than on any statistical cluster analysis.

8 Diversity and democracy

1. *Baragouiner* derives from how Breton destitute were forced on to the streets in France to beg, and, not speaking French, sought pity in their mother tongue asking for 'bara' (bread) and 'gwin' (wine).

Bibliography

Aarbakke, V. (2001). *The Turkish Minority of Thrace, Greece*. Unpublished Ph.D. Thesis, University of Bergen.

Achard, P. (1982a). En finir avec la Francophonie. *Tiers Monde*. Vol. xxiii, No. 90, April–June, pp. 419–22.

Achard, P. (1982b). 'Sociologie du Développement' ou Sociologie du 'Développment'. *Révue Tiers Monde*. Vol. xxiii, No. 90, pp. 257–78.

Achard, P. (1988). The Development of Language Empires. In U. Ammon, N. Ditmar et al. eds. *Sociolinguistics: A Handbook*. Vol. 2, Berlin, de Gruyter, pp. 1541–51.

Achard, P. (1993). *La Sociologie du langage*. Paris, PUF.

Achard, P. (n.d.). *Linguistique et sciences sociales: Après le structuralisme*. Unpublished paper.

Aikio, P. and H. J. Hyrvarinen (1995). A Review of Finnish Legislation on the Sami in 1993. In E. Gayim and K. Myntti eds. *Indigenous and Tribal People's Rights – 1993 and After*. Rovaniemi, University of Lapland.

Aikio, S., U. Aikio-Puoskari and J. Helander (1994). *The Sami Culture in Finland*, Helsinki, Lapin Sivistysseura.

Aixpurua, Xavier (1995). *Euskaren Jarraipena*. Vitoria, Eusko Jaurlaritzaren Argitalpen-Zerbitzu Nagusia.

Alcaraz Ramos, M. (1999). *El pluralismo lingüístico en la Constitución Española*. Madrid, Congreso de los Diputados.

Alexander, J. C. (1998). Bifurcating Discourses. In J. C. Alexander ed. *Real Civil Societies*. London, Sage, pp. 96–115.

Althusser, L. (1976). *Positions*. Paris, Éditions Sociales.

Ar Mogn, O. and M. Stuijt (1998). *Breton: The Breton Language in Education in France*. Ljouwert, Mercator-Education.

Aracil, L. (1983). *Dir la Realitat*. Barcelona, Paisos Catalans.

Arendt, H. (1967). *Essai sur la Révolution*. Paris, Gallimard.

Arendt, H. (1968). Imperialism. In *The Origins of Totalitarianism*. Vol. ii. San Diego, Harcourt, Brace and Jovanich.

Areny, M. and A. Van Der Schaaf (2000). *Catalan, The Catalan Language in Education in Catalonia, Spain*. Ljouwert, Fryske Akademy.

Aufschnaiter, W. (1994). Die Sicherung des Rechts auf Gebrauch der Muttersprache in der Verwaltung in Sudtirol. In W. Holzer and U. Proll eds. *Mit Sprachen leben: praxis der Mehrsprachigkeit*. Klagenfurt, Cedvoc.

Auroux, S. (1994). *La révolution technologique de la grammatisation*. Paris, Mardaga.

Austrian Centre for Ethnic Groups (ACEG) (1994). *Austria Ethnica: State and Perspectives*. Vol. 7, Vienna, ACEG.

Austrian Centre for Ethnic Groups (ACEG) (1996). *Ethnic Group Report*. Vienna, ACEG.

Baggioni, Daniel (1997). *Langues et Nations en Europe*. Paris, Payot.

Bagnasco, A. and M. Oberti (1998). Italy: 'le trompe-l'oeil' of regions. In P. Le Gales and C. Lequesne eds. *Regions in Europe*. London, Routledge.

Balibar, R. (1985). *Institution du Français*. Paris, PUF.

Balibar, R. (1993). *Le Colinguisime*. Paris, PUF.

Basque Regional Government (1989). *Soziolinguitikazko Mapa I.* Vitoria, Eusko Jaurlaritzaren Argitalpen-Zerbitzu Nagusia.

Basque Regional Government (1996). *Soziolinguitikazko Mapa II.* 3 Vols, Vitoria, Eusko Jaurlaritzaren Argitalpen-Zerbitzu Nagusia.

Bauer, R. (1999). *Sprachsoziologische Studien zur Mehrsprachigkeit im Aostatal.* Tubingen, Niemeyer.

Bauman, Z. (1987). *Legislators and Interpreters: On Modernity, Post-modernity and Intellectuals.* Oxford, Polity.

Bauman, Z. (1992). *Postmodern Ethics.* Oxford, Blackwell.

Bauman, Z. (2000). *Liquid Modernity.* Oxford, Polity.

Baumgartner, G. (2001). *Croatian: The Croatian Language in Austria.* Ljouwert, Fryske Akademy.

Bauske, B. (1998). *Planificación lingüística del asturiano.* Gijon, VTP.

Becat, J. (2000). *La situacio del catala a Franca: aspectes juridic i docents i estudis sobre la materia.* Barcelona, IEC.

Beck, U. (1986). *Risk Society.* Cambridge, Polity.

Berlin, I. (1999). *The Roots of Romanticism.* Princeton University Press.

Bernal, M. (1987). *Black Athena: The Afroasiatic Roots of Classical Civilisation. Vol. 1: The Fabrication of Ancient Greece, 1785–1985.* New Brunswick, Rutgers University Press.

Berthoumieus, M. and A. Willemsma (1997). *Occitan.* Ljouwert, Fryske Akademy.

Boltanski, L. (1984). *Prime education et morale de classe.* Paris, EHESS.

Boltanski, L. (1993). *La Souffrance à distance.* Paris, Metailie.

Boltanski, L. and E. Chiapello (1999). *Le Nouvel Espirit du Capitalisme,* Paris, Gallimard.

Boltanski, L. and L. Thevenot (1991). *De la Justificacion. Les Économies de la Grandeur.* Paris, Gallimad.

Bonacich, E. (1972). A Theory of Ethnic Antagonism: The Split Labour Market. *American Sociological Review,* 37. 547–59.

Bonald, Louis de (1985). *Demonstration philosophique du principe constitutif de la société.* Paris, Vrin.

Bossuyt, Marc. (1975). La distinction juridique entre les droits civils et politique et les droits économiques, sociaux et culturels. *Révue des droits de l'homme,* Vol. 8. pp. 783–820.

Bourdieu, P. (1982). *Ce que parler veut dire.* Paris, Fayard.

Boutet, J. (1994). *Construir le sens.* Paris, Lang.

Bouzada, X. M. and A. M. Lorenzo Suarez (1997). *O Futuro da Lingua: Elementos Socio-linguísticos para un Achegamento Prospectivo da Lingua Galega.* Santiago de Compostelo, Conselo da Cultura Galega.

Broudic, F. (2000). Le Breton. *TILV,* No. 27. pp. 53–8.

Busch, B. (1998). *Slovenian. The Slovenian Language in Education in Austria.* Ljouwert, Fryske Akademy.

Busquet, J. and J. Sort (1999). Communication, Minority Languages, and the Information Society: Steps for the Competitive Cooperation (Cooptition) of the Catalan Audio-Visual Sector. In G. Williams ed. *Towards an Integrated European Minority Language Television Service.* Report submitted to DGXIII (Contract: 98–06-AUT-0092-00) August 1999.

Calvet, L. J. (1974). *Linguistique et Colonialisme.* Paris, Payot.

Calvet, L. J. (1987). *La guerre des langues et les politiques linguistiques.* Paris, Payot.

Carrithers, M., S. Collins and S. Lukes eds (1985). *The Category of the Person*. Cambridge University Press.

Carrozza, P. (1992). Situation juridique des minorites en Italie. In H. Giordan ed. *Les Minorites en Europe*. Paris, Ki me, pp. 215–33.

Cenoz, J. (2001). Basque in Spain and France. In G. Extra and D. Goerter eds. *The Other Languages of Europe*. Clevedon, Multilingual Matters.

Chambers, J. K. and P. Trudgill (1980). *Dialectology*. Cambridge University Press.

Chauvel, L. (1995). L'Europe des régions? Valeurs régionales et nationales en Europe. *Futuribles*, 54.

Chistiansen, E. M. and A. Teebken eds (2001). *Living Together: The Minorities in the German-Danish Border Regions*. Flensburg, ECMI.

Christopoulos, D. and C. Tsitseilikis eds (1997). *The Minority Phenomenon in Greece*. Athens, Kritiki.

Costas, X.-H. (2001). *Galician: The Galician Language in Education in Spain*. Ljouwert, Fryske Akademy.

Dahrendorf, R. (1974). Citizenship and Beyond: The Social Dynamics of an Idea. *Social Research*, Vol. 41, No. 4. pp. 673–701.

Denney, D., J. Borland and R. Fevre (1992). Nationalism and Community in North-West Wales. *Sociological Review*, 1. 49–72.

Descartes, R. (1970). *Descartes: Philosophical Writings*. London, Nelson.

Descartes, R. (1979). *The World*. Trans. M. S. Mahoney. New York, Abaris.

Donzelot, J. (1984). *L'Invention du Social*. Paris, Minuit.

Donzelot, J. (1991). The Mobilization of Society. In G. Burchell, C. Gordon and P. Miller eds. *The Foucault Effect: Studies in Governmentality*. Hemel Hempstead, Harvester, pp. 169–74.

Durkheim, E. (1912). *Les forms élémentaire de la vie réligieuse*. Paris, Alcan.

Durkheim, E. (1979). *Essays on Morals and Education*. RKP, London, (ed. W. S. F. Pickering).

Dworkin, R. M. (1977). *Taking Rights Seriously*. London, Duckworth.

Egger, K. and M. L. McLean (2001). *Dreisprachig werden in Groden*. Bolzano, Institut Pedagogich Ladin.

Ela, L. (2000). Die heutige situation der sorbsichen sprache und konzepte zu ihre revitalisierung. In Serbski Institut eds. *Zdzer enje rewitalizacija a wuwiaee mjen inowych rieow*. Serbski Institut.

Elias, N. (1991). *The Symbol Theory*. London, Sage.

Elias, N. and J. L. Scotson (1994). *The Established and the Outsiders*. Sage, London.

Elle, L. (1995). *Sprachenpolitik in der Lausitz. Eine Dokumentation 1949–1989*. Bauzen, Domowina.

EURYDICE (1990). *Structure of the Education and Initial Training Systems in the Member States of the EC*. Brussels, Eurydice.

EURYDICE (1994). *Organisation of School Time in the Member States of the EC*. Brussels, Eurydice.

European Commission (1996). *EUROMOSAIC: The Production and Reproduction of the Minority Language Groups in the European Union*. Luxembourg, OOPEC.

European Parliament (2002). *The European Union and Lesser-Used Languages*. Brussels, DG Research, Education and Culture Series.

Farras, J., J. Torres and F. Xavier Vila (2000). El coneixement del catala. 1996. Mapa Sociolinguístic de Catalunya. Analisi de l'enquesta oficial de poblacio de 1996. *Serie Estudis 7*. Barcelona, Generalitat de Catalunya.

Febvre, L. et al. (1930). *Civilisation, le môt et l'idée*. Paris, Le Rénaissance du Livre.

Fehlen, F. et al. (n.d.) *Le Sondage 'Baleine': Une étude sociologique sur les trajectories migratoires, les langues et la vie associative au Luxembourg*. Luxembourg, Recherche Etude Documentation, Hors Serie, 1.

Fereira, M. B. (1999). Licao de Mirandes. In F. Fernandez Rei e A. Santamarina eds. *Estudios de Sociolinguística Romanica. Linguas e variedades minorizadas*. Santiago, University of Santiago de Compostella, pp. 133–53.

Foucault, M. (1966). *Les Môts et les choses*. Paris, Gallimard.

Foucault, M. (1969). *The Archaeology of Knowledge*. New York, Random House.

Foucault, M. (1972). *Folie et déraison: Histoire de la folie a l'age classique*. 2nd edn, Paris, Gallimard.

Foucault, M. (1991). Governmentality. In G. Burchell, C. Gordon and P. Miller eds. *The Foucualt Effect: Studies in Governmentality*. Chicago, University of Chicago Press.

Friedman, V. (1997). Macedonian. In Goebl et al. eds. *Kontaktlinguistik Ein Internationales Handbüch zeitgenössischer Forschung*. Berlin and New York, de Gruyter. pp. 1442–50.

Fusina, J. (1999). Media audio-visuel el langue locale: le cas du corse. In: n.a. *Bretagne et peuples d'Europe. Mélanges a Per Dennez*. Rennes.

Fusina, J. (2000). *Corsican: The Corsican Language in Education in France*. Ljouwert, Fryske Akademy.

Gaffard, J. L., S. Bruno, C. Longhi and M. Quere (1993). *Cohérence et diversité des systêmes d'innovation en Europe*. FAST, Brussels: EU.

Gardner, N. (2000). *The Basque Language in Education in Spain*. Leouwert, Fryske Akademy.

Garcia Negro, M. P. (2000). *Dereitos Linguísticos e Control Politico*. Santiago, Ediciónes Laiovento.

Gargallo, J. E. (1999). Unha Encrucillada pirenaica: a variedade occitana do Val d'Aran. In F. Ferandez Rei and A. Santamarina Fernandez eds. *Estudios de Sociolinguística Romanica*. Santiago, University of Santiago de Compostella Press.

Generalitat de Catalunya (n.d.). *L'us de la Llengua Catalana a les Empreses de Catalunya*. Barcelona, Dpto. De Cultura.

Generalitat de Catalunya (1978). *Els Sistems Delectius A Europa: Elements per a Una Descirpcio*. Barcelona, Generalitat de Catalunya.

Generalitat Valenciana (1992). *Enquesta sobre l'us del Valencia*. Valencia.

Giddens, A. (1994). *Beyond Left and Right*. Cambridge, Polity.

Giordan, H. (1992). *Les Minorités en Europe*. Paris, Kime.

Gonzales Riano, Xose A (2002). *Asturian: The Asturian Language in Education in Spain*. Ljouwert, Fryske Akademy.

Gordon, C. (1991). Governmental Rationality: An Introduction. In C. Gordon and P. Miller eds. *The Foucault Effect: Studies in Governmentality*. Hemel Hempstead, Harvester.

Gorter, D. et al. (1984). *Language in Frysland*. Ljouwers, Fryske Akademy.

Gorter, D. and R. J. Jonkma (1995). *Taal Yn Fryslan*. Ljouwert, Fryske Akademy.

Govern Balear (1988). *La Lengua de las Islas Baleares*. Palma, Institut Balear D'Estadistica.

Gramsci, A. (1978). *Selections from Prison Notebooks*. Lawrence & Wishart, London.

Grin, F. (1999). *Compétences et récompenses: La valuer des langues en Suisse*. Friboug University Press.

Habermas, J. (1996). An Interview with Jürgen Habermas. *Theory, Culture and Society*, Vol. 13, No. 3, 1–17.

Harre, R. (1986). *The Social Construction of Emotions*. Oxford, Blackwell.

Hegel, G. W. F. (1971). *The Philosophy of Right*. Oxford University Press.

Hemminga, P. (2001). *Sorbian: The Sorbian Language in Education in Germany*. Ljouwert, Fryske Akademy.

Heraud, G. (1982). Les Slovenes d'Autriche et d'Italie. *Language Planning and Language Problems*, Vol. 4, No. 2, pp. 137–53.

Herder, J. G. von (1966). *Essays on the Origins of Language*. Trans. J. H. Morou and A. Gode. University of Chicago Press.

Hirvonen, V. (1995). The Sami People in Finland. In n.a. *Cultural Minorities in Finland*. Heslinki, Unesco Commission, p. 66.

Hobsbawn, E. (1992). *Nations and Nationalism, since 1780: Programme, Myth, Reality*. Cambridge University Press.

Hollander, R. K. and T. Steensen eds (1991). *Friesen und Sorben: Beitrage zu einer Tagung unber zwei Minderheiten in Deutscheland*. Bredstedt, Braist.

Hudlett, A. (2000). Le bilingualisme français/allemande en Alsace. *TILV*, No. 27, pp. 32–5.

Hut, A. (2001). *Cornish: The Cornish Language in Education in the UK*. Ljouwert, Fryske Akademy.

Jennings, H. (1991). *De huidige situatie von her Duitstalig gebied in Belgie*. Vortraksmanuskript.

Jowitt, K. (1992). *New World Disorder*. Berkeley, University of California Press.

Kahl, T. (1999). Ethnizitat und raumliche Verteilung des Aromunen in Sudosteuropa. *Munstersche Geographische Arbetien*, 43.

Kant, I. (1946). *What is Enlightenment? Introduction to Contemporary Civilisation in the West*. Vol. I, Columbia University Press, New York.

Kattenbusch, D. (1996). Ladinien. In R. Hinderling and L. M. Eichinger eds. *Handbüch der mitteleuropaische Sprach minderheiten*. Tubingen, Narr, pp. 311–34.

Kloss, H. (1967). Abstand Languages and Ausbau Languages. *Anthropological Linguistics*, 9, pp. 29–41.

Kostopolos, T. (2000). *The Forbidden Language*. Athens, Black List.

Kymlicka, W. (1996). *Multicultural Citizenship: A Liberal Theory of Minority Rights*. Oxford, Clarendon.

Lainio, J. (2001). *Meankieli and Sweden Finnish: The Finnic languages in Education in Sweden*. Ljouwert, Fryske Akademy.

Ledo Andion, M. (1997). *Television e Interculturalidade en Bretana, Galicia e Pais de Gales*. Santiango de Compostela, University of Santiago Press.

Ledo Andion, M. (1999). Galicia. In G. Williams ed. *Towards an Integrated European Minority Language Television Service*. Report Presented to EC, Brussels (contract no: 98-06-AUT-0092-00).

Lenoble-Pinson, M. (1997). Grandeur et misère du plurilinguisme en Belgique. In N. Labrie, ed. *Etudes récentes en linguistique de contact*. Bonn, Dummler, pp. 240–9.

Liebkind, K., R. Broo and F. Finnas (1995). The Swedish-Speaking Minority in Finland: A Case Study. In J. Pentikainen and M. Hitunen eds. *Cultural Minorities in Finland*. Helsinki, Finnish National Commission for UNESCO, pp. 48–84.

Losurdo, D. (1992). La 'philosophie allemande' entre les idéologies, 1789–1848. *Genesis*, 9, pp. 60–92.

Luhmann, N. (1998). *Observations on Modernity*. Stanford, CA, Stanford University Press.

Luna, C. E da Cruz (2001). *O ensino do Portuges em Olivenca*. Unpublished m.s.

Macherey, P. (1992). Aux sources des rapports sociaux: Bonald, Saint-Simon, Guizot. *Genesis*, 9. pp. 25–44.

Mari, I. (1991). La Politica Linguística de la Generalitat de Catalunya. In I. Mari and I. Castell eds. *Processos de normalizacio linguística: l'extensio d'us social i la normalizacio*. Barcelona.

Marin, M. J. (1996). Language Planning in the Valencian Autonomous Community. In M. Nic Craith ed. *Watching One's Tongue: Aspects of Romance and Celtic Language*s. Liverpool, Liverpool University Press.

Marteel, J.-L. (2000). Le flamand dialectal du nord de la France. *TILV*, No. 27. pp. 72–5.

Martinez, M. (2004). *Catala en Arago*. Calaceit, Associacio Cultural de Matarranya.

Marx, K. (1976). *Capital*. Vol. I (Trans. B. Fowkes), Penguin, Harmondsworth.

McLeod, J. et al. (1996). Community Integration, Local Media Use and the Democratic Process. *Communication Research*, Vol. 23, No. 2, pp. 179–209.

Milner, J. C. (1978). *L'amour de la langue*. Paris, Seuil.

Modeen, T. (1995). The Cultural Rights of the Swedish minority in Finland. In S. Gustavsson and H. Runblom eds. *Language, Minority, Migration*. University of Uppsala Press.

Moll, A. (1994). L'amenagement linguistique aux Iles Balears. In P. Martel and J. Maurais eds. *Langues et Sociétés en contact. Mélanges offerts a Jean-Claude Corbeil*. Tubingen, Niemeyer, pp. 95–106.

Montgomery, C. (1998). *Fragmented Voices: Language, Community and Rights*. Unpublished Ph.D. Thesis. Université de Montréal.

Myntti, K. (1997). *Suomen Saamelaisten Yhteiskunnallinen Osallistuminen ja Kultuuuuri – Itsehallinto*. Helsinki, Hakapino Oy.

Nagore Lain, F. (1998). *Los Territorios linguísticos en Aragon. Seminario sobre normalización linguística de las lenguas minoritarias en Aragon*. Vol. 3.

Ogris, T. and T. Domej eds (1998). *Landesschulrat fur Karnten*. Klagenfurt.

Ostern, A. L. (1997). *Swedish, The Swedish Language in Education in Finland*. Ljouwert, Fryske Akademy.

O'Murchu, H. (2001). *Irish: The Irish Language in Education in the Republic of Ireland*. Ljouwert, Fryske Akademy.

O'Riagain, P. (1997). *Language Policy and Social Reproduction: Ireland 1893–1993*. Oxford, Clarendon Press.

O'Riagain, P. and H. Tovey (1998). Language Use Surveys in the Language Planning Process: Ireland. In G. Williams ed. *Language Planning in a European Context*. Final Report presented to DGXXII. (Project No: 97-06-NOR0040-00).

Pecheux, M. (1982). Sur le '(de)-construction des théories linguistique. *DRLAV*, No. 27, pp. 1–24.

Pentikainen, J. and M. Hiltunen eds (1995). *Cultural Minorities in Finland*. Helsinki, Finnish National Commission for UNESCO.

Picco, L. (2001). *Ricerje su la condizion sociolenghistiche dal furlan*. Udine, Forum.

Pieterson, L. (1969). *De Friezen en hun taal*. Drachten, Laverman.

Pircher, K., U. Huber and H. Taschler (2002). *German: The German Language in Education in South Tyrol (Italy)*. Leeouwert, Fryske Akademy.

Pusey, M. (1998). Between Economic Dissolution and the Return of the Social: The Contest for Civil Society in Australia. In J. C. Alexander ed. *Real Civil Societies*. London, Sage, pp. 40–66.

Putnam, R. (1993). *Making Democracy Work*. Princeton University Press.

Quijano, A. (1974). The Marginal Role of the Economy and the Marginalised Labour Force. *Economy and Society*, Vol. 3, No. 4.

Rei-Doval, G. (2001). *A Lingua Galega no Medio Urbano: Unha Visión desde a Macrosociolingüístico*. Unpublished Ph.D. thesis. University of Santiago de Compostela.

Rei Doval, G. and F. Ramallo (1995). *Publicidade e lingua galega*. Santiago de Compostela, Consello da Cultura Galega.

Reiterer, A. F. (1996). *Kartner Slowenen: Minderheit oder Elite?* Klagenfurt, Drava.

Renkema, W. J., J. Ytsma and A. Willemsma (1996). *Frisian: The Frisian language in Education in the Netherlands*. Ljouwert, Fryske Akademy.

Rindler Schjerve, R. (1996). Sardaigne. In H. Goebl, P. Nelde, S. Zdenek and W. Wolfgang eds. *Contact Linguistics*. New York, De Gruyter, pp. 1376–83.

Ritaine, E. (1998). The Political Capacity of Southern European Regions. In P. Le Gales and C. Lesquene eds. *Regions in Europe*. London, Routledge, pp. 67–88.

Robertson, B. (2001). *Gaelic: The Gaelic Language in Education in the UK*. Ljouwert, Fryske Akademy.

Rose, N. (1995). Towards a Critical Sociology of Freedom. In P. Joyce ed. *Class*. Oxford University Press, pp. 213–25.

Rynck, S. de (1998). Civic Culture and Institutional Performance of the Belgian Regions. In P. Le Gales and C. Lequesne eds. *Regions in Europe*. London, Routledge, pp. 199–218.

Sassoon, D. (1999). European Social Democracy and New Labour: Unity in Diversity? In A. Gamble and T. Wright eds. *The New Social Democracy*. Oxford, Blackwell, pp. 19–37.

Saxenian, A. (1999). *Silicon Valley's New Immigrant Entrepreneurs*. Working Paper, San Jose, Public Policy Institute of California.

Schumpeter, J. A. (1947). *Capitalism, Socialism and Democracy*. New York, Harper.

Seriot, P. (ed). (1996). *N. S. Troubetzkoy, L'Europe et l'humanité, écrits linguistique et paralinguistique*. Paris, Mardaga.

Seriot, P. (1997). *Ethnos* et *Demos*: la construction discursive de l'identité collective. *Langage et Société*, No. 79, pp. 39–53.

Siedentop, Larry (2000). *Democracy in Europe*. London, Allen Lane.

Siguan, M. (1993). *The Languages of Spain*. Amsterdam, Swets and Zeitlinger.

Stuijt, M., M. Garay, M. Basmoreau and T. Delbel (1998). *Basque: The Basque Language in Education in France*. Ljouwert, Fryske Akademy.

Svonni, M. (2001). *Sami: The Sami language in Education in Sweden*. Ljouwert, Fryske Akademy.

Taylor, Charles (1992). *Multiculturalism and 'The Politics of Recognition'*. Princeton University Press.

Telmon, T. (1992). *Le minoranze linguistiche in Italia*. Alessandria, Dell Orso.

Thevenot, L. and L. Boltanski (1987). *Les économies de la grandeur*. Paris, PUF.

Toqueville, Alexis de (1998). *Democracy in America*. Ware, Wordsworth.

Tosi, A. (2001). *Language and Society in a Changing Italy*. Clevedon, Multilingual Matters.

Touraine, A. (1989). Is Sociology Still the Study of Society? *Thesis Eleven*, 23, pp. 174–86.

Touraine, A. (1994). *Qu'est-ce que la Démocratie*. Paris, Fayard.

Touraine, A. (1997). *Pourrons-Nous Vivre Ensemble?* Paris, Fayard.

Tovey, H. (1988). The State and the Irish Language: The Role of Bord na Gaelige. *International Journal of the Sociology of Language*, 70, pp. 53–68.

Trudgill, P. (2000). Greece and European Turkey: From Religious to Linguistic Identity. In S. Barbour and C. Carmichael eds. *Language and Nationalism in Europe.* Oxford University Press, pp. 240–63.

Tsitsipis, L. (1998). *A Linguistic Anthropology of Praxis and Language Shift: Arvanitika (Albanian) and Greek in Contact.* Oxford, Clarendon.

Tsitselikis, K. and G. Mavrommatis (2003). *Turkish: The Turkish Language in Education in Greece.* Ljouwert, Frsyke Akademy (revised by D. Morelli).

Tucker, R. C. ed. (1972). *The Marx-Engels Reader.* New York, Norton.

Turell, M. T. ed. (2001). *Multilingualism in Spain – Sociolinguistics and Psycholinguistic Aspects of Linguistic Minority Groups.* Clevedon, Multilingual Matters.

Turner, B. (1988). *Status.* Oxford University Press.

Valku-Poustovaia, I. (1997). Lecture(s) recursive(s): analysé et interpretations. *Langage et Société,* 79, pp. 75–106.

Van Der Schaaf, A. and D. Morgon (2001). *German: The German Language in Education in Alsace, France.* Ljouwert, Fryske Akademy.

Van der Schaaf, A. and R. Verra (2001). *Ladin: The Ladin Language in Education in Italy.* Ljouwert, Fryske Akademy.

Vaniscotte, F. (1989). *70 Million d'Elèves: L'Europe de L'Education.* Paris, Hatier.

Voltaire (1879). *Histoire du Siècle du Louis XIV.* Cambridge University Press.

Walker, A. (1997). *North Frisian.* Ljouwert, Frsyke Akademy.

Walzer, M. (1992). *What it Means to be an American.* New York, Marsilio.

Weber, M. (1978). *Economy and Society.* Berkeley, University of California Press.

Welsh Language Board (1993). *A Strategy for the Welsh Language.* Cardiff, Welsh Language Board.

Willemsma, A. and A. MacPoilin (2001). *Irish: The Irish Language in Education in Northern Ireland.* Ljouwert, Fryske Akadmey.

Williams, G. (1987a). Bilingualism, Class Dialect and Social Reproduction. In G. Williams ed. *The Sociology of Welsh.* The Hague, Mouton, pp. 85–98.

Williams, G. (1987b). Policy as Containment within Democracy: The Welsh Language Act. In G. Williams ed. *The Sociology of Welsh.* The Hague, Mouton, pp. 49–60.

Williams, G. (1992a). *The Welsh in Patagonia: The State and the Ethnic Community.* Cardiff, University of Wales Press.

Williams, G. (1992b). *Sociolinguistics: A Sociological Critique.* London, Routledge.

Williams, G. (1998). Modernity, Normativity and Social Order: The Problem of Ethnicity. In R. Bombi and G. Graffi eds. *Ethnicity and Language Community: An Interdisciplinary and Methodological Comparison.* Atti del Convergo Internatzionale, Udine: Forum, pp. 517–38.

Williams, G. (1999a). *French Discourse Analysis: The Method of Poststructuralism.* London, Routledge.

Williams, G. (1999b). Sociology. In J. Fishman ed. *Language and Ethnicity.* Oxford University Press, pp. 164–81.

Williams, G. ed. (1999c). *Towards an Integrated European Minority Language Television Service.* Report Presented to EC, Brussels (contract no: 98-06-AUT-0092-00).

Williams, G. (2000a). The Digital Value Chain and Economic Transformation: Rethinking Regional Development in the New Economy. *Contemporary Wales,* No. 13, pp. 94–116.

Williams, G. (2000b). *Developing Digital Democracy.* Final Report to ISPO, DGXIII of the European Commission (Project No: IS 97206).

Williams, G. (2001). Developing Digital Democracy: From Reperesentative to Participatory Democracy. *Plarilingua,* pp. 123–34.

Williams, G. and C. Roberts (1982). Institutional Centralisation and Linguistic Discrimination. In G. Braga and E. Monti Civelli eds. *Linguistic Problems and European Unity*. Milan, Franco Angeli Editore, pp. 75–104.

Williams, G. and C. Roberts (1983). Language, Education and Reproduction in Wales. In B. Bain ed. *The Sociogenesis of Language and Human Conduct*. New York, Plenum, pp. 497–517.

Williams, G. and D. Morris (2000). *Language Planning and Language Use: Welsh in a Global Age*. Cardiff, University of Wales Press.

Williams, G., E. Roberts and R. Isaac (1978). Language and Aspirations for Upward Social Mobility. In G. Williams ed. *Social and Cultural Change in Contemporary Wales*. London, Routledge & Kegan Paul, pp. 193–206.

Wolpe, H. ed. (1979). *The Articulation of Modes of Production*. London, Routledge & Kegan Paul.

Xambo, R. (1996). *El sistema comunicatiu Valencià*. Unpublished Ph.D. thesis, University of Valencia.

Index